# SOCIAL WORK RESEARCH IN THE HUMAN SERVICES

*Second Edition*

# SOCIAL WORK RESEARCH IN THE HUMAN SERVICES

*Second Edition*

*Edited By*

**Henry Wechsler, Ph.D.
Helen Z. Reinherz, M.S.W.,
M.S. Hyg., Sc.D.
Donald D. Dobbin, M.S.W.**

**HUMAN SCIENCES PRESS**

72 Fifth Avenue    3 Henrietta Street
NEW YORK, NY 10011  ●  LONDON, WC2E 8LU

Copyright © 1981 by Human Sciences Press, Inc.
72 Fifth Avenue, New York, New York 10011

Printed in the United States of America
123456789      987654321

**Library of Congress Cataloging in Publication Data**
Main entry under title:

Social work research in the human services

Includes index.
1. Social service–Research–Addresses, essays, lectures. 2. Evaluation research (Social action programs)–Addresses, essays, lectures.
I. Wechsler, Henry, 1932-       II. Reinherz, Helen Z. III. Dobbin, Donald D.
HV11.S592   1981      361'.0072      81-1760
ISBN 0-89885-038-X (case)      AACR2
ISBN 0-89885-039-8 (pbk.)

# CONTENTS

# ABOUT THE EDITORS

HENRY WECHSLER, PH.D., Director of Research, The Medical
Foundation, Inc.; Adjunct Professor, Simmons College School
of Social Work; Lecturer in Social Psychology, Harvard School
of Public Health, Boston, Mass.

HELEN Z. REINHERZ, SC.D.., Professor of Social Work and Chair-
person of Research Sequence, Simmons College School of Social
Work, Boston, Mass.

DONALD D. DOBBIN, M.S.W., Senior Researcher and Planner,
United Community Planning Corporation, Boston, Mass.

# CONTRIBUTORS

The affiliations listed below are the most recent available on each of the contributors.

EUGENE M. CAFFEY, M.D., Assistant Chief Medical Director for Professional Services, VA Central Office, Washington, D.C.

JOY CAMP, M.S.W., Special Instructor in Social Work Research, Simmons College School of Social Work, Boston, Mass.

HAROLD W. DEMONE, JR., PH.D., Dean, Graduate School of Social Work, Rutgers University, New Brunswick, N.J.

SELMA FRAIBERG, M.S.W., Professor of Child Psychoanalysis, Department of Psychiatry; Director, Child Development Project, University of Michigan, Ann Arbor, Mich.

NELL H. GOTTLIEB, M.A., Community Health Associate, The Medical Foundation, Inc., Boston, Mass.

SUSAN E. HANKS, S.M., Clinical Social Worker, The Ombudsman Project; Private Psychotherapist, San Leandro, Calif.

MARGUERITE HEYWOOD, M.S.W., Psychiatric Social Worker, Cutler Counseling Center, Norwood, Mass.

GERARD E. HOGARTY, M.S.W., Associate Professor of Psychiatry, Western Psychiatric Institute, University of Pittsburgh School of Medicine, Pittsburgh, Pa.

BERNARD HOROWITZ, PH.D., Assistant Professor, Graduate School of Social Work, Rutgers University, New Brunswick, N.J.

ROSALIE A. KANE, D.S.W., Research Consultant, Rand Corporation, Santa Monica, Calif.

C. JAMES KLETT, PH.D., Chief, VA Cooperative Studies Coordinating Center, Perry Point, Md.

RICHARD LAMB, M.D., Associate Professor of Psychiatry, University of Southern California School of Medicine, Los Angeles, Calif.

HARRY LAWRENCE, D.S.W., Associate Professor, School of Social Work, Arizona State University, Tempe, Ariz.

MARGARET W. LINN, M.S.W., PH.D., Director, Social Science Research, VA Medical Center; Associate Professor of Psychiatry, University of Miami School of Medicine, Miami, Fla.

SUSAN MERCER, D.S.W., Associate Professor, Little Rock Graduate School of Social Work, University of Arkansas, Little Rock, Ark.

STEPHEN J. PEDI, M.S.W., Behavior Modification Specialist, Catholic Social Services, Diocese of Grand Rapids, Grand Rapids, Mich.

ELIZABETH MOORE PLIONIS, D.S.W., Assistant Professor, National Catholic School of Social Service, Catholic University of America, Washington, D.C.

JOSEPH M. REGAN, M.S.W., PH.D., Assistant Professor of Social Work, Simmons College School of Social Work, Boston, Mass.

SONYA L. RHODES, D.S.W., Adjunct Assistant Professor, Hunter College School of Social Work, New York, N.Y.

JOAN F. ROBERTSON, PH.D., Associate Professor, School of Social Work, University of Wisconsin, Madison, Wisc.

C. PETER ROSENBAUM, M.D., Professor of Psychitary and Behavioral Sciences, School of Medicine, Stanford University, Stanford, Calif.

ALLEN RUBIN, PH.D., Director, Project on Research Utilization in Social Work Education, Council on Social Work Education, New York, N.Y.

LAWRENCE SHULMAN, M.S.W., ED.D., Professor, School of Social Work, University of British Columbia, Vancouver, B.C.

CLAUDE L. WALTER, D.S.W., Assistant Professor, George Warren Brown School of Social Work, Washington University, St. Louis, Mo.

JOHN S. WODARSKI, PH.D., Director, Research Center, School of Social Work, University of Georgia, Athens, Ga.

ISABEL WOLOCK, PH.D., Associate Professor, Graduate School of Social Work, Rutgers University, New Brunswick, N.J.

# ACKNOWLEDGMENTS

*Chapter*

2. From *Smith College Studies in Social Work,* 1970, *40*(2), 101–115. Reprinted by permission of the author and the Smith College School of Social Work.
3. From *American Journal of Orthopsychiatry,* Vol. 47, No. 2 (1977), pp. 250–263. Copyright © 1977 the American Orthopsychiatric Association, Inc. Reproduced by permission.
4. From *Journal of Gerontological Social Work,* Vol. 1, No. 2 (1978), pp. 95–109. Reprinted by permission of The Haworth Press, Inc.
7. From *American Journal of Orthopsychiatry,* Vol. 47, No. 2 (1977), pp. 291–306 Copyright © 1977 the American Orthopsychiatric Association, Inc. Reproduced by permission.
8. From *Social Service Review,* Vol. 53, No. 2 (1979), pp. 175–194. Reprinted by permission of the author and The University of Chicago Press.
9. From *Health & Social Work,* Vol. 4, No. 1 (February 1979), pp. 91–116. Reprinted by permission of the author and the National Association of Social Workers.

12. From *Social Work,* Vol. 22, No. 4 (July 1977), pp. 290–296. Reprinted by permission of the author and the National Association of Social Workers.

13. From *Social Service Review,* Vol. 51, No. 1 (1977), pp. 125–140. Reprinted by permission of the author and The University of Chicago Press.

14. From *Social Work,* Vol. 23, No. 4 (July 1978), pp. 274–280. Reprinted by permission of the author and the National Association of Social Workers.

17. From *Adolescence,* Vol. 11, No. 42 (Summer 1976), pp. 167–179. Reprinted by permission of the authors and Libra Publishers, Inc.

18. From *Social Work,* Vol. 23, No. 2 (March 1978), pp. 127–133. Reprinted by permission of the author and the National Association of Social Workers.

19. From *Archives of General Psychiatry,* Vol. 36, No. 10 (1979), pp. 1055–1066. Reprinted by permission of the author and the American Medical Association. Copyright 1979, American Medical Association.

22. From The muse in the kitchen: A case study in clinical research. *Smith College Studies in Social Work,* 1970, *40*(2), 115–134. Reprinted by permission of the author and the Smith College School of Social Work. Readers should remember that the first part of this study appears in Chapter 2 ("The Muse in the Kitchen: A Case Study in Clinical Research").

23. From *Public Health Reports,* Vol. 94, No. 5 (1979), pp. 477–482. Reprinted by permission of the authors and *Public Health Reports.*

24. From *Community Mental Health Journal,* Vol. 14, No. 3 (1978), pp. 199–208. Reprinted by permission of Human Sciences Press.

# INTRODUCTION

This revised edition provides social work students with the basic materials necessary to understand the different phases of research in the human services. Selected articles from recent social work journals and human service journals have been brought together to give the student, teacher, and practitioner examples of the different aspects of social work research. The book first examines the process of selecting a worthwhile research problem, of determining when and when not to do research, of selecting from among the various different types of study, and of formulating a specific question for research.

The book also includes articles that will help the student to select a workable research design and a valid study sample. Exploratory, descriptive, experimental, and "quasi-experimental" studies are discussed. Emphasis is given to the optimal use of research tools, especially data-collection techniques such as questionnaires and interviews, and the use of unobtrusive methods. Evaluative research is given special treatment by the editors, as it is a major current focus in human services research. The last section deals exclusively with problems in the analysis and interpretation of results.

All of the articles are preceded by detailed issue-oriented introductions, including suggestions for further technical reading. The articles have been chosen to provide a balanced coverage of major issues and viewpoints in social work. The linkages between chapters are provided by cross-references to the articles in other parts of the book, and by citations from research methodology texts.

It is recommended that the instructor should use this reader in conjunction with standard social science research and statistics texts. This combination of content and technology should provide students of the human services not only with the ability to become critical consumers of the literature in their field, but also with a basic understanding of the crucial choices and decisions that govern the processes of research in the human services.

Part I

# PROBLEM FORMULATION: THE KEYSTONE

*Chapter 1*

# THE ROLE OF RESEARCH IN SOCIAL WORK PRACTICE

## Problem Formulation, The First Step

### Helen Z. Reinherz
### Joseph M. Regan

This chapter will define social work research, its mandate, evolution, and current status. In addition, the chapter will systematically outline the process of formulating a problem for social work research. The reader will also be able to apply these guidelines to three studies that have different objectives and methods, in order to assess their authors' approach to the formulation of appropriate social work research questions.

## SOCIAL WORK RESEARCH: A DEFINITION

Social work research establishes its identity from its unique position as the connecting link between two different orientations. There is the perspective of science, which emphasizes the ideals of objectivity, logical thinking, and the use of explicit rational techniques in the orderly pursuit of systematic and generalizable knowledge. Along side of this, however, are those elements intrinsic to the social work profession such as the importance of values, the view of practice as an "art" relying on insight and creativity, and the involvement with complex individual and social problems that do not always lend themselves to a particular formal research strategy.

The history of research (Zimbalist, 1977) in social work can be described as the interaction and integration of these two orientations. Both must come together in its development. Social work research must be, after all, research in the service of the social work profession. Social work practice raises the issues and problems that become the focus of research endeavors. This is true not only in an examination of current topics chosen for research as exemplified in the articles chosen for this book, but also, and perhaps even more strikingly, in the way the research problems are formulated for study. It is seen again in the methodologies that are used. Today there is much discussion on the increased need for single subject designs offering a potential for practitioners to examine and evaluate their own work (Howe, 1974). Even the more traditional survey and experimental designs, however, have always required considerable adjustment to the particular social work problem and setting.

In spite of efforts to integrate applied and scientific orientations, the role of research in social work education is not always clearly defined and in many programs remains peripheral. There are indications that social work practitioners do not sufficiently rely on research to inform their practice (Rosenblatt, 1968) and that social work agencies do not engage in or encourage research endeavors as a regular part of their program activity (Kirk, Ozmalov, & Fisher 1976). The main question that social work faces is the best way to proceed in facilitating and promoting the joining of research and practice to advance the interests of the profession and the groups it serves.

It is clear that to advance our objectives the research priorities must reflect the priorities of the social work profession. The formulation of research problems must be attuned to needs deriving from real practice issues involving policies and programs for children, the elderly, minorities, the handicapped, and other vulnerable groups. Methodologies in the areas of general design, sample selection, and instrumentation need to be continually refined and developed so that they both satisfy the requirements of reliability, validity, and generalizability, and still allow for the real nature of the social work problem areas to be addressed. Strategies must be developed that permit more sophisticated methods of analysis on the one hand and facilitate interpretability and application of results on the other.

It may seem that the imperative to adapt lies more heavily on the scientific aspects of this process. In actuality, progress must proceed from both directions. It is from this philosophy that this book is written. Illustrative articles are not presented as models ideal in every respect but as attempts to address social work problems and through the use of the research process to promote our understanding and to increase our options for action. Social work practitioners need to develop the skill that will enable them to have influence in the research process by redefining and reshaping their concerns so that research techniques can address them. The complaint that practitioners find so many of the results of social work research irrelevant is often presented as if researchers should recast their findings in ways that more clearly spell out their implications (Kirk et al., 1976). Even when this is done, the problem of utilization of results often still remains. Social work practitioners must develop their own skills for establishing meaning and application. For social work research to develop, integration of research and practice efforts must proceed on all levels involving practitioners and administrators of social agencies as well as social work researchers.

The current issues of accountability and professional credibility aside, the central role of research in the social work profession stems from its function in facilitating and structuring systematic thinking about practice. It becomes one tool that a data-based profession can use to generate empirically valid principles for policy and practice and ultimately service to our clientele.

## THE PROCESS OF PROBLEM FORMULATION

At this, the earliest stage of research, given a significant issue for study, a framework for systematic procedure provides an invaluable aid to the research worker. The steps will be presented in a sequence that often occurs. The most important issue is not the specific order of each step, however, but the careful consideration of each of these areas. None of the procedures must be omitted when one is setting the stage for a piece of meaningful research formulated in a manner that will result in a study producing relevant knowledge for the field of social work.

### A Felt Need: The First Consideration

Problems for social work research often arise from the concern of an agency, the community, or professional social workers over a group that is not served, or is served inadequately or inappropriately. These issues whether around strategy for planning for the elderly, planning for deinstitutionalization of mental patients, or treatment approaches to disturbed children constitute the "felt needs" prompting research. Problems in social work research should *ideally* have two purposes: first, to have results for policy and practice that will lead to better services for clients, and second, to add to knowledge and theory for the social work field. These are difficult goals to balance. Some of the best work in the field fulfills the two criteria, however. The Fraiberg study (Part I) in which the felt need was to serve a client population (children blind from birth) fulfilled that specific need by developing methods of work with that client group. In addition, however, it contributed significantly to the theory of development of the ego in the visually impaired infant.

At the initial stage at which a need for study emerges, before the further steps of problem formulation take place, a thorough review of the literature should be undertaken to identify other studies in the topic area or relevant theoretical literature. In searching through literature specific to the topic of interest care should be taken to include work in allied areas as well. The study, of Family Functioning and Childhood Accident Occurrence, by Plionis, reprinted in Part I, presents a comprehensive literature survey concerning the relationship of repetitive accidents and familial characteristics. The author also surveyed literature concerning major health problems and health functioning in addition to that on accidents in childhood to aid in focusing her study.

At this early stage of problem formulation, the researcher should also interview those who have had actual experience with the anticipated problem area. Additionally, one's own creativity and insight are valuable and opportunity should exist for observation and reflection upon individual experiences with the problem areas.

*Focus: Reduction of the Problem to Manageable Size*

In the early stages of problem formulation just described, it is useful to view the topic (potential problem area) broadly from multiple perspectives. After the initial stages, however, a focusing and specific narrowing must take place so that the topic can be studied empirically. Most researchers first conceptualize a problem in broad ranging or global terms. Thus, it becomes crucial to narrow and focus so that the problem is amenable to study and later interpretation.

Fraiberg's wide-ranging, yet far from random, observations of blind "normal" and developmentally problematic children led her to focus on ego formation in blind infants (Part I). Ultimately, she phrased more specific questions and hypotheses on adaptive behavior in blind infants, and specifically on the role of the mother in facilitating the adaptation of these children.

## DEFINING CONCEPTS: CONCEPTUAL AND OPERATIONAL DEFINITIONS

The definition of the major concepts of the study and their translation into observable empirical operations is part of the process of progressive narrowing of the scope of a study. The concepts for study must be such that they can be represented by evidence that can be gathered by observation, interviewing, or some other means of data collection (Selltiz, Wrightsman, & Cook, 1976).

The importance of this stage of problem formulation should not be underestimated. Clear, well formulated, and well-operationalized concepts for study set the stage for later creation of appropriate data-gathering instruments as well as eventual analysis, summary, and organization of the results of the study. The article of Plionis (reprinted in Part I) utilized a scale comprised of eight significant aspects of family adequacy to represent the major concept of "family functioning." Utilization of a previously published instrument not only provided a useful (feasible) means of studying a highly abstract concept, it also allowed for detailed examination of important components of the concept such as "family relationships" and "use of community resources." Time spent in clearly defining and operationalizing concepts is well spent for its potential impact on further steps of the study.

## The Feasibility of the Proposed Study

At each stage of the problem formulation, the researcher must continuously face the very practical issue of feasibility. Granted there is need for the study and concepts are clear, will there be appropriate subjects? Even if the topic is relevant to the field and an important addition to knowledge, where can it be carried out? Finally, there are questions of an ethical nature affecting the privacy or well-being of potential subjects. Each of the above issues require early and constant consideration.

Also important are the technical and informational backgrounds of the individuals who are undertaking research in a particular problem area. Does the research and/or project staff have the requisite expertise and time to complete the study? Another point for examination is whether predesigned research tools exist or will have to be created. Good research is expensive. The elaborateness, cost, and funding needs are further issues.

## Examination of the Problem in Relation to Appropriate Design

This aspect of problem formulation relates to the amount of knowledge that already exists around the problem, and availability of studies that have been done before in this field. If no information is available and variables are not clearly defined, an exploratory study is indicated before a descriptive survey or carefully controlled experimental study can be launched.

As will become clear, each stage of the study should be organically related to the earlier aspects of the study. Especially in the problem formulation phase, the researcher should be aware of the further steps of the process including sampling and study design, data collection, and analysis.

A study may test a hypothesis, have the formulation of a hypothesis as a goal, or simply ask and answer a descriptive question. The first part of the Fraiberg study was primarily directed toward establishing what were the important variables to be studied, and it was only in the second portion of the study (reprinted in Part V) that hypotheses could be posited and examined. Furthermore, some studies based upon hypotheses may explicitly state the hypothesis to be tested. The Plionis study reprinted in this section tests a hypothesis relating specified areas of family functioning and repetitive accidents of children. In contrast, the Robertson study of the aged, also in this section, describes the preferences of aged persons living in the community. The ultimate goal of this descriptive study is to provide a guide to practitioners working with the elderly based on the client group's own view.

## THE ULTIMATE QUESTION: THE ANTICIPATED VALUE OF THE RESULTS

If the researcher has been guided by the dual objectives of selecting a problem of anticipated usefulness for policy and practice as well as potentially adding to the body of knowledge in the field, the importance of the study is clear. Many of the studies reprinted in this book fulfill these criteria.

In the next section of this book studies that have been chosen specifically to illustrate some of the areas of problem formulation will be represented. For the guidance of the reader, it is suggested that these studies should be examined specifically for their approach to the problem formulation process. Each of the guidelines listed should be utilized in assessing the writers' handling of this portion of the research process. Other aspects of these studies may be viewed in subsequent sections of the book.

## References

Howe, M. Casework self-evaluation: A single subject approach. *Social Service Review*, 1974, *48*, 1–23.

Kirk, S., Ozmalov, M., & Fisher, J. Social workers' involvement in research. *Social Work*, 1976, *21*, 121–124.

Rosenblatt, A. The practitioner's use and evaluation of research. *Social Work*, 1968, *13*, 53–59.

Selltiz, C., Wrightsman, L. S., & Cook, S. W. *Research methods in social relations*, 3rd ed. New York: Holt, Rinehart and Winston, 1976.

Zimbalist, S. *Historic themes and landmarks in social welfare research*. New York: Harper and Row, 1977.

*Chapter 2*

# THE MUSE IN THE KITCHEN

## A Case Study in Clinical Research (Part A)

## Selma Fraiberg

Our subject today is a consideration of problems of clinical research.

Those of us who are old enough to have followed the literature in this area for twenty-five years or more have witnessed a growing estrangement between clinical practice and clinical research. A marriage that should have brought mutually enriching rewards in human science and its applications seems to be drifting apart. The clinician has taken to minding the pots in the kitchen and the researcher is conducting an affair with a computer.

In the session we have planned for today I have agreed to bring in a case history of a clinical research project with some typical and some atypical marriage problems. I propose that we use this case history for discussion of the clinical problems that invited the research, the methods that were designed to get the answers, and finally the application of these findings to a program of prevention and rehabilitation.

This paper was presented at an institute sponsored by the New England Chapter of the Smith College School for Social Work Alumni Association March 27, 1969 in Boston, Massachusetts.

This research has been supported since 1966 by Grant #HD01–444 from the National Institute of Child Health and Development and funds from the Department of Psychiatry of the University of Michigan Medical School and since 1969 by Grant #OEG–0–9–322108–2469(032) from the Office of Education.

## The Clinical Problem

The story begins, very simply, as a clinical problem in a social agency. In 1960 I was consultant to the Family Service Society of New Orleans when we were asked to take on a caseload of twenty-seven blind children between the ages of three and fourteen years. Viola Weiss, as chief supervisor of the F.S.S., asked me to give some time to the new work with blind children. Neither I nor any other member of the staff had ever worked with blind children. We were in no way prepared for the impact of these blind children on our eyes.

Of the twenty-seven blind children, at least seven presented a clinical picture that closely resembled autism in the sighted. There were stereotyped hand behaviors, rocking, swaying, mutism or echolalic speech. These were children who were content to sit for hours, sucking on a clothespin or a pot lid, rocking, detached, vacant, virtually unresponsive to the mother or to any other human being. The striking feature of these cases was uniformity. We had the uncanny feeling that we were were seeing the same case over and over again. In reading our cases we had to provide ourselves with mnemonic cues to distinguish one case from the other. ("Martin is the one who likes to suck on clothespins; Martha is the one who chews rubber jar rings; Jane is the hand-banger; Chrissey bangs her bottom against the wall.")

Of the remaining twenty children, nearly all showed one or another form of stereotyped motility, but speech was organized and there were demonstrable ties to human objects.

When I first saw these autistic blind children I was convinced that they suffered brain damage. I think I would have rather believed anything than to consider that something in human experience could produce these automatons. We asked Dr. David Freedman, a neurologist and psychoanalyst, to consult with us. He reviewed the medical findings which included EEG's on several cases and personally examined certain children. In the end he confessed himself as baffled as we were. He found no evidence of neurological damage. This did not, in itself, rule out the possibility of brain damage of unknown causes, but in the absence of positive signs we were certainly free to consider other possibilities.

We reviewed the birth histories of each of the children and found no correlation between birth weight, length of time in oxygen (in the case of the premature baby), and the clinical picture of autism. Later, we were to find as Keeler did in his Toronto study (1958), that the autistic patterns were not correlated with any specific disease or cause of blindness but were seen most commonly in children who were blind from birth, who were totally blind or had no pattern vision and who had received inadequate stimulation in infancy. From Keeler's studies and others we learned also that our population at the Family Service Society was more typical than we had guessed. Approximately one-quarter of Keeler's metropolitan sample presented the clinical picture of autism. The incidence of autism in his group was, then, as high as our own.

The question of possible brain damage is still debated in the literature of the sighted and blind autistic child. It is still neither proved nor disproved by any scientific studies. However, we have learned since 1960 in our own work that if we can identify the autistic blind child in the early years, preferably under two years of age, we can bring this child to normal functioning. This means that whether or not there is a primary neurologic defect, other factors in the environment or in the unique adaptive problems of a blind infant must play a decisive role.

## Clinical Observations

As clinicians, Dr. Freedman and I asked ourselves certain questions. First of all, we were impressed by the picture of developmental arrest in the autistic blind child, of personalities frozen on the level of mouth-centeredness and nondifferentiation. There was no "I" or "you," but there was also no "me" or "other," no sense of a body self and "something out there."

All of this was of a piece with the most distinguishing characteristic of these children—the absence of human connections. The mother was barely distinguished from other persons; her comings and goings went unnoticed. There were no cries to summon her, no sounds of greeting when she appeared, no signs of distress when she left. We know, of course, that in the absence of a human partner the baby cannot acquire a sense of self and other, of "me" and "you." But should blindness be an impediment to the establishment of human object relations? How about our other blind children, the twenty children who had demonstrable human ties? How did these children make their human partnerships? The sighted child in the first year makes increasingly selective and highly differentiated responses to his mother. So far as we knew from psychoanalytic studies, the differential smile, the discrimination of mother and stranger, and indeed the whole sequence of differential human responses are predicated upon visual recognitory experiences. In the absence of vision how does the blind baby differentiate, recognize, become bound through love? There must be an adaptive substitution for vision. The mother of a blind baby must find some ways of helping the baby find the route. How? And if she does not?

We observed that in all of these autistic children, perception was largely centered in the mouth. The hand itself seemed to have no autonomy from the mouth. The cliché, "The hands are the eyes of the blind," had become a terrible irony in the case of these children. They had blind hands, too. The hands did not reach out for objects to attain them. The hands were not used to get information about objects. Most striking, the hands had remained in a kind of morbid alliance with the mouth. They could bring objects to the mouth to be sucked. And when the hands were not serving the mouth in some way they were typically held at shoulder height with stereotyped inutile movements of the fingers.

These children had virtually no independent mobility. Even walking with support was a late achievement, in some instances as late as five years of age; in one instance at the age of nine! In the literature these children are classified as "the blind mentally retarded." If we are interested only in developmental measurement, this is certainly indisuputable. But to the psychoanalytic investigator these blind mentally retarded children presented some inexplicable problems. If the systems for receiving nonvisual stimuli were intact (and this was demonstrable in the neurological examination) how could we explain this extraordinary picture of developmental arrest, this freezing of personality on the eight-to-twelve month level with virtually no gains, no small increments of learning thereafter?

### INFERENCES FROM THE CLINICAL PICTURE

As clinicians we were accustomed to reading and interpreting behavior signs and there were a number of signs in the clinical pictures of these children that led our thinking along certain paths.

It is immediately apparent that the body schemas which normally lead to adaptive hand behavior had failed to integrate in these children. Normally, vision insures that at five months the thing seen can be grasped and attained. In the absence of vision other sense modalities must be coordinated with grasping. How is the adaptive substitution found in the case of the blind infant? And if it isn't found?

Next, our attention was drawn to the delay in locomotion. Were all motor achievements delayed in the case of these deviant blind children? No. A puzzle appeared in the developmental histories. Rolling over, sitting with support, sitting independently were not markedly delayed. But creeping, walking with support, and of course, walking independently were markedly delayed or never achieved. If the histories were reliable, there was neuromuscular adequacy demonstrated in the gross motor achievements during the first six months. Why the impasse in creeping and later locomotion?

As you can see, our first questions were addressed to the unique adaptive problems of a child blind from birth. In the case of the autistic blind child the sensory deficit and unknown factors in early experience had produced a picture that suggested adaptive failure. But what about the twenty other children in our sample who had found the adaptive routes with varying degrees of success?

As a group, the remaining twenty children demonstrated human attachments with some variability in the quality of these ties or the capacity in later childhood to function independently. The range in adaptive hand abilities I cannot give you because in those days we did not yet know how to "read" hand behavior in blind children. But for most of these children, too, the achievement of independent mobility was very late by sighted child standards, between two and three years for independent walking. Typically, too, there was no mention of creeping in the developmental histories. But strangely enough in this "normal" group of blind children nearly all the children demonstrated one or another kind of stereotyped motility, rocking, swaying, hand-waving, eye-rubbing, or idiosyncratic movements. These behaviors were long known to workers with the blind, and have been called "blindisms." With the exception of eye-rubbing, all of these behaviors can be found in the sighted autistic child. These children were not autistic. What did this mean?

If we now looked at the entire group of twenty-seven children it appeared that certain characteristics such as the delay in locomotion and the stereotyped motility were found in both groups with qualitative and quantitative differences. The range for the achievement of independent mobility was not nearly so great for the "normal" group as for the autistic group. The stereotyped motility constituted a large part of the repertory of the autistic group and a small part of the repertory of the "normal" group. If we had known how to "read hands" in those days we might have learned through the study of the "normal" group what I have since learned through study of children in the general blind population. A large number of blind children who are not autistic and who have differentiated personalities may still have "blind hands," hands that do not serve as sensitive perceptual organs. But this brings us ahead of the story and we should really stay with what we knew at this point in our investigation.

At this point our observations and questions provided some kind of framework for our thinking. We were reasonably sure that what we saw in the range of personalities available to us in this sample of twenty-seven children was a range of adaptive behaviors to the problem of blindness during the first eighteen months of life. The picture of developmental arrest in the autistic blind child showed failure to find the adaptive routes on the six- to twelve-month level. We inferred this from the clinical picture of an undifferentiated self—not self, from the arrest in locomotor achievements and language, and from the absence of coordinated hand behavior to an external stimulus. *We reasoned that for every developmental failure in the blind autistic child there should be a correlate in the development of all blind babies in the form of a unique adaptive problem posed by blindness.* The difference between the autistic blind child and the child in the normal group might, then, appear in developmental studies in which one group found the adaptive solutions and the other group met a developmental impasse.

## A NEED FOR OBSERVATION OF A BLIND INFANT

Our own group of twenty-seven children could not help us in searching for clues. They had come to us with poor developmental histories from a variety of agencies that had no clinical interest in the problems with which we were concerned. The differences between the autistic blind children and the "normal" group in the first year of life could not be discerned from the records. In both groups the babies were described as "quiet" babies, content to lie in their cribs for the best part of the twenty-four hour day. In both groups the mothers were described as "depressed." In both groups there were the delays in gross motor achievements during the last quarter of the first year.

We then turned to the literature to find longitudinal studies of blind infants which could provide us with the detailed descriptive information on the blind baby's development. Then, to our surprise, we learned that no detailed longitudinal studies of blind babies existed. We found Norris' volume (1957), which described the developmental achievements of 200 blind children as measured by a modified Cattell scale. We found five useful case histories in this volume which gave some picture of the developmental achievements of a selected sample. But our problems were different from those of the Norris group when they undertook their study. We needed to know in fine detail how the blind baby finds the adaptive routes and how ego formation takes place in the absence of vision.

Until this point we had not intended to engage in research. We wanted to inform ourselves and be useful to caseworkers who were working with vast unknowns in their responsibilities for blind children. Yes—and something more, too. We were already excited by certain ideas that were beginning to emerge in our minds. The high incidence of autism in the blind might provide vital clues to autism in the sighted. Also, we knew that the blind baby could teach us about the role of vision in early ego formation.

If research begins at any one point I suppose our research began here. We waited for the first new baby to be referred to our Family Service Society program for blind children, and the baby turned out to be Toni, a five-month-old girl, blind from birth due to ophthalmia neonatorum. We ascertained that Toni was otherwise intact and healthy. The agency obtained the mother's interest and consent and we arranged to set up regular monthly observation sessions.

We had no research plan beyond observing and recording. We would use cinema film for documentation of certain behavior samples. We had no money or any hopes of getting any. Nobody liked our research proposal, such as it was, and at least two foundations questioned our qualifications for the study of blind infants. They were quite right, I think.

So, at the start, we were both unqualified and unfunded. It is possible, I suppose, to be either unqualified or unfunded and still conduct research. But to be *both* unqualified and unfunded is normally discouraging to an investigator. We agreed to support our venture out of pocket and to divide the bill for film and processing on the first of every month. We would, of course, give our own time. As for our lack of qualifications, this proved to be no deterrent.

On July 22, 1961, we borrowed a 16 millimeter movie camera from the man next door, packed ourselves and our equipment into an old VW, and like two innocents in a fairy tale, we set out for a journey to the land of the blind. The New Orleans map led us to a slum, to a tiny brown house on a dirt road, and there we met the first blind baby we had ever seen.

### OBSERVATIONS OF TONI

What can we learn from one case?

When David Freedman and I set out to visit Toni we brought with us a number of hypotheses. We had hypotheses regarding blindness as an impediment to the establishment of libidinal object relations. We had a hypothesis regarding the adaptive substitution of sound for vision. We had another hypothesis regarding the role of sound in prehension. And there were others which are fortunately obliterated by time. In the next eighteen months Toni threw out each of our hypotheses one by one, like so many boring toys over the rail of a crib.

Since Toni was selected with no other criteria than her blindness and her age, we were quite fortunate in our first baby. She was a healthy, robust little girl, the youngest of six children. She was the illegitimate child of a young Negro woman in her early thirties. Toni's mother was an experienced mother. In spite of her feelings of guilt and fears for the future of her blind child, she was a woman whose motherliness was called forth by need and this baby who needed her in special ways evoked deep tenderness in her.

Toni tossed out one of our hypotheses on the first visit. She was five months old, making pleasant noises in her crib as we talked with her mother. When her mother went over to her and called her name, Toni's face broke into a gorgeous smile and she made agreeable responsive noises. I called her name and waited. There was no smile. Dr. Freedman called her name. There was no smile. Mother called her name and once again evoked the joyful smile and cooing sounds. Her mother said, a little apologetically, "She won't smile for anyone. Not even her sisters and brothers. Only me. She's been smiling when I talk to her since three months."

Now since it is written in all our books, including my own, that it is the *visual* stimulus of the human face that elicits smiling in the baby at three months, Toni's smile had just shattered a major theory, which shows you what one case can do. Seven years later I can give you a long list of blind babies who smiled in response to mother's or father's voices at ages under three months. But it doesn't really matter. If only one blind baby smiles in response to mother's voice, there is something wrong with our theory.

In our notes of this session we recorded a number of observations showing the selective response of Toni to her mother, paralleling in all significant ways that of a sighted child at five months. Three months later, at eight months, Toni demonstrated another achievement in the scale of human object relations. Soon after she heard our voices, strange voices, she became sober, almost frozen in her posture. Later, when I held Toni briefly to test her reactions to a stranger, she began to cry, she squirmed in my arms, and strained away from my body. It was a classic demonstration of "stranger anxiety." Yet it is written in all our books, including my own, that stranger anxiety appears at eight months on the basis of the visual discrimination of mother's face and stranger's face.

We were good sports about it. We conceded that under favorable environmental conditions blindness need not be an impediment to the establishment of human object relations. Anyway, we still had a lot of other hypotheses tucked away.

One of these hypotheses had to do with the adaptive substitution of sound for vision. We all know that around five months of age the sighted child can reach and attain an object on sight. In the case of the blind child we expected that a coordination of sound and grasping would take place at approximately the same time. But at five months, at six months, and, astonishingly, even at nine months, Toni made no gesture of reach toward any of the sound objects we presented to her. We sneaked around with jangling keys, rattles, squeaky toys, always in a range where Toni could easily reach them. She looked alert and attentive. She made no gesture of reach. It did not matter whether we used her own familiar toys or Freedman's car keys; there was not a gesture of reach. Was the baby deaf? Certainly not. As soon as she heard the sound of the camera motor, for example, she would startle or wince. She could discriminate voices. She could imitate sounds at seven months. What was it then?

At ten months Toni demonstrated for the first time her ability to reach and attain an object on sound cue alone. Thereafter she became expert in grabbing sound objects within arm's range. As we drove back from Toni's house that day we were stunned by the implications of this observation. Toni had given her first demonstration of a direct reach for a sound object at ten months. The sighted baby coordinates vision and grasping at five months. But how did Toni solve the problem? We knew perfectly well that no developmental achievement appears overnight. A coordinated action of hand and external stimulus is the result of complex sensorimotor learning. There were antecedents which must have been present for months, unrecognized by us.

Now we were obsessed by the problem and its implications. Since memory could not serve us we went back over thousands of feet of film, frame by frame, to try to reconstruct the sequence. But the story was not there. And we knew why. Film and film processing is expensive. Since we were financing this research out of pocket we had to be thrifty in our use of film. We devoted only a small amount of footage to each of the areas we were sampling and we had thought that our sampling was adequate. In order to pick up our lapse we would have needed generous and unprejudiced samples. The story of Toni's coordinated reach on sound cue was lost to us and we already knew that this story would prove to be a vital clue in the study of the blind baby's development. (Three years later at the University of Michigan we got the answer. A generous department supported a highly unthrifty film study which made the work possible.)

To return now to Toni and to go back a bit in the story: At eight months Toni had excellent control of her trunk and was indisputably moving toward an upright posture. She could support her weight on hands and knees, she could elevate herself to a standing position and let herself down easily. There was no question, from our knowledge of babies, that Toni was getting ready to creep. As we were leaving Toni's house at the end of the eight-month visit, I said to the mother, "Well, I'll bet when we come back next month Toni will really be into everything!" These were foolish words and I came to regret them.

At nine months Toni was not creeping. Nor at ten months or twelve months. This is what we saw: Toni, with demonstrated postural readiness for creeping, was unable to propel herself forward. On the floor in prone position she executed a kind of radial crawl, navigating in a circle.

Why couldn't Toni propel herself forward? Clearly there needed to be an external stimulus for the initiating of the creeping pattern. What happens in the case of the sighted child? The sighted child at nine months, let us say, is supporting himself ably on hands and knees. He sees an out-of-range object. He reaches for the object. And what we see now is a reach and a collapse, a reach and a collapse, each time moving forward until the object is attained. Within a few days the motor pattern begins to smooth out and becomes a coordinated action of hands and legs in what we call "creeping."

Why didn't Toni creep? Clearly because no external stimulus was present to initiate the creeping pattern. Even eight years later, I can still remember the stunning impact of that discovery. Toni had brought a brand new insight into the understanding of motor development in sighted children. We—all of us—had never had occasion to question the assumption that locomotion in infancy follows maturational patterns that are laid down in a biological sequence. Toni demonstrated that motor maturation follows the biological pattern but in the absence of an external stimulus for reaching, the creeping pattern will not emerge. It was risky to generalize on the basis of only one case, but we reminded ourselves that in the retrospective histories of all blind children it is common to find that creeping was never achieved, and, in fact, there is a marked delay in the achievement of all locomotor skills from this point on, with independent walking a very late achievement in the second and third years.

Between eight and ten months we begin to see something in Toni that roused our own anxieties. At times during the observational session we would see Toni stretch out on the floor, face down on the rug, and for long periods of time lie quite still, smiling softly to herself. The passive pleasure in immobility was chilling to watch. Her mother, watching this with us, looked strained and anxious. "She does that all the time," she told us. She was an experienced mother, you remember, and she knew as well as we did that no healthy baby at nine months will lie on the floor for long periods of time, smiling softly to herself. And when did Toni assume this posture? At any time, we observed, when external sources of stimulation were not available to her, i.e., if no one was talking to her, playing with her, feeding her. In these moments of non-stimulation she would fall back on this form of self-stimulation in which the ventral surface of the body was in contact with the rug.

Did this mean that Toni's mother was neglecting her? We thought not. During the same period, pleasure in mother's voice, pleasure in being held by mother were clearly seen whenever mother resumed contact with her. But in a normal busy household, where five other children must make their claims upon a mother, there were, inevitably, periods when Toni was not being played with, talked to, held in mother's arms. It happens to sighted children too.

What does a sighted child do at nine months when he is "by himself?" He occupies himself with toys, or, if he is creeping, he goes on excursions to visit the underside of the dining table or the top side of the living room couch, or the inside of the kitchen cupboard. And if he has no toy handy, and if he can't creep, he will occupy himself by looking, just plain looking around. Visual experience creates its own appetite for repetition; the hunger to see and the functional pleasure of vision are among the great entertainments of a baby after the first days of life. Vision keeps the baby "in touch" with his mother and with the world of things, giving continuity to experience. The sighted child at nine months does not have to be continually held by his mother or talked to by her in order to "be in touch" with her.

But when Toni could not touch her mother or hear her mother's voice, she was robbed of her mother and robbed of a large measure of the sensory experience that linked her to the world outside of her body. In this insubstantial, impermanent world, her own body and body sensations became at times the only certainty, the only continuous source of sensory experience in the discontinuous experience of darkness. And because proprioceptive experience provided the chief means for "keeping in touch" in the near void of blindness, and the only means for experiencing continuity of self feelings, Toni stretched out on the floor, face down upon the rug. In this posture, which afforded maximal contact between the body surface and the rug, she might obtain feelings of comfort, safety, pleasurable tactile sensations and a sense of body awareness. We are reminded too that the ventral surface of the baby's body is normally eroticized in the posture of being held against the mother's body and that pleasure, intimacy, comfort and safety are united for a lifetime in this posture —the embrace. What we saw in Toni, face down, nuzzling a rug was a form of stimulus hunger. Where vision would have insured abundant sources of stimuli and the visual alternatives to contact hunger for the mother, blindness caused this child in periods of external nonstimulation to fall back upon the poverty of body sensations. Like a starving organism that will finally ingest anything where there is not enough food, the stimulus hunger of this child led her to ingest the meager proprioceptive experience of body contact with a rug.

Later in my experience, I was to see variations of this posture in blind children. But when we first saw this in Toni we found it a chilling experience. We had not foreseen such a development in an otherwise healthy child. And remember, too, that during this period, at nine months, we were also sobered by the fact that Toni was unable to locomote in spite of the fact that she had maturational readiness for creeping. In other respects, too, Toni seemed to have reached a developmental impasse. Although she was still lively and responsive to her mother and her sisters and her brothers, there was almost no interest in toys, and at nine months she was not reaching for objects. Her mother, we observed, seemed anxious and discouraged. For the first time we saw a number of instances in which mother was manifestly out of rapport with her baby.

When we returned at ten months, the entire picture had changed. Toni's mother, entirely on her own, had purchased a walker, and within a short time Toni had become expert in getting around in it. She was still unable to creep but the walker provided mobility and Toni was cruising around the house with tremendous energy and making discoveries and rediscoveries at every port. Did she still lie down on the rug, we asked, concealing our own anxiety. Oh, no, the mother assured us. In fact, she absolutely refused to get into the prone position. Mother took Toni out of her walker and gave us a demonstration. The moment Toni was placed on the floor in the prone position, she yelled in protest and uprighted herself. This was now the posture of immobility and Toni had found mobility. The moment she was put back in her walker she stopped crying and took off like a hot rodder.

We never saw this passive prone posture again in Toni. Within three months, at thirteen months of age, Toni began walking with support, and now also creeping (!). Toni was "into everything," exploring the cupboards, the drawers, and getting into mischief. At thirteen months Toni had a small and useful vocabulary, she was using her hands for fine discriminations, and she was now expert in reaching and attaining objects on sound cue. From this point on, Toni's development progressed without any major impediments. (Only one pathological behavior appeared in the second year, and I will describe it later.)

But now what about the stereotyped prone behavior which had so alarmed us at eight and nine months? It is clear from the sequence that once Toni acquired mobility she could not even be persuaded to get back into the prone position on the floor. Mobility provided functional motor pleasure, of course, but mobility also put her in touch with a world beyond her body and a world that she could act upon: mobility gave her for the first time a sense of autonomy.

Here, we thought we had found another clue to the ego deviations encountered among blind children. If we understand that the blind child lives in a near-void for much of his waking day, he can make few discoveries about the world around him until he becomes mobile. And if mobility itself is delayed until well into the second year, he will live for a perilously long time in this near-void in which the presence of the mother or other persons, or ministrations to his own body become the only experiences which give meaning to existence. In those periods where neither sound nor touch, feeding, bath or play occur there is nothing except his own body. Now we began to understand how some blind babies may never find the adaptive routes and remain frozen in the state of body centeredness, passivity, immobility, and ultimately nondifferentiation.

I mentioned that one pathological trait was observed in Toni, beginning in the second year. Let me briefly describe it. When Toni became anxious, when she was separated even briefly from her mother or when a strange person or a strange situation signaled danger to her, she would fall into a stuporous sleep. We observed this ourselves. It was as if a light were switched off. As far as we can reconstruct the onset of this symptom, it was first manifest in connection with a brief separation from her mother. She retained this symptom as late as the fourth year when we obtained reports on her. In all other respects she was a healthy, active little girl, able to ride a trike, play ball, join in children's games. Her speech was very good; eating and sleeping were entirely satisfactory. There was only this. We asked ourselves when we would find an otherwise healthy sighted child who defended against danger by falling into a pathologic sleep. Never, of course. But then, one should ask, what defenses against danger does a blind child possess? I did not understand this until several years later.

This is a brief sketch of Toni and what Toni taught us. I should also tell you that during the same period that we were observing Toni, we took on the joint treatment of an autistic blind child and his mother. I was the child's therapist; Dr. Freedman analyzed the mother. I wish there was time to give you a report of this case as well (Fraiberg and Freedman, 1964). Perhaps it will suffice to say that Peter, the autistic nine-year-old child, taught us how blindness can lead to adaptive failure and Toni taught us how the route to successful adaptation is a perilous one for a blind baby. I worked with Peter for two years and saw him five times a week. There was considerable improvement but he never became a normal child. Today, when we get a Peter in the second year or even the third year, we know how to help him and we can bring about normal functioning. Much of what we now know we learned from Toni and from Peter.

Yet, it is worth mentioning that even with the small amount of knowledge we gained through the study of one healthy baby and one autistic blind boy we were able to help two blind babies in our Family Service Society caseload who were well on their way to autism by the time they were referred in the second year. Since we knew the danger signs and now had some pretty good hunches regarding the con- tributing causes, we worked out some simple guidance procedures which brought both babies to normal functioning within a matter of months.

In 1963 I moved from New Orleans and came to the University of Michigan. David Freedman also moved shortly afterwards to Baylor University. Since then, each of us, following his own special interests, has continued research in the area of sensory deficits.

In Ann Arbor, I received support and generous funds from my department to continue pilot work in the development of blind in- fants. Two years later we received a grant from the National Insti- tutes of Child Health and Development to expand these studies. From this point on we were in a position to study the development of blind babies on a larger scale.

## REFERENCES

Fraiberg, S., and Freedman, D. A. Studies in the ego development of the congeni- tally blind child. In *Psychoanalytic study of the child,* Vol. XIX. New York: International Universities Press, 1964, pp. 113–169.

Keeler, W. R. Autistic patterns and defective communication in blind children with retrolental fibroplasma. In P. H. Hoch and J. Zubin (Eds.), *Psychopathology of communication.* New York: Grune and Stratton, 1958.

Norris, M., Spaulding, P. J., and Brodie, F. *Blindness in children.* Chicago: Univer- sity of Chicago Press, 1957.

*Chapter 3*


# FAMILY FUNCTIONING AND CHILDHOOD ACCIDENT OCCURRENCE

## Elizabeth Moore Plionis


Accident occurrence constitutes a major health problem. It is the leading cause of morbidity and mortality for all children in the United States from birth to age fifteen.[14,15] Until recently, accidents were conceptualized from a chance perspective and were assumed to fall outside the parameters of scientific investigation.[62] Unable to influence chance as a causative agent, health practitioners directed their interventions toward mitigating the consequences of accident occurrence. Chance caused accidents. Accidents caused injuries. Injuries were treated medically. Today, accidental injuries are still treated medically as isolated episodes caused by chance.

The evidence for accident repetitiveness[4,28,34,42,47] suggests that such an approach is a mistake. Accidents appear to be both medical and behavioral. The diagnostic determination of whether a given accident is a single event or part of a repetitive pattern is critical in determining the intervention focus in order to prevent recurrence.

Indeed, it has been observed that the strict application of medical procedures to certain medical problems is often not enough to produce a healthy outcome and prevent recurrence.[58] Chaiklin and associates[13] found this the case in lead poisoning recidivism among children. Psychosocial factors have been found to form significant etiological parameters, which appear to be necessary but not sufficient precipitants of major health changes.[40,50,55,57,58] Consequently, the need for a diagnostic system capable of assessing not only presenting medical symptomatology but also the psychosocial context of that symptomatology has been recognized as essential in producing health outcome and preventing recurrence.

## REVIEW OF THE LITERATURE

Initially, researchers observed that accident frequencies varied for different subgroups in the population beyond that expected by chance.[5,62] Thus, the conceptualization of accident occurrence as an irrational act of fate falling outside the parameters of scientific investigation was called into question.

Researchers next conceptualized accident occurrence from an epidemiological perspective, in which accidents were viewed as a form of disease subject to the etiological factors of host, agent, and environment. In establishing small homogeneous groupings, this approach organized the search for factors etiologically associated with increased incidence. While serving a useful function as a simple descriptive scheme for classifying various factors associated with accidents, such a methodology proved insufficient to analyze why accidents happen.[62]

It was then hypothesized that hazards[14,20,64] caused accidents and efforts were aimed at safety-proofing the environment. A series of studies[7,14,21,60] revealed that accidents continued to occur despite environmental control programs. Subtle human causal factors were estimated to be involved in at least 70% of all accidental injuries.[28] The premise that human factors played a part in accident occurrence led to the formulation of the clinical concept of accident-proneness.

Two concepts have been used to explain individual differences in accident frequencies: accident-proneness and accident repetitiveness.[29,60] Accident-proneness assumes that differences in individual accident liabilities are due to a psychological trait characterized by inward-turning aggression. Numerous research findings have challenged the monocausal nature of this concept. Subsequently, the concept of accident repetitiveness was adopted because it could encompass a multicausal explanation. Accident repetitiveness simply denotes that some individuals have "many" accidents, while others have "few" accidents.

Indeed, two schools of thought are evident in the literature as to whether accident repetitiveness does or does not exist.[4,34,42,47] The validity of this concept for research purposes depends upon whether or not one accepts the premise that individuals differ in their accident liabilities and, if so, whether these differences are stable over time. Though the theoretical and empirical evidence for accident repetitiveness is tentative and inconclusive, this study accepted the premise of accident repetitiveness, which was found to be supported by the literature.

Those who accept accident repetitiveness as a valid research entity adopt a behavioral perspective that assumes that an accident progresses through a series of stages of development.[5,62] The difficulty in using this model for research purposes lies in the determination of just where to cut the accident developmental sequence in order to establish operational definitions and indices. Researchers first cut the developmental sequence at physical and maturational factors. Studies indicated however that children with repetitive accident histories did not differ significantly from children with non-repetitive accident histories on a variety of physical indices.[19,38,42,60]

Similarly, the presence of hazards *per se* was found to be un-related to repetitiveness.[7,14,21,60.] Demographic variables, though associated with group variations in accident frequencies, appeared to make no difference when individuals with repetitive accident histories were compared with each other or with their accident-free counterparts.[33,60]

Researchers next looked at individual adjustment. Assuming normality, some researchers identified "being-a-dare devil" and high activity level with frequent accident occurrence.[21,36,38,42,60] Those who assumed some type of pathology, found an association between aggressive behavior and repetitiveness,[1,2,17,35,48] though no cause-effect relationship between aggressive personality type and accident repetitiveness was conclusively substantiated.[36]

A wide range of psychological indices indicative of individual maladjustment have been found to be associated with accident repetitiveness.[9,21,36,38,42,43,46,60,61] So many, in fact, that Mellinger and Manheimer,[46] regarding them as virtually useless, attempted to explain them away altogether by using an exposure/coping model of accident occurrence. Unsuccessful, the authors concluded that individual maladjustment is an important variable in accident liability.

Researchers also explored the child with a repetitive accident history within the context of his or her social network. Associations were found to exist between repetitive childhood accident occurrence and indices of parental pathology.[16,19,39,43,60] Associations were also observed between repetitiveness and the quality of the parental marital relationship, as well as the degree of family cohesion.[6,33, 36,37,41,60,61,63] A correlation was found between the absence of the father from the home and frequent accident occurrence among children.[60,61,65]

It has generally been acknowledged that a relationship exists between stress and psychosomatic illness.[16,50,57] More recently, researchers have found a relationship between stress and the onset of physical illness.[40,55] Individuals with repetitive accident histories have also been found to have a history of psychosomatic illness or a history of numerous physical illnesses.[33,38,42,60] Studies indicate that stress is an important variable to consider, but the evidence as to its temporary or chronic nature in relation to accident causation is inconclusive.[16,38,60]

Accident repetitiveness is an empirical generalization still in need of explanation. Though numerous associations have been found between psychosocial variables and accident occurrence, the results have been generally inconclusive. A parsimonious unit of analysis, capable of integrating and giving theoretical relevance to those findings, was needed. The study to be reported in this paper looked to the family as that viable unit of analysis.

## THE FAMILY AS A DIAGNOSTIC UNIT

Researchers have found that the family is a primary diagnostic unit in health and medical care. The family has been shown to be a contributory factor in the etiology, care, and treatment of both physical and mental illness, as well as a basic unit of interaction and transaction in health care.[40] It constitutes the most important psychosocial context within which health problems occur and are resolved. The premise that individual pathology and familial pathology are interrelated underscores a major portion of the literature and research drawn from marital and family therapy.[51]

The use of the family as a diagnostic unit in health care, however, has been plagued by methodological imprecision, limited empirical inquiry, and minimal involvement or integration with theory. While some studies have looked at the family,[37,60] no study has investigated accident repetitiveness where the family has been conceptually and methodologically clear. This study chose to conceptualize the family from a structure-functional perspective because its theoretical propositions seemed to be compatible with the empirical data reported in the accident literature.

## STUDY RATIONALE

THEORETICAL FRAMEWORK.[45,52,53] Structure-functionalism is distinct as a theory in that it assumes causal priority of the whole over the part. The concept "system" is given explicit central theoretical status, becoming the point from which all analyses of structure and process are made. It borrows from Gestalt theory the premise that, in any behavorial system, the best equilibrium will be achieved, and from anthropology the premise that all units are system-determined and system-relevant. It brings the problem of interaction into central focus, analyzing the conditions under which eunomia or dysnomia exist.

From these more general propositions, Pareto and Parsons derived the concept of the "social system," a new whole composed of a plurality of interacting persons. Fundamental to this concept, is the premise that individuals attempt to meet their personal and social needs through prescribed interaction roles with others.

According to Parsons, a given social system can exist only if a sufficient proportion of its members perform the essential roles required to maintain it with an adequate degree of effectiveness. So conceived, role, not the individual actor, is the proper unit of analysis of the social system.

Consistent with this perspective, Bell and Vogel[8] conceptualized the family as a (semi) social system, which is under various internal and external pressures toward dissolution or maintenance. So conceived, it is maintained that individual behavior can be best analyzed in terms of the system's structural shaping of the behavior or the behavior's functional contribution to the system. The family is primary over the individual.

Geismar's family assessment schedule/scale[23] constitutes the major effort to define family functioning in a manner theoretically consistent with the structure-functional perspective. Consistent with Parson's premise of system maintenance, Geismar operationally defines thirty-two tasks corresponding to the role expectations designated by society as essential for the family to perform in order to maintain itself as a functional system within the community. By assessing the amount of discrepancy existing between these role expectations and a family's actual role performance, Geismar obtains a measure of adequacy of family functioning.

This study is based on the assertion that structural-functional theory provides a rationale, consistent with the data, that is capable of making the terms and relationship variables of accident repetitiveness more abstract, *i.e.,* capable of theoretically conceptualizing these terms and relationships. Accordingly, the empirically documented phenomenon of accident occurrence is transformed into the more abstract concept of individual functioning, to form the explanadum. Similarly, the developmental accident sequence, found to be associated with numerous psychosocial factors, is transformed into the more abstract concept of family functioning, to form the explanans.

Following from this argument is the proposition that family functioning is causally influential[12] in individual functioning, which gives rise to the hypothesis to be tested in this study—that there is an association between the adequacy of family functioning and the index child's accident rate.

## PROCEDURE

The study set out to examine the relationship between family functioning and childhood repetitive accident occurrence. Family functioning, the independent variable, was viewed from a structure-functional theoretical perspective, and assessed by Geismar's scale.[23] (A pretest to determine reliability yielded results consistent with those reported elsewhere in the literature.[24,35]) Accident occurrence, the dependent variable, was viewed, from a behavioral perspective, as a form of human behavior susceptible to the same kinds of scientific investigation as are other forms of human behavior.[29,62]

An accident was defined operationally as a bodily injury that requires medical attention and is not the product of disease or deliberate conscious intent (*e.g.,* abuse, suicide). Frequency of accident occurrence was determined by the index child's accident rate (the number of accidents in the child's medical record divided by the child's age). The literature supports the use of medical records as a data source[41] and number of accidents as an indicator of accident liability.[4,47] To avoid any arbitrary determination of "repetitiveness," accident rates were used and ranked throughout all analyses.

A survey design was established to test the hypothesis that there is an association between adequacy of family functioning and the index child's accident rate. An alternative variable, family stress, was also explored, using the Holmes-Rahe Social Readjustment Rating Scale.[31] The design employed a semi-structured interview approach on a small clinical sample ($N$=15) of families with children hospitalized at a major Eastern hospital during a five-month study period. Participation in the study was completely voluntary, and based upon informed consent. Of twenty families meeting the selection criteria, one interview could not be completed and four families declined to participate. Since it is not known to what extent the decision not to participate biased the sample, homogeneous groups were formed on the basis of collected demographic data for purposes of analysis.

Table 1   Characteristics of Sample (N = 15)

| Variable | N | Variable | N |
|---|---|---|---|
| Age of Child | | Race of Child | |
| Infants (2 and under) | 5 | Black | 11 |
| Children (3–11) | 10 | White | 4 |
| Interview Source | | Sex of Child | |
| Both parents | 4 | Male | 12 |
| Mother only | 10 | Female | 3 |
| Father only | 1 | | |
| Family Structure | | Type of Injury | |
| Single-parent | 5 | Infants: | |
| Two-parent[a] | 10 | Burns | 2 |
| | | Fractures | 3 |
| Family Size | | Children: | |
| Two members | 1 | Fractures | 1 |
| Three members | 2 | Perforations/lacerations | 4 |
| Four members | 5 | Concussions | 2 |
| Five members | 4 | Other | 3 |
| Six members | 1 | | |
| Seven members | 1 | Agent of Injury | |
| Eight members | 0 | Infants: | |
| Nine members | 1 | Falls | 3 |
| | | Other | 2 |
| Socioeconomic Class | | Children: | |
| I | 0 | Falls | 1 |
| II | 2 | Auto | 2 |
| III | 3 | Collision—object, person | 2 |
| IV | 2 | Struck by flying object | 3 |
| V | 8 | Other | 2 |

[a] Includes stepparent.

Hospitalization served to standardize the sample subjects on the basis of the severity of the injury. A family was assessed and given a functioning score prior to the search of the medical record to obtain the child's accident history. Spearman's rank order correlation coefficient $r_s$ and the Mann-Whitney U test were used to analyze the data.

## FINDINGS

RESEARCH HYPOTHESIS.  Relevant sample characteristics are summarized in Table 1. Using Spearman's correlation coefficient to test the hypothesis, relationship between family functioning and accident occurrence for the entire sample was found to be not significant. However, when the sample was split into two age groups, infants (birth through two years, $N=5$) and children (ages three through eleven, $N=10$), a highly significant relationship was found for the latter group.*

AGE: SUPPRESSOR VARIABLE.  Reflection on the possible nature of age as a suppressor variable[56] led to the conjecture that the accident rate observed in the case of the infants was not necessarily their true accident rate. In fact, the younger the child is when the index accident occurs, the higher the accident liability implied. If infants were observed over a full three- or four-year period, an observation norm used in most accident research studies,[33,36,38,41,42] their accident rates would probably average out at a level lower than that observed by dividing the one observed accident over their short life span. According to this reasoning, the suppressor variable is one that distinguishes between sample subjects where the observed accident rates are true rates (children) and those sample subjects (infants) where the observed accident rates are not necessarily the true rates, due to lack of adequate observation time. In order to control this suppressor variable, analyses were conducted on split samples: infants and children. The balance of this discussion is based on analysis of the sample of children.

*Statistical elaboration of family functioning scores and index child's accident rates for the full sample, and broken down separately for infants and for children, is available from the author.

EXTRANEOUS VARIABLES.    Race, sex, and socioeconomic class were indicated in the accident literature to be extraneous variables. Holding these variables constant, statistical analysis revealed that the correlation between family functioning and accident occurrence held for the subgroups of seven males ($p=.028$, controlling on sex), seven blacks ($p=.028$, controlling on race), and six black males ($p=.05$, controlling on race and sex). Inspection of the subgroup "black males" showed that all are members of socioeconomic classes IV and V (Hollingshead two-factor socioeconomic class index).

## Component Variable Specification

Family functioning is a global concept. As such, it is unspecific. Rosenberg's technique of specification[56] attempts to enhance understanding of a global concept by specifying its decisive components. To answer the question, "What is it about family functioning that gives rise to repetitive or nonrepetitive accident patterns?", each of the eight major categories and each of the twenty-five subcategories of Geismar's schedule were tested to determine whether an association existed between any category or subcategory score and the accident rates of the children. Results of this analysis are summarized in Table 2, and will be elaborated upon in the following discussion.

FAMILY RELATIONSHIPS.    As a major category, "family relationships" reflect the adequacy of interpersonal interaction among family members. The pattern of relationships found in this category and its four subcategories suggests that the greater the disturbance in the marital solidarity, the higher the index child's accident rate. These findings are compatible with those of others.[6,33,36,37,41,60,61,63]

The failure to find a significant relationship for the subcategory of "parent-child relationship" suggests that repetitiveness is more indicative of disturbed family relationships than a disturbed parent-child relationship. This finding challenges the view that accident repetitiveness reflects a parent-child struggle over the discipline/punishment or dependency/independency clusters associated with child rearing practices.[5,60]

IINDIVIDUAL BEHAVIOR AND ADJUSTMENT.    This study did not find an association between repetitive accident patterns among the index children and indices of individual behavior and adjustment problems

Table 2    Relationship of Family Functioning to Accident
Patterns of Index Children

| Variable | Signif- icance | Variable | Signif- icance |
|---|---|---|---|
| Family Relationships | 0.004 | Economic Practices | NS |
| Marital relationship | 0.004 | Source and amount of income | NS |
| Parent-child relationship | NS | Job situation | b |
| Sibling relationship | NS | Use of money | NS |
| Family solidarity | 0.004 | | |
| | | Home and Household Practices | 0.033 |
| Individual Behavior | NS | Physical facilities | NS |
| Mother | NS | Housekeeping standards | NS |
| Father | 0.033a | | |
| Children | NS | Health Conditions and Practices | 0.033 |
| Index child | NS | Health conditions | 0.048 |
| | | Health practices | 0.033 |
| Child Care and Training | NS | | |
| Physical care | b | Use of Community Resources | b |
| Training methods | 0.017 | School | b |
| | | Church | b |
| Social Activities | 0.016 | Health resources | b |
| Informal associations | 0.016 | Social agencies | b |
| Formal associations | b | Recreational agencies | b |

a Father's presence or absence in the home.
b Probabilities could not be determined either because of too few sample points, or because all sample points clustered in the same functioning class (i.e., "above" or "below" average).

among their mothers or their fathers. This is contrary to findings reported by others.[19,39,43,60] Reassessment of the fathers' behavior in terms of their presence or absence from the home did reveal a significant correlation between the fathers' absence from the home and high accident rates among the index children. This corresponds to findings reported elsewhere in the literature.[60,61,65]

The presence or absence of a child with a repetitive accident history did not appear to be predictive of sibling behavior and adjustment. Though others[19,33] have found disturbed behavior among the siblings of children with repetitive accident histories, this study found that children with repetitive accident histories sometimes had siblings who manifested disturbed behavior and sometimes had siblings whose behavior was normal, as did the children with nonrepetitive accident histories.

Contradictory findings have been reported in the literature as to whether[36,46,60] or not[38] individual maladjustment plays a part in accident repetitiveness. This study found that the presence or absence of a repetitive accident history did not appear to be indicative of the overall behavior and adjustment of the index child. As was the case with sibling behavior, it was found that some children manifested individual behavior independently of their accident histories.

CARE AND TRAINING. All parents were found to give adequate care to their children. While some disagreement and inconsistency was found to exist between parents on how to discipline their children, the parents of those children with the highest accident rates felt they lost control over their ability to effectively discipline their children. This corresponds to similar findings reported by Langford.[38]

SOCIAL ACTIVITIES. This major category reflects the relationship found in its subcategory, "informal associations." Parents of children with repetitive accident histories were generally found to be devoid of informal supportive interpersonal relationships both within and without the family structure. Similar findings are reported by Holter and Friedman in their study of child abuse,[32] while contradictory findings are reported by Sobel.[60]

ECONOMIC PRACTICES. No association was found between accident rate rankings and the major category, "economic practices," and its three subcategories. The most likely explanation of this lies in the fact that the sample of children was fairly homogeneous regarding socioeconomic class.

HOME AND HOUSEHOLD PRACTICES. A significant association was found between the children's accident rate rankings and this major category, although no such association was found to exist for either of its two subcategories. The relationship is due, therefore, primarily to a weighting, which took into account a family's subjective feeling about their living facilities. Whether or not a family lived in public housing was not predictive of.accident patterns; however, intensely hating to live there, as represented by the weighting of the major category score, was found to be predictive. Everyone interviewed who lived in high-rise public housing did not want to live there; however, some were desperately distressed about it (e.g., "Get me out. They only put bad people there or crazy people." "It's like a prison." "You don't live there, you just exist." "I hate it.") This finding is similar to that reported by Holter and Friedman.[32]

HEALTH CONDITIONS AND PRACTICES. Children with repetitive accident histories were found to have a history of numerous physical and psychosomatic illnesses when compared to children with nonrepetitive accident histories. This corroborates similar findings made by others.[33,38,42] There appears to be some relationship between the sick-prone and the accident-prone child.

USE OF COMMUNITY RESOURCES. No comparative analysis was possible for this major category and its five subcategories.

## Family Stress: An Alternative Hypothesis

The Holmes-Rahe social readjustment rating scale was used to test the alternative hypothesis that circumscribed family dysfunctioning due to a temporarily stressful period or event, rather than ongoing systemic family dysfunctioning, was the more powerful explanatory concept. Analysis showed that accident rate rankings appeared to be independent of high or low family stress in the two-year period preceding the index accident. This suggests that: 1) the accident event did not cause the family stress, and 2) the presence or absence of stress *per se* cannot explain repetitive accident occurrence.

Furthermore, no association was found between families' scores on the Holmes-Rahe scale and the families' scores on the family functioning assessment scale. This suggests that something about family functioning is either able to mitigate or not able to mitigate stress. The fact that many families function adequately in the presence of high stress is indicative of the power of internal family processes to overcome overwhelming external pressures. Family functioning, not family stress, is the more powerful explanatory concept.

## THEORETICAL INTERPRETATION

Accidents need to be understood in the context of the family as a system of interpersonal relationships involving all family members. Dysfunctioning in one part of the system leads inevitably to disturbance elsewhere. Should disequilibrium occur in the system, the system's components act to restore equilibrium. It is impossible, for example, for a mother to be unhappily married without imposing serious strain on the husband and children, or for the father to be absent from the home without imposing a similar strain.

A member affects the functioning of the family system in direct proportion to his or her role importance to the family unit. It follows therefore, and the evidence supports it, that the causal flow in childhood repetitive accident occurrence proceeds from a disturbance in the marital relationship, such that family solidarity is threatened. Parental roles are key to maintaining the family system. As parents attempt to cope with marital problems, their interactions and roles with the children experience a shift. Some children react to this disturbance by developing repetitive accident patterns.

In such cases, the family seems to legitimize accidents. One is permitted to be hurt and dependent if it is a result of an accident—after all, no one is to blame. This ties in with the observation that children with repetitive accident histories also have a history of high incidence of illness. Most likely this high incidence of illness tends to have a desensitizing effect on the family, resulting in decreased legitimization of the sick role. Also, families may wish to avoid the implication inherent in high illness incidence, that they are responsible for the child's failure to get well and stay well. Accidents are caused by chance; thus no blame is assumed or assigned.

This interpretation is consistent with the findings that the children's accident rate rankings were associated with family functioning and not associated with indices of individual maladjustment. Accident repetitivenss appears to be due to family disorganization, rather than to the personality characteristics of the child or a disturbed parent-child relationship.

It has been observed that illnesses tend to bring a family closer together. Accidents probably serve the same function. Not only do they reflect a child's way of coping—attempting to meet his or her needs within a disorganized family—they also serve to affect the family structure and functioning through role and interaction shifts such that a new equilibrium can be established. An accident allows a mother to redirect her attention from preoccupation with other family problems to the nurturing role. This is compatible with the findings that both the mother's psychic depletion[39] and lack of parent-child closeness[43,61] are associated with childhood repetitive poisonings. An accident allows the child to meet his or her needs for meaningful contact with the mother.

The accident also shifts responsibility for the child's welfare from the family to the hospital or health care system. This shift frequently allows a parent, who is coping with other problems in the family system, some relief and support. This is particularly beneficial, if not crucial, for those parents who are severely stressed and lack an interpersonal support system. Holter and Friedman noted that troubled families often seek medical care at a time when family stresses, other than illnesses, are too much to tolerate.[32]

Indeed, this study showed that parents of children with repetitive accident histories made frequent use of the emergency room for their children, who suffered a variety of illnesses as well as injuries.

## IMPLICATIONS

ACCIDENT SEQUENCE.   Treatment intervention is contingent upon how one views the etiology of an injury. An accident is an *ex post facto* determination. Traditionally, health practitioners have relied upon the credence of the accident sequence, the age of the child at the time of injury onset, and the type of injury as diagnostic criteria for classifying an injury as an accident. Child abuse further complicates the diagnostic process when a child appears in an emergency room with an injury.

When the accident sequences, the scores on the assessment scale, and the children's accident histories were all compared, it was discovered that the accident sequence, in and of itself, appeared to have little diagnostic power, if any. It was found that sequences essentially the same: 1) could be accepted or questioned by health practitioners, 2) could be associated with either a single accident history or a repetitive accident history, and 3) showed no association with family functioning scores.

AGE.   Reliance on the age of the child at the onset of injury does not appear to be a very powerful diagnostic indicator either. As stated previously, statistical analysis of the group of infants in this study was not possible because of the inability to determine their true accident rates due to an inadequate period of observation. Inspection of this sample of infants showed, however, that in four out of five cases family functioning was judged to be above average, and in the one remaining family to be marginal. This observation suggests that infants do have true accidents despite the adequacy of care given by well functioning families. Elmer and associates[18] offer corroborative evidence for this observation in their study of infant injuries.

TYPE OF INJURY. Holter and Friedman[32] attempted to distinguish abuse from accidents by looking at the type of incurred injury. Subsequently, they empirically labeled those injuries found to be associated with abuse as "high-risk" and all other injuries as "low-risk." According to their injury typology, 87 percent of the injuries in this study would be classified as "high-risk," yet in no instance were the injuries found to be due to abuse or neglect. Furthermore, their typology was found to be incapable of distinguishing between single and repetitive accident occurrence, as both types of accidents are found in both "low" and "high-risk" injury categories.

CHILD ABUSE. Child abuse and repetitive accident occurrence parallel each other in that, for each, the syndrome does not occur with the presenting incident of injury. A history of previous injuries could be indicative of either abuse or repetitive accident occurrence. This study did not address, nor did it intend to address, the issues inherent in defining an injury as abuse or accident. Cognizance of this issue emerged as a result of the study. Its resolution requires research that is conceptually and methodologically designed toward that end. However, it has been observed elsewhere,[18] as in this study, that frequently health practitioners confuse abuse and accident occurrence, since neither phenomenon is well understood. Successful treatment of each requires their differentiation.

## CONCLUSIONS

These findings should not be interpreted to mean that where there is family dysfunctioning there will be repetitive accident occurrence. As a global concept, family dysfunctioning can be manifested in a variety of individual dysfunctioning behaviors. This study simply states that an accident should be regarded as a possible recurring symptom requiring further assessment. The study offers some evidence that family assessment could be used to increase the therapeutic potential of those diagnostic indicators currently used to assess the etiology of childhood injuries. As such, it could be used to guide the intervention focus in order to produce health outcome and prevent recurrence. This would appear to be important, as marked incongruence was observed between the family and health practitioners, as well as among the health practitioners themselves, in defining a childhood injury as abuse, neglect, repetitive or single accident occurrence.

To the extent that accident repetitiveness is defined as a family problem, effective treatment must include measures designed to strengthen the family unit. Medical treatment of the injury is not enough. Husband and Hinton[33] offered evidence that families who have a child with a repetitive accident history can be helped by defining with them the areas in which they are having difficulty, and by helping them understand the connection between these difficulties and the accident patterns of their child. When such an approach is used, children frequently stop injuring themselves.[33]

## REFERENCES

1. Ackerman, N. And Chidester, L. 1963. Accidental self-injury in children. Arch. Pediat. 53(11):711–721.

2. Alexander. F. 1949. The accident-prone individual. Pub. Hlth Rep. 64(2): 357–362

3. American Humane Association (Childrens Division). 1971. National Symposium on Child Abuse. Denver, Colorado.

4. Arbous, A. and Kerrich, J. 1951. Accident statistics and the concept of accident proneness. Biometrics 7(4):340–432

5. Association for the Aid of Crippled Children. 1961. Behavioral Approaches to Accident Research. Association for the Aid of Crippled Children. New York.

6. Backett, E. 1959. Social patterns of road accidents to children. Brit. Med. J. 1:409–413.

7. Baltimore, C. and Meyer, R. 1968. A study of storage, child behavorial traits, and mothers' knowledge in fifty-two poisoned families and fifty-two comparison families. Pediatrics 42(2):312–317.

8. Bell, N. and Vogel, E., eds. 1968. A Modern Introduction to the Family. Free Press, New York.

9. Birnback, S. 1947. A comparative study of accident-repeaters and accident-free pupils. Doctoral Dissertation, New York School of Education, New York.

10. Bonjean, C., Hill, R. and McLemore, D. 1967. Sociological Measurement: An Inventory of Scales and Indices. Chandler Publishing Co., San Francisco.

11. Brown, C. and Ghisell, E. 1948. Accident proneness among street car motormen and motor coach operators. J. Appl. Psychol. 32(1):20–24.

12. Burr, W. 1973. Theory Construction and the Sociology of the Family. John Wiley, New York.

13. Chaiklin, H. et al. 1974. Recurrence of lead poisoning in children. Soc. Wk 19(2): 196–201

14. Department of Health, Education and Welfare. 1971. Children and Youth: Selected Health Statistics United States: 1958–1968. National Health Survey Series 10. Government Printing Office, Washington, D.C.

15. Department of Health, Education and Welfare. 1970. The Health of Children —1970. Public Health Service. Government Printing Office, Washington, D.C.

16. Dunbar, H. 1943. Psychosomatic Diagnosis. Hoeber, New York.

17. Dunbar, H. 1947. Mind and Body: Psychosomatic Medicine. Random House, New York.

18. Elmer, E. et al. 1971. Studies of child abuse and infant accidents. *In* Mental Health Program Report–5, National Institutes of Mental Health, eds. Government Printing Office. Washington, D.C.

19. Fabian, A. and Bender, J. 1947. Head injury in children: predisposing factors. Amer. J. Orthopsychiat. 17(1):68–79

20. Foote, N. 1961. Sociological factors in childhood accidents. In Behavioral Approaches to Accident Research. Association for the Aid of Crippled Children, eds. Association for the Aid of Crippled Children, New York.

21. Fuller, E. 1948. Injury-prone children. Amer. J. Orthopsychiat. 18(4):708–723.

22. Fuller, E. and Baune, H. 1951. Injury proneness and adjustment in second grade: sociometric study. Sociometry 14(2):210–225.

23. Geismar, L. 1971. Family and Community Functioning: A Manual of Measurement for Social Work Practice and Policy. Scarecrow Press, Metuchen, N.J.

24. Geismar, L. and Ayres, B. 1959. A method for evaluating the social functioning of families under treatment. Soc. Wk 4(1):102–108.

25. Geismar, L., Lasorte, M. and Ayres, B. 1962. Measuring family disorganization. Marr. Fam. Living 24(1):51–56.

26. Greenwood, M. and Yule, G. 1920. An enquiry into the nature of frequency distributions representative of multiple happenings, with particular reference to the occurance of multiple attacks of disease or of repeated accidents. J. Royal Statist. Society 83:255–279.

27. Gregg, G. and Elmer, E. 1969. Infant injuries: accident or abuse? Pediatrics 44 (3):434–439.

28. Hacker, H. and Suchman, E. 1963. A sociological approach to accident research. Soc. Problems 10(4):383–389.

29. Haddon, W., Suchman, F. and Klein, D. 1964. Accident Research: Methods and Approaches. Harper and Row, New York.

30. Hill, R. and Hansen, D. 1965. The identification of conceptual frameworks utilized in family study. In Sourcebook in Marriage and the Family, M. Sussman ed. Houghton-Mifflin, Boston.

31. Holmes, T. and Rahe, R. 1967. The social readjustment rating scale. J. Psychosomat. Res. 11(2):213–218.

32. Holter, J. and Friedman, S. 1969. Child abuse: early case finding in the emergency department. Pediatrics 42(1):128–138.

33. Husband, P. and Hinton, P. 1972. Families of children with repeated accidents. Arch. Dis. Childhd 47(6):396–400.

34. Jacobs, H. 1960. Conceptual and methodological problems in accident research. *In* Behavioral Approaches to Accident Research, Association for the aid of Crippled Children eds. Association for the Aid of Crippled Children, New York.

35. Klein, M. 1937. Psycho-Analysis of Children. Hogarth, London.

36. Krall, V. 1953. Personality characteristics of accident-repeating children. J. Abnorm. Soc. Psychol. 48(1)99–107.

37. Kurokawa, M. 1966. Childhood accidents as a measure of sociol integration. Canad. Rev. Sociol. Anthropol. 3:67–83.

38. Langford, W. et al. 1952. Pilot study of childhood accidents: preliminary report. Pediatrics 11(10):405–413.

39. Lewis, M. et al. 1966. An exploration study of accidental ingestion of poison in young children. J. Amer. Acad. Child Psychiat. 5(1–4):255–271.

40. Litman, T. 1974. The family as a basic unit in health and medical care: a social-behavioral overview. Soc. Sci. Med. 8(9):495–519.

41. Manheimer, D. et al. 1966. 50,000 child-years of accidental injuries. Pub. Hlth Rep. 81(3):519–533.

42. Manheimer, D. and Mellinger, G. 1967. Personality characteristics of the child accident repeater. Child Develpm. 38(2):491–513.

43. Marcus, I. et al. 1960–1961. An interdisciplinary approach to accident patterns in children. Monogr. Soc. Res. Child Develpm. 25–26(2):1–79.

44. Maritz, J. 1950. On the validity of inferences drawn from the fitting of poisson and negative binomial distributions to observed accident data. Psychol. Bull. 47(5):434–443.

45. Martindale, D. 1960. The Nature and Type of Sociological Theory. Houghton-Mifflin, Boston.

46. Mellinger, G. and Manheimer, D. 1967. An exposure coping model of accident liability among children. J. Hlth Soc. Behav. 8(2):96–106.

47. Mellinger, G. et al. 1965. A mathematical model with applications to a study of accident repeatedness among children. J. Amer. Statist. Assoc. 60:1046–1059.

48. Menninger, K. 1938. Man Against Himself. Harcourt Brace, New York.

49. Newbold, E. 1927. Practical applications to the statistics of repeated events, particularly of industrial accidents. J. Royal Statist. Society 90(3):487–535.

50. Myres, J. et al. 1972. Life events and mental status: a longitudinal study. J. Hlth Soc. Behav. 13(4):398–406.

51. Olson, D. 1970. Marital and family therapy: integrative review and critique. J. Marr. Fam. 32(4):501–538.

52. Parsons, T. 1951. The Social System. Free Press, Glencoe, Ill.

53. Parsons, T. et al. 1955. Family, Socialization and Interaction Process. Free Press, New York.

54. Porterfield, A. 1960. Traffic fatalities, suicides and homocide. Amer. Sociol. Rev. 25(6):897–901.

55. Rahe, R. et al. 1964. Social stress and illness onset. J. Psychosomat. Res. 8(4):35–44.

56. Rosenberg, M. 1968. The Logic of Survey Analysis. Basic Books, New York.

57. Selye, H. 1956. The Stress of Life. McGraw-Hill, New York.

58. Shochet, B. and Lisansky, E. 1968. Making the 'double diagnosis': technique of comprehensive medical diagnosis. Psychosomatics 9(4):12–15.

59. Siegel, S. 1956. Nonparametric Statistics for the Behavioral Sciences. McGraw-Hill, New York.

60. Sobel, R. 1970. The psychiatry implications of accidental poisoning in childhood. Pediat. Clin. N.A. 17(3):653–685.

61. Sobel, R. and Margolis, J. 1965. Repetitive poisoning in children: a psychological study. Pediatrics 30(10):641–651.

62. Suchman, E. 1961. A conceptual analysis of the accident phenomenon. Soc. Problems 8(3):241–253.

63. Suchman, E. 1965. Cultural and social factors in accident occurrence and control. J. Occupational Med. 7(10):487–492.

64. Suchman, E. 1970. Accidents and social deviance. J. Hlth Soc. Behav. 11(1): 4–15.

65. Wehrle, P. et al. 1961. The epidemiology of accidental poisoning in an urban population: the repeater problem in accidental poisoning. Pediatrics 27(10): 614–620.

*Chapter 4*

# ACTIVITY PREFERENCES OF COMMUNITY-RESIDING AGED AS A GUIDE FOR PRACTICE EMPHASES

## Joan F. Robertson

Given the contradictory theoretical and empirical literature, it is difficult, if not impossible, to assess adequately the activity preferences of older adults, particularly those relating to types and frequency of activities with families and friends, and in organizations. The intent of this writer is to challenge the criticism that practitioners have "oversimplified the problems of the aged" (Rosow, 1967) and have been insensitive to their needs. Unfortunately, in the absence of data or caught in the substantial time lag between the acquisition of research and the dissemination of that knowledge for use, professionals have had to practice on the basis of sound judgment and intuition. This does not imply a lack of concern with the subtler social needs and interests of the aged, but rather a capacity and compelling need to deal with the exigencies of the present.

Dr. Robertson is Associate Professor, School of Social Work, University of Wisconsin-Madison, 425 Henry Mall, Madison, Wisconsin 53706. This research was partially supported by Small Grant MH19773 from the National Institute of Mental Health. The author is especially grateful to Jan Greenberg for his helpful advice and assistance with the practice component of this manuscript. His current practice experience provided the substance from which it was possible to bridge research and practice.

The phenomenon of a large aging population has been described as one of the most dramatic and influential developments of the 20th century. Never before in history have there been so many older people, nor have we had so many people live for so long (Brody, 1970). Whereas at the turn of the century people aged 65 and over represented roughly 4% of the total population (3 million), they now approximate 10% of the overall population (20 million). Combined with projections for drastic changes in the population structure, these figures pose challenging and complex problems for human services professions, and specifically for the functions and roles of practitioners. (For a detailed analysis of the changing U.S. age distribution and the complex service and planning issues for current and future age cohorts see Cutler & Hartootyan, 1975, pp. 31–69.)

More and more, practitioners serving present and future cohorts of aged persons will look to research and educational communities for a knowledge base that they can translate into practice specifics and utilize in meeting human needs. Recognizing that the elderly face a unique clustering and abruptness of problems resulting from the inevitable decrements of natural aging, professionals are constantly plagued with the need to identify what types of supportive or linking services might help older persons relate and adapt to the changes of late life. This is particularly evident in the social arena where practitioners have been criticized for concentrating on the more obvious material and medical problems of the elderly and neglecting their subtler social needs which are less apparent but no less compelling (Rosow, 1967).

Service-oriented professionals are constantly grappling with decisions as to what kind of direct services and programs should be developed to ensure participation and membership in social groups for individuals who desire such an outlet. On the other hand, some do not wish to pursue such outlets, leaving practitioners with the challenging question of deciphering how else they might best facilitate the inevitable readjustment processes of late life because of major role changes due to death, retirement, loneliness, isolation, or transition roles (e.g., a shift from being healthy to being partially disabled or from being married to being divorced or widowed). Generally, professionals resort to three kinds of support systems: families, friends, and community involvement. However, a number of questions have yet to be answered! Are these supports the ones most desired by the aged to meet their needs? Are they realistic? Do they make any difference in terms of the morale or life satisfaction of aged persons?

The literature presents conflicting evidence as to the kinds of support systems desired by the aged, their involvement in activity patterns with each, whether participation in activities is a correlate of life satisfaction, or if activity levels vary on the basis of such factors as age, sex, or marital and work status. Proponents of disengagement theory, for example, would argue that as a result of aging, individuals inevitably and voluntarily withdraw from social participation in society to conserve energy and have time for introspection (Cumming, & Henry, 1961; Henry, 1964, pp. 415–418). From this perspective, one would predict that many community-residing older persons would not be interested in more than a limited degree of social participation and group membership but still indicate positive life satisfaction. Activity theorists, on the other hand, challenge the disengagement position and posit that life satisfaction, self-esteem, and health are significantly related to opportunities for maintaining a high frequency of diverse activities (Maddox, 1963). If this is the case, one would predict that the elderly within the community would desire and take advantage of a variety of activities that would ensure social participation and group membership, and if these were not available, one would predict a low life satisfaction. This perspective is not unlike the views of social integration theorists who claim that high life satisfaction occurs when the aged are afforded opportunities for social participation and group membership (Rosow, 1967). This, they say, ensures social integration, which is a correlate of life satisfaction and is maintained when the aged can preserve desired activity levels that are continuations of middle-aged behavior patterns.

The gap between theory and reality is equally inconclusive as one tries to obtain information on the preferred activity patterns of older adults and the relationship between involvement in these activities and life satisfaction. The author reviewed the literature to assess four spheres of activity: family, friends, organizations, and work. Each of these spheres of activity may be regarded as primary, alternative, or compensatory opportunities for social participation and group membership that may be related to life satisfaction and that were deemed reflective of the preferred activity level of community-residing older adults. Empirical findings are as contradictory as the previously detailed theoretical perspectives in rendering specific information as to the preferred activity patterns of the aged and the relationship between involvement in family, friendship, organizational, and work activities and life satisfaction. (For a more detailed review of the contradictory evidence of the relationship between family and friendship interactions and life satisfaction see Wood & Robertson.)

Blau (1973), for example, reports that peer friendships are more valuable than family relationships to the older individual who makes shifts from work to retirement or from being a spouse to being a widow. In making her case, she cites a number of other studies that revealed no positive relationship between frequency of involvement with families and life satisfaction; in fact, in some cases, there were indications of an inverse relationship (Blau, 1957; Gravatt, 1953; Kerckhoff, 1966, pp. 139–159; Kutner et al., 1956, pp. 267–269). Riley and Foner, on the other hand, believe that families are far more important to the elderly than are friends (Riley & Foner, 1968, p. 61; Riley, Foner, Hess, & Toby, 1969, pp. 951–982). Friends, they say, are no more than a substitute for kinship associations.

The evidence pointing to the value of friendship activities is slightly less problematic, but it, too, suffers from some degree of confusion, particularly as it relates to types of activities friends share and the frequency of involvement in those activities. Empirical sources indicate that friends act as valuable sources or effective buffers against personal pains produced by major role losses such as widowhood, retirement, divorce, or decreased social participation (Blau, 1973; Lopata, 1971a, 1971b; Lowenthal & Haven, 1968; Rosow, 1967, pp. 79–128). A colleague and I have reported on the higher value placed on friendships in adult life than on kinship interaction (Wood & Robertson, 1977). A number of other studies demonstrate a positive relationship between interaction with friends and life satisfaction or happiness (Blau, 1973; Lemon et al., 1972; Lowenthal & Haven, 1968; B. Phillips, 1961; D. Phillips, 1973, pp. 245–253).

The evidence pointing to the value and use of organizational activities to older adults is, indeed, scarce. There have been studies that indicate that older individuals react to widowhood by immersing themselves in community or work activities (Rosow, 1967; Shanas et al., 1968). On the other hand, the literature indicates that there are other older adults who have maintained a lifelong commitment to work and organizational associations on a par with family involvements (Kutner et al., 1956, pp. 267–269; Wood, 1963).

## THE PRESENT STUDY

The objective of this paper is to report the results of a study that addresses some of the subtler social needs and interests of community-residing aged. The author examined older individuals' preferences for social participation and group membership in four spheres of activity; family, friends, organizations, and work. A second goal was to assess whether there was variation in the expressed activity patterns on the basis of such factors as age, sex, marital status, and life satisfaction. More specifically, answers were sought to four questions:

1.  With increasing age, are older individuals less involved in family, friendship, and organizational groups and/or activities?
2.  Is there variation in the preferred amount or frequency of activity on the basis of such factors as sex and marital status?
3.  Do retired individuals have a higher or lower level of activity with family, friends, and in organizations than do working individuals?
4.  What is the relationship between family, friendship, organizational, and work or nonwork activity patterns and life satisfaction?

## METHOD

### Sample

The study population consisted of an all-white cross-sectional area probability sample of 257 older adults, 132 males and 125 females. All of the subjects in the sample were grandparents. Forty-two of the men were husbands of women in the study population. The average age of the men and the women was approximately the same—around 65. Nearly a third of the subjects were aged 70 and over, whereas only 4% were aged 45 or younger. Slightly more than two-thirds of the respondents were married and living with spouses. Almost 90% of the men, but slightly fewer than half of the women, were married.

More than two-thirds of the men were working or had worked

at skilled or semiskilled blue-collar jobs. Slightly less than 20% were or had been in professional or managerial positions. Close to two-thirds of the women were or had been employed—for the most part in service or clerical jobs. Of the working women, over a fourth reported that they were retired. Nearly two-thirds of the women and a little over half of the males did not finish high school. Slightly over 10% of the respondents had some college. They were predominantly Lutheran Protestants and Catholics of German and Scandinavian backgrounds. The average family size of the respondents was three children and six grandchildren. Close to one-fourth of them had great-grandchildren.

## Measurement Indices and Scoring Procedures

Data regarding activity patterns were obtained from the descriptions subjects gave to trained interviewers in their own homes. The instrument was approximately 50 minutes in length and was administered by trained interviewers from the University of Wisconsin Survey Research Laboratory. The present author worked closely with this research organization in the development, pretesting, and administration of the interview schedule. (For a more detailed description and analysis of the specific items on family friendship and organizational activities of the study population, and a copy of the interview schedule, see Robertson, 1971, Appendixes C, D, E.)

Interval scales were used to measure types, number of, and frequency of activities for the spheres of family, friends, and organizations. Nominal classifications were used to separate the working retired, and never employed.

FAMILY ACTIVITY PATTERNS. These were measured by 14 different types of behaviors that older persons engage in with their grandchildren. Given findings that reveal that elders voluntarily seek out family activities in exchange for love and attention (Robertson, 1977) and crossnational data corroborating a high frequency of intergenerational interactions (Shanas et al., 1968, pp. 184–206), involvement with grandchildren was reasoned to be a good index of the older person's preference for family activity patterns. Behaviors with grandchildren are free from economic and child-rearing constraints and are viewed as pleasurable activities of choice (Robertson, 1977). Grandchildren also may assure the older individual a continued opportunity to be in contact with their adult children without seeming to be meddlesome or intruders in family life. Some examples of family activity pattern questions were: "Have you babysat with your grandchildren? Do you ever take grandchildren out shopping, on trips, or to the zoo, etc.? Do you read to your grandchildren? Do you provide them with advice on personal problems, work, religion, or information about family history, etc.?" For each of the 14 items, the subjects were asked if they engaged in the activity, how frequently, and whether they initiated it or if it was initiated by their adult child or the grandchild.

The subjects were assigned a score of 1 for each of the family activity behaviors they engaged in and 0 for those that they did not engage in. Thereafter, these scores were summed to yield a family activity pattern score ranging from a low of 0 to a high of 13.

FRIENDSHIP ACTIVITY PATTERNS. These were measured by a series of questions related to 13 different types of friendship activities. The subjects were asked, for example, "How often do you engage in any of the following with your friends: attend social functions, talk over phone, drink coffee, write letters, visit in their homes, talk over personal problems, play cards, help in time of sickness or death, etc." They were also asked how frequently they engaged in each activity.

The subjects were assigned a score for each friendship item ranging from 5 points if they engaged in the friendship activity frequently, to a score of 1 point if they never engaged in the activity. Subsequently, each individual's scores for the 13 items were summed to obtain a raw score for friendship activity patterns ranging from a low of 0 to a high of 65.

ORGANIZATIONAL ACTIVITY PATTERNS. These were measured by asking the degree to which respondents were involved in 13 different types of community and fraternal organizations, labor unions, and so on. The subjects were asked: "Would you tell me if you belong to any of the following groups or organizations? How long have you been a member? How often do you attend their functions?"

The subjects were assigned a score of 1 if they belonged to and participated in an organization for 5 years or less and 2 if they belonged to and participated in an organization for 6 years or more. Subsequently, each subject's scores for the 13 items were summed to yield a raw score for organizational activity patterns ranging from a low of 0 to a high of 26.

WORK VERSUS RETIREMENT PATTERNS.  The respondents were asked if they were working, retired, or had never been employed. They were placed in nominal classifications and activity patterns for family and friends, and organizational involvements were run against work or nonwork status.

LIFE SATISFACTION.  A life satisfaction score was obtained by the use of 13 items comprising the Life Satisfaction Index A (Wood Wylie, & Sheafor, 1969). For each of these items the subject was assigned a score of 1 for a correct response and 0 for an incorrect or a "depends" response. Subsequently, each respondent's scores for the 13 items were summed to obtain a life satisfaction score ranging from a low of 0 to a high of 13.

Analysis of variance techniques were used to test the relationship between activity patterns and age, sex, marital, and work status and life satisfaction.

## RESULTS

The findings are presented in terms of the four questions posed at the beginning of the paper.

### Do an Older Person's Activities with Family, Friends, and in Organizations Decrease with Age?

More precisely, since these data are cross-sectional, do the older respondents report fewer activities than their younger counterparts? To address this question, the subjects were categorized into five distinct age groups ranging from the 40s through 80 and over.

Table 1    Activity Patterns and Life Satisfaction by Age*

| | Age | | | | | |
|---|---|---|---|---|---|---|
| Activity patterns | 40–49 $N = 16$ | 50–59 $N = 69$ | 60–69 $N = 81$ | 70–79 $N = 70$ | 80+ $N = 21$ | Significance level |
| Family | 4.49 | 6.01 | 6.77 | 7.30 | 5.86 | .001 |
| Friendship | 34.91 | 34.25 | 33.14 | 33.10 | 24.10 | .0001 |
| Organizational | 2.25 | 2.30 | 2.01 | 2.41 | 1.29 | NS |
| Life Satisfaction | 9.93 | 10.07 | 9.14 | 9.36 | 8.00 | .04 |

*Analysis of variance: group means: N–257

The data indicate that family and friendship activities are related to age at the .001 and .0001 levels, respectively, but the amount of activities in organizations is not (Table 1). There is, however, a decided drop in organizational activity for the age group 80 and over. Friendship activities show a slight decrease as one moves from the 40s to the 50s, 60s, and 70s, and a decided decrease for the group in their 80s and older. Family activity patterns increase steadily as one goes from the youngest age group through the 70s, but again, there is quite a definite decrease for the age group 80 and over. Undoubtedly, a higher proportion of the 80 and over age group has health and disability problems than is true of the younger age groups —a thesis that cannot adequately be answered at this time with these data. Unfortunately, these data do not contain adequate measures that would permit a comparison of the healthy with the not-so-healthy to ascertain whether health is a more salient determinant of an older person's activity patterns than age per se. These findings do indicate that family activity patterns steadily *increase* as one moves from the 40s through the 70s, with a distinct drop-off in all activities after that. Further, they reveal that friendship activities gradually *decrease* with age and that organizational activities remain relatively *constant.*

### Is There Variation in the Amount or Level of Activity by Sex and Marital Status of the Older Person?

Findings indicate that women are more involved in family and friendship activities than are men (Table 2). On the other hand, males are decidedly more involved in organizational activities than are women. It is important to note that membership in organizations of any kind is very minimal, possibly an artifact of a predominantly working-class sample where organizational involvement is not a norm. The organizational activities that respondents were involved in were limited for the most part to such organizations as church groups, labor unions, and recreational groups. Interestingly, women belonged only to the first group, for the most part.

Since almost all the widowed individuals in the study population were women, the findings relating to differential involvement in all activities are not relevant for males. Contrary to the predictions of the author, widowed women were no more involved in family or friendship activities than were married women, and only slightly less involved in organizational activities, the level of activity being low for all women relative to the men.

## Do Retired Individuals Have a Higher or Lower Level of Activity with Family, Friends, and in Organizations Than Do Working Individuals?

This question was answered by comparing the activity levels of working individuals with levels of those who were not working—retired men and women and one-third of the women who were not working and had never worked. These data indicate that the nonworking group had a significantly higher level of family activity and a significantly lower level of friendship activity (Table 2). The nonworking group also had fewer organizational activities than the working group, but the difference between the groups was not statistically significant.

## What Is the Relationship Between Family, Friendship, Organizational, and Work Activity Patterns and Life Satisfaction?

Findings indicate that there is a very definite and positive relationship between the amount of activity in friendship and organizational roles and life satisfaction, but that family activity patterns, as measured by behaviors with grandchildren, are unrelated (Table 3).

Table 2   Activity Patterns by Sex, Marital, and Work Status*

|  | Activity patterns | | |
| Variables | Family | Friendship | Organizational |
| --- | --- | --- | --- |
| *Sex* | | | |
| Males (N = 132) | 6.18 | 32.05 | 2.73 |
| Females (N = 125) | 6.82 | 34.20 | 1.55 |
| Significance Level | .07 | .04 | .00 |
| *Marital Status* | | | |
| Married (N = 177) | 6.63 | 33.10 | 2.47 |
| Single (N = 80) | 6.19 | 33.08 | 1.46 |
| Significance Level | NS | NS | .003 |
| *Work Status* | | | |
| Employed (N = 113) | 5.19 | 34.42 | 2.31 |
| Nonemployed (N = 144) | 6.94 | 32.06 | 2.06 |
| Significance Level | .004 | .031 | NS |

*Analysis of Variance: group means: N–257

Table 3   Activity Patterns by Life Satisfaction Level*

| Activity patterns | Life satisfaction | | | |
|---|---|---|---|---|
| | Low $N = 81$ | Medium $N = 112$ | High $N = 64$ | Significance level |
| Family | 6.02 | 6.55 | 6.47 | NS |
| Friendship | 29.41 | 33.79 | 36.67 | .000 |
| Organizational | 1.72 | 2.04 | 2.91 | .015 |

*Analysis of Variance: group means: N = 257

## DISCUSSION

The data indicate rather clearly that older adults place much emphasis on friendship activities. The reader is reminded that the study population comes from a predominantly blue-collar working-class area. Since it includes only grandparents, this discussion does not address the preferences and behaviors of that 20% of the population who have no children.

For the most part, stable blue-collar community-residing older persons are only minimally involved in organizational and group activities outside the family. But whatever organizational activities they do participate in are at a fairly constant level of all age groups except those at the advanced age of 80 and over. Organizational involvement is not related to age. Tradition prevails; that is, males belong to labor unions and recreational groups, and women belong to church groups. The nonworking have fewer organizational activities than those who work, suggesting that aside from work-related activities, older individuals are not motivated to become involved in commitments of this sort. It is noteworthy that involvement in organizational and group activities, however minimal, is related to life satisfaction. A second significant piece of information, which may be of value to professionals, has to do with the number and types of organizations these individuals actually participated in and their very limited frequency of participation when they did belong. Given a possibility of participating in 13 types of groups ranging from labor unions to church groups, fraternal organizations, neighborhood clubs, ethnic groups, recreational clubs, business and civic clubs, political organizations, and charity and welfare groups, most of these subjects belonged only to one or two organizations. Given these choices, working-class older adults of both sexes tend not to be joiners in organizations. Furthermore, when they do join, it appears to be related to work activities, and attendance is infrequent.

Although community-residing aged are more involved in family activity patterns than they are in organizational or group activities, family activities are not related to their life satisfaction. Nonetheless, these activities steadily increase with age until 80 or over. As might be expected, women and the unemployed were far more involved in family activities, but contrary to expectations, widows were not prone to family activities. This is not surprising in view of Rosow's (1967, p. 315) data, which indicate that widows do not resort to families as compensatory and/or functional support systems for coping with loss of spouses. Widows turn to friends more often, and the marrieds and nonworking continue to be involved in family activities. It appears that the latter two groups may still use spouses as primary support systems, but widows seek out friends to replace spouses—something that is not terribly difficult to do, given the fact that women outnumber men in the population and there is a large circle of widowed women one can turn to.

One of the most significant pieces of information these data point to is the value of friendship activities in adult life and the need for professionals to develop services that put older individuals in touch with their peers. Friendship activities are more salient to the life satisfaction of these community-residing elders than are family activities, even those activities that are considered joyous and free from the constraints and responsibilities of child rearing. Within the family one's spouse and siblings are age peers, but if neither of these is available for the older person, other age peers need to be found.

A woman who is widowed, especially if widowhood occurs relatively early in middle age, may suffer the loss of friends as well as the loss of her husband. As Lopata (1971b) has pointed out, this is because couples tend to have other couples as friends,. and when her spouse dies, a widow is apt to feel like a fifth wheel with these couples. Social interaction with them is apt to be discontinued or significantly altered. Women who are widowed later in life are more likely to have friends who are already widowed, and they join this widows' circle of age peers. Lopata points out that we have no mechanisms in our society for getting widows back into the social network. Since the majority of women are eventually widowed, widows should be a major concern of practitioners, as a special set of supportive or linking services may be needed to help them maintain their psychological well-being.

Rosow (1967, p. 295) has shown that satisfaction and activity levels are both related to neighborhood age-density. That is, individuals who live in neighborhoods where there are large numbers of age peers have more friends, a higher level of social interaction, and, consequently, higher satisfaction. This is true for working-class neighborhoods but not necessarily for upper middle-class residential areas. Because of the propensity to make friends only among persons of like age, persons living in working-class neighborhoods where there are few age peers are more likely to have low levels of social interaction and satisfaction.

In sum, it seems clear that activity and social integration perspectives are useful frameworks for understanding aging phenomena, in particular as they relate to the relationship of involvement in friendship and organizational activities and life satisfaction. Although these elderly do not participate regularly in organizational activity patterns, family and friendship activities are steadily maintained. Given the high priority placed on friendship activities as a determinant of life satisfaction, professionals should strive to find ways to help the aged maintain regular social interaction with peers. Families, although important, seem to be less preferred.

The findings of this research have a number of practice implications. Social workers should strive to put older persons in touch with age peers. This might be done by focusing on *individual* patterns of social relations. We might start with the elderly person and work toward preferred types of friends and activities. A specific treatment goal could be to find accessible and desired friends. This suggests that social workers should formulate programs and interventions that meet the psychosocial needs of the elderly. Realizing that the aged person wants friends, a social worker in a nursing home might deliberately choose group counseling as an intervention modality to work on problems of adjustment rather than individual counseling. Nursing home staff could encourage and find ways for aged residents to remain integrated in community activities. One way to accomplish this would be for the social workers to approach members of a senior citizen group with the idea of setting up a one-to-one volunteer visiting program whereby community-residing elderly visit nursing home elderly regularly. Or the social worker could work with senior citizens' clubs to develop joint activities with nursing home residents such as a monthly dinner at the senior center.

Groups at senior centers are formed usually around an instrumental activity such as weaving, ceramics, bowling, or woodworking. Since as an individual ages, he/she is forced to experience a series of role changes, groups could be developed around certain psychological problems such as a widow-to-widow group, or a retired men's group. In coordinating programs between a variety of organizations serving the elderly and in developing a greater variety of groups within their organizations, the practitioner will maximize the individual's chance for meaningful social interaction with age peers. Given our finding that psychological well-being is influenced by friendship activities, these program innovations will result in a higher level of life satisfaction among the aged population.

Furthermore, this research should help social workers advise family members who are in the process of selecting a nursing home for an aged parent. Frequently, they approach the medical social worker when they begin a search for a nursing home for a hospitalized parent. Given the general lack of knowledge, the practitioner advises the family to consider such factors as the nursing staff-patient ratio, the type of social activities available, and the proximity of the nursing home to the family. This research suggests that the family consider the accessibility of the nursing home to the friends of the older individual and also evaluate the level of social interaction between residents at the nursing home. Is there public transportation to the nursing home so that it is easily accessible to friends of the resident? Do the residents gather in small groups to talk with one another, or do they sit alone in their rooms? Is there a welcoming committee for new residents? Does the physical design of the nursing home offer residents the opportunity to talk privately with one another? Given my findings on the relationship between friendship and life satisfaction, the practitioner needs to advise the family that is in the process of evaluating nursing homes to consider not only quantitative factors, such as the nursing staff-patient ratio, but also qualitative factors, such as the potential for friendships to form between residents.

Most importantly, this research suggests that outreach workers could utilize family members as resource links between the aged and programs designed for them. In the past, outreach workers have concentrated their efforts on one-to-one contact with the elderly. Since there is frequent contact between the aged and their families, practitioners should focus their outreach programs not only on direct attempts to reach the elderly in need of services but also on developing programs aimed at educating family members as to the community services available for the elderly. Social workers might send out newsletters that describe the senior citizen programs to families in the community. Senior center and nursing home staff could hold family nights which could serve both an educational and social function for the elderly and their families. By taking advantage of the natural visiting patterns between family members, practitioners could concentrate their one-to-one contacts on the 20% of the elderly population without adult children.

## REFERENCES

Blau, Z. S. *Old age: A study of change in status.* Unpublished doctoral dissertation, Columbia University, 1957.

Blau, Z. S. *Old age in a changing society.* New York: New Viewpoints, a Division of Franklin Watts, 1973.

Brody, E. M. Serving the aged: Educational needs as viewed by practice. *Social Work,* 1970, *1,* 42–51.

Cumming, E., & Henry W. *Growing old: The process of disengagement.* New York: Free Press, 1961.

Cutler, N. E. & Hartootyan, R. A. Demography of the aged. In D. S. Woodruff & J. Birren (Eds.), *Aging.* New York: D. Van Nostrand, 1975.

Gravatt, A. E. Family relations in middle and old age: A review. *Journal of Gerontology,* 1953, *8,* 197–201.

Henry, W. E. The theory of intrinsic disengagement. In P. From hansen (Ed.), *Age with a future.* Copenhagen: Munksgaard, 1964.

Kerckhoff, A. C. Norm-value clusters and the strain toward consistency among older married couples. In I. H. Simpson & J. C. McKinneys (Eds.), *Social aspects of aging.* Durham, N.C.: 1966.

Kutner, B., et al. *Five hundred over sixty.* New York: Russell Sage Foundation, 1956.

Lemon, B., et al. An exploration of the activity theory of aging: Activity types and life satisfaction among in-movers to a retirement community. *Journal of Gerontology,* 1972. *27,* 511–523.

Lopata, H. Z. *Occupation housewife.* New York: Oxford University Press, 1971. (a)

Lopata, H. Z. Widows as a minority group. *Gerontologist,* 1971, *11,* 67–77. (b)

Lowenthal, M. F., & Haven, C. Interaction and adaptation: Intimacy as a critical variable. *American Sociological Review,* 1968, *33,* 20–30.

Maddox, G. L. Activity and morale: A longitudinal study of selected elderly subjects. *Social Forces,* 1963, *42,* 195–204.

Phillips, B. S. Role change, subjective age and adjustment: A correlational analysis. *Journal of Gerontology,* 1961, *16,* 347–352.

Phillips, D. L. Social participation and happiness. In J. N. Edwards & A. Booth (Eds.), *Social participation in urban society.* Cambridge, Mass.: Schenkman, 1973.

Riley, M. W., & Foner, A. *Aging and society.* Vol. 1, *An inventory of research findings.* New York: Russell Sage Foundation, 1968.

Riley, M. W., Foner, A., Hess, B., & Toby, M. Socialization for the middle and later years. In D. Goslin (Ed.), *Handbook of socialization theory and research.* Chicago: Rand McNally, 1969.

Robertson, J. F. *Grandparenthood: A study of role conceptions of grandmothers.* Unpublished doctoral dissertation, University of Wisconsin-Madison, June 1971.

Robertson, J. F. Grandmotherhood: A study of role conceptions. *Journal of Marriage and the Family.* February 1977, pp. 171–172.

Rosow, I. *Social integration of the aged.* New York: Free Press, 1967.

Shanas, E., et al. *Old people in three industrial societies.* New York: Atherton Press, 1968.

Wood, V. *Role change and life styles of middle-age women.* Unpublished doctoral dissertation, University of Chicago, June 1963.

Wood, V., & Robertson, J. F. *Friendship and kinship interaction: Differential effect on the morale of the elderly.* Unpublished manuscript, May 1977.

Wood, V., Wylie, M., & Sheafor, B. An analysis of a short self-report measure of life satisfaction: Correlation with rater judgements. *Journal of Gerontology,* 1969, *24,* 465–469.

Chapter 5

# DISCUSSION OF THE SELECTED STUDIES

## Helen Z. Reinherz
## Joseph M. Regan

In this chapter we will discuss the chapters in Part I, in particular for the light they shed on various aspects of problem formulation.

### FRAIBERG: THE MUSE IN THE KITCHEN (PART A)*

This study emerged from a practical problem: how to treat blind autistic children within an agency's clientele. It grew into a theory-generating exploratory study that provided many insights. Thus, it fulfills both applied and theoretical criteria.

As phrased by Fraiberg, the problem that demands solution (the felt need) is this: "In the absence of vision, how does the blind baby differentiate, recognize, become bound through love?" In other, more technical words, the article presents a search for the important adaptive solutions in the establishment of object relations by blind infants.

Fraiberg's initial decision to study one child intensively narrowed the focus of the work. Even so, the observers had to study a

*The second part of Fraiberg's study is reprinted and discussed in Part V of this volume.

large number of variables of the child's behavior and interaction of this child and her mother as well as others in the environment including the researchers.

In the study of Toni, the initial hypotheses of the observers were refuted. Concepts were clarified and reformulated in the process of an intensive study of one child, and resulted in the planning of future studies to examine the process of adaptation of blind children in a more comprehensive manner.

The anticipated value and consequences of the study are clearly presented by the author: it led to useful clinical practice with blind children and also to the building of new theories so that clinicians could further develop understanding of visually impaired infants.

### PLIONIS: FAMILY FUNCTIONING AND CHILDHOOD ACCIDENT OCCURRENCE

The author addressed the important issue of understanding the psychosocial context within which repetitive accidents of children occur. The "felt need" was established by the documentation that accidents are the leading causes of morbidity and mortality for children below the age of fifteen.

This chapter is noteworthy for an extensive review of the literature of the phenomenon under study (accident occurrence) but also of social and behavioral factors associated with accident occurrence. Through the literature search, the author identified a group of familial indices related to repetitive accidents in children including poor family cohesion and marital conflict. Proceeding from a theoretical orientation viewing the family from a structure-functional perspective the author selected a scale developed for social work research by Geismar (1971). Family functioning was assessed through the role expectations designated by society and essential for family maintenance and the family's actual role performance.

The use of this methodology allowed Plionis to clearly focus her study and test the hypothesis; there is an association between the adequacy of family, functioning, and the index child's accident rate. The feasibility of the study was insured by utilization of a small hospital-based sample of children (fifteen) whose parents gave permission to participate in the study.

The study is descriptive by nature as variables were carefully defined before the study. The implications of this study could have wide ranging impact on both differential diagnoses of repetitive accidents and their treatment with a total family framework.

## ROBERTSON: ACTIVITY PREFERENCE OF COMMUNITY-RESIDING AGED AS A GUIDE FOR PRACTICE EMPHASES

The author establishes the need for this study on the basis of three interconnected issues: the growing demand for social work practitioners to design treatment plans and to develop programs responsive to the increasing number of aged requiring service. Moreover, they must do this in a situation in which the theories about the essential activity requirements of the elderly lead to conflicting practice implications. The empirical evidence supporting any one of these theories is also either inconclusive or contradictory. The study develops each one of these issues from the available literature. Although the felt need of the study is to establish a knowledge base for practitioners, it also illustrates how this knowledge requires both theory refinement and empirical data to be firmly established.

Focus is developed gradually. From an initial general concern about what types of programs the elderly need to ensure participation and membership in social groups and the requirement to strike a balance between medical and psychological problems, the author identifies three specific support systems: family, friends, and organizational membership and connects these with the maintenance of life satisfaction. The study narrows this further by directly examining older individuals' preferences for social participation in the four spheres of 1) work, 2) formal organizations, 3) family, and 4) friends. It addresses four subquestions relating the main study objective to variation in age, sex, retirement status, and life satisfaction.

Given the nature of this problem formulation, the author chooses a descriptive design requiring a sizeable number of subjects and collects information by means of a detailed interview administered by trained interviewers. The measurements used in each specific content area indicate how each variable is operationalized and scored.

The results are presented in a fashion that answers each element of the initial question formulated specifically and in order. In the discussion the author attempts to reconnect the study's results to specific theoretical positions and to spell out precise practice implications.

## Articles Reprinted

Fraiberg, S. The muse in the kitchen: A case study in clinical research. *Smith College Studies in Social Work,* 1970, *40*(2), 101–115.

Plionis, E. M. Family functioning and childhood accident occurrence. *American Journal of Orthopsychiatry,* 1977, *47*(2), 250–263.

Robertson, J. F. Activity preferences of community-residing aged as a guide for practice emphasis. *Journal of Gerontological Social Work,* 1978, *1*(2), 95–109.

## Reference

Geismar, L. *Family and community functioning: A manual of measurement for social work practice and policy.* Metuchen, N.J.: Scarecrow Press, 1971.

Part II

# RESEARCH DESIGN AND SAMPLE SELECTION

*Chapter 6*

# CHOOSING A RESEARCH DESIGN AND A STUDY SAMPLE

## Henry Wechsler

In the research process each decision made influences the next. The way in which a problem is formulated sets the stage for the next step, the choice of a design. The research design is the basic plan of the study. It should follow logically from the particular manner in which the problem is framed. The most important factors in the ultimate choice of a design are the present level of knowledge about the phenomenon to be studied, and concomitantly, the degree to which one wishes to generalize the findings of a particular study to encompass other, similar phenomena (e.g., people, agencies, or programs).

The research designs of the studies presented in this book may be classified as exploratory, descriptive, or experimental (Selltiz, Wrightsman, & Cook, 1976). There can be, and there often are, mixed types of designs, particularly those in the "exploratory-descriptive" category. For purposes of classification, however, designs can be arrayed according to their goals, levels of precision, and degrees of flexibility, as will be demonstrated by the examples provided.

## DESIGNS

### Exploratory

Exploratory designs are appropriate when little is known from prior research of the phenomenon, group, or program to be investigated. The aim of the study may be simply to identify the important variables or its ultimate aim may be to develop (not test) specific hypotheses. Precision of measurement is not an issue in this type of design, which leaves much freedom in the choice of methodology. Sampling is less formal as well, with less concern for the representative character and general significance of the sample than descriptive and experimental designs require.

### Descriptive

Descriptive designs are used to provide detailed information about the interrelationship of certain variables concerning the phenomenon in question. The relevant variables are known with some precision, but their interrelationship has not previously been measured. Descriptive studies can link two variables and establish correlations, such as between poverty and certain types of social problems or between alcoholism and family background. Cause and effect cannot, however, be specified.

Surveys are a major type of descriptive research in the human services. Descriptive designs require more precise and accurate measurement than do exploratory designs, and necessitate concern over issues of the reliability and validity of data. Sampling procedures must also be constructed with an eye toward the representative nature of the sample, since the aims of the study may include generalization to broader populations. In all events, accuracy and specificity are important features of studies of this kind.

### Experimental

When relationships of cause and effect are to be determined, experimental designs are necessary. In this kind of study, independent variables (possible causes) are controlled by the researchers, so that they can study their effect on the dependent variable. Evaluative research is often of this design, using measurements of outcome as the dependent variables. A sound experimental design must include means of measuring the impact of the experimental variable or intervention, and adequate controls must be present to ensure that the effects measured are not due to factors other than this experimental variable.

An experimental design often used has the following requirements: 1) baseline pretest measures on all persons in the study; 2) randon assignment of persons to either an experimental or control group; 3) introduction of a clearly defined intervention or experimental variable, which is applied only to the experimental group; 4) conditions for the control group that are identical in all ways to those of the experimental group, except for exposure to the experimental condition; and 5) posttest measures.

This kind of design may not be possible for many studies in the human services field. In such cases the procedures undertaken in place of any of the five requirements will influence the general significance of the research. For example, in studies that do not provide the opportunity for baseline pretest measures, it may still be assumed that the experimental and control groups are equivalent if they are large enough and if individuals are assigned at random to either group. On the other hand, if random assignment cannot be used owing to ethical or legal considerations, the experimental and control groups should be carefully pretested before the treatment. If no differences are found, this procedure may be substituted for the random assignment. If neither device is used, however, unequal selection is likely to result and any posttest differences between the experimental and control groups may be a function either of the intervention or of pretest differences due to unequal selection. The researcher would not be able to distinguish between these effects.

Because of the difficulty of meeting all the conditions of experimental design in educational research on humans, Campbell and Stanley (1963) and Cook and Campbell (1979) have conceived a number of "quasi-experimental" methods for use in this area. The same types of problems exist in human services research. Part IV of this book, on evaluation research, considers alternative designs for cases where ethical or other considerations prohibit random assignment of persons to control and experimental groups.

Research studies are susceptible to a number of problems that may affect their usefulness. One major type of problem is the contamination of the relationship between the independent and dependent variables, through the presence of a third variable. Thus, for example, persons treated in an intensive casework intervention program may improve after two years not because of the program, but rather because of factors such as maturation (they are now two years older, and past a critical age) or other changes in their environment (e.g., an economic recession may have ended). The presence of a control group exposed to the same extraneous variables but not to the extensive casework permits the elimination of these variables as sources of contamination.

Another major problem area relates to the selective inclusion of persons in the experimental or action program of the study. The random assignment of people included in the study to an experimental or control group helps to eliminate this form of selectivity as a contaminating factor. Another form of selectivity, however, that of selective dropout rates from the study, must still be examined. Thus, persons may be randomly assigned to one of two groups, but those in the active treatment group may, because of extensive demands on their time, drop out of the study more readily than those in the control group. If the dropout rate is so high that only the most psychologically healthy remain in the treatment group, we can expect that the treatment group will score more highly on psychological health in the posttest than the control group. This would be due to selective attrition rather than to successful intervention.

## SAMPLING

One of the aspects of research design most often taken for granted is sampling. If a study has covered a large population, it appears to be more credible than a study with a smaller sample. But what is more important than the number of subjects is the way the sample is drawn. Even total population studies do not always guarantee accuracy. A striking example often cited is the underenumeration of young black men by the United States Census in recent years. On the other hand, small samples carefully and systematically selected can be used to find out about the total populations from which they are drawn.

Perhaps the strongest argument for the use of samples in research is that if sampling is appropriate to the investigation and is properly carried out, it works. Carefully drawn samples of people, organizations, programs, and so on, can be used to answer questions regarding the larger constellation—the population, census, or universe—from which they are drawn, or can provide useful information, although the sample may well differ somewhat from the true population.

Working with samples, with some of the clients or some of the workers, saves time; and where time is saved, costs are reduced. The rigorous sampling plans developed in survey research have reached such a point of sophistication that surveys of less than one per cent of the voters can be used to forecast accurately the outcome of national elections.

Obviously, sampling also allows the researcher to carry out experiments by selecting comparable groups from a universe, or population, and testing hypotheses with these groups.

## Probability

Probability sampling, one of the two basic types of sampling, gives every member of a population an equal chance to be selected. If the probability sample is large enough and is correctly drawn, it should be representative of the total population. This kind of sample, most often a simple random sample, is usually selected if the aim of a study is to provide information about the total population.

If, however, a study requires separate analyses for certain population subgroups, stratified random sampling may be employed. In this procedure, the general population is subdivided into two or more strata, and each individual's chance of being selected is equal to any other's within the same stratum. However, an individual in one stratum may have a smaller or greater chance of being selected for the study than someone in another stratum. Stratified random sampling would be used if, for instance, one wanted to examine the effects of intensive casework in the aftercare of mental hospital patients but believed that the effects would be different for men and women and for different age groups. Such a study would require a sample with sufficient numbers of discharged male and female patients in different age groups. Since there may be fewer discharged patients below age 25, one would have to oversample this age group to obtain a sufficiently large sample for detailed study. Also, since there are fewer men than women over age 65, one would need to oversample men in that age category.

A form of probability sampling that is often used for reasons of economy is *cluster sampling*. In this technique the basic unit to be sampled is not the individual but larger units or clusters of individuals. One might, for instance, sample social agencies or classes in

schools of social work. Cluster sampling is often a multistage procedure, with a sample of the larger unit drawn first and followed by
a sampling of the individuals in the clusters selected. One might, as
an example, select every tenth client coming to the sample of social
agencies that had been selected. Public opinion polls often use a
three-stage sampling technique. First, they select a sample of blocks
within a city or town; then they select a sample of housing units
within that block; finally they select an individual within each housing unit.

A study is efficient to the degree it employs the minimum sample
size capable of adequately representing the population it seeks to
describe. Public opinion polls using mail samples to predict election
outcomes must seek to negotiate between the conflicting demands for
lower costs and accurate results. Statistical texts such as those by
Blalock (1972) or Colton (1974) provide methods of calculating the
sample size needed in a particular study.

## Nonprobability

Unlike probability sampling, nonprobability sampling does not
provide an equal chance for inclusion to each member of the population. Everyone present in a particular location on a particular day
may be chosen. The ease of drawing such samples explains why
much psychological research is done on students attending psychology classes. If certain numbers of persons with special characteristics are needed, quotas may be established. Interviewers may be
told to get so many men, so many women, so many elderly. Another
method of nonprobability sampling is selecting only "average" respondents. None of these techniques assures a representative sample.
Findings of a study using nonprobability sampling may not be generalized to the whole population.

For more detailed discussions of survey research designs, the
reader may consult Selltiz et al. (1976). A discussion of sampling
techniques can be found in Suchman (1967).

## Protecting the Rights of Human Subjects

Social work research by its nature involves the use of humans
as subjects. In so doing, it must comply with legal and ethical requirements to safeguard the rights of these subjects. As a first step,

informed consent must be secured before someone is included in a sample. This means that the person must know what the research is about, what his or her participation will mean, and what will be the risks in the research. Furthermore, the benefits of the research must outweigh the individual risks involved. Nowadays most research projects require approval by an institutional review committee. A good discussion from a number of different perspectives of the issues involved in human experimentation is available in Bogomolny (1976).

## References

Blalock, H. M., Jr. *Social statistics.* New York: McGraw-Hill, 1972.
Bogomolny, R. L. (Ed.). *Human experimentation.* Dallas: Southern Methodist University Press, 1976.
Campbell, D. T., & Stanley, J. C. *Experimental and quasi-experimental designs for research.* Chicago: Rand McNally, 1963.
Colton, T. *Statistics in medicine.* Boston: Little, Brown, 1974.
Cook, T. D., & Campbell, D. T. *Quasi-experimentation: design and analysis issues for field settings.* Chicago: Rand McNally, 1979.
Selltiz, C., Wrightsman, L. S., & Cook, S. W. *Research methods in social relations,* 3rd ed. New York: Holt, Rinehart and Winston, 1976.
Suchman, E. A. *Evaluative research.* New York: Russell Sage Foundation, 1967.

*Chapter 7*

# BATTERED WOMEN
## A Study of Women Who Live with Violent Alcohol-Abusing Men

### Susan E. Hanks
### C. Peter Rosenbaum

Although much has been written about the impact of alcohol abuse on the family and it is commonly known that some women are physically abused by their mates, relatively little research has been done on the dynamics of both violence and alcohol use in conjugal interactions. This paper describes 22 women who lived with violence-prone alcohol-abusing men and who were physically abused by them.

An attempt was made to elucidate who these women were, how they became involved with violence-prone alcohol abusers, why they remained in potentially lethal relationships, and what their contribution was, if any, to the violent episodes. The women were not found to be a homogeneous group. They originated from three different family background types (characterized by either a Subtly Controlling Mother/Figurehead Father, Submissive Mother/Dictatorial Father, or Disturbed Mother/Multiple Fathers) and were currently involved in three correspondingly different types of conjugal rela-

*A revised version of a paper submitted to the Journal in November 1975. Research was supported by NIAAA grant AA498. Authors are at: Family Service of Berkeley, Berkeley, Calif. (Hanks); and Stanford University Department of Psychiatry and Behavioral Sciences (Rosenbaum).*

tionships. Similarly, within each different type of conjugal relationship, the character of the violent interactions differed in meeting a variety of needs for the couple. The alcohol abuse played a catalytic but secondary role in relation to the violence. The women were found to be neither innocent victims nor sole precipitators of the violent episodes; rather, they were unwitting collaborators with their mates in the creation, enactment, and resolution of the violent episodes.

## THE ALCOHOL AND VIOLENCE CLINIC STUDY

The 22 women participated conjointly with their male partners (the primary patients) in the Alcohol and Violence Clinic, Department of Psychiatry and Behavioral Sciences, Stanford University Medical Center. The clinic investigated the relationship between violent behavior and alcohol use, and it explored and evaluated possible treatment approaches to the problem during the three years of its existence (1972–1975). Because these women were often the chief target of the violence, they were viewed as an integral part of the program.

EVALUATION PROCEDURES   Of the 32 male subjects, 24 were or had recently been involved significantly with women when they entered the clinic ("significant" was defined as important to both parties and assumed to be of long-term duration). These women were either wives or girlfriends. The women were asked to participate in the evaluation and, if willing, treatment phases of the program. Of the 24 women, two have been eliminated from consideration in this research; one refused to complete the total evaluation, and one was later discovered to be the primary violent alcohol abuser.

The evaluation of the women consisted on an initial conjoint interview with the patient and the clinic staff, and approximately three individual sessions with the clinic social worker. During the semistructured interviews with the 22 women, and from therapy material from the eleven who entered treatment, information was elicited on the following topics:

1.   Childhood and family of origin: marital stability and instability; parental communication and role structures; alcohol use and abuse; discipline and violence; stability of father's and mother's role as parent and financial provider; evidence

of psychological disturbance in the woman and her siblings; educational attainments.

2. Recent and current history: relationship with male subject and other relationships with men; communication patterns and role structures; predispositions to drinking and violent interactions; the meaning of violence in the relationship; evidence of psychological disturbance in the woman and her male partner.

DESCRIPTIVE DATA. The 22 women ranged in age from 20–52, half being 30 years of age and under. All were caucasian and from a variety of culturally mixed backgrounds. Families of origin were an even mixture of middle and lower socioeconomic classes. The women were currently involved in relationships with men from comparable socioeconomic and ethnic backgrounds. Over two-thirds of the women were raised in Catholic homes; none came from Jewish homes. Six women had less than a high school education, twelve had completed high school, and four had some college education.

Twenty women were legally married to their partner. This was the first marriage for fourteen women (average length of marriage, seven years), and the second marriage for five women (average 10.8 years); one woman was in the fourth year of her third marriage. Both women in common-law marriages (average length 1.5 years) had been divorced from their first husbands. Financially, only three of the 22 women were totally dependent on their mates. Two of the women were the sole support of themselves and their mates.

## A TYPOLOGY OF FAMILIES OF ORIGIN

When the data on the women's childhoods and families of origin were examined, it became apparent that they came from three different and describable kinds of families. The nature of the family interaction patterns in childhood paralleled in many interesting ways the women's contemporary relationships to men, including the primary subjects of the study. The women will be described first by family of origin, then by their current conjugal relationships. The three types of families of origin are 1) the Subtly Controlling Mother/Figurehead Father family, 2) the Submissive Mother/Dictatorial Father family, and 3) the Disturbed Mother/Multiple Fathers family.

## Subtly Controlling Mother/Figurehead Father

Ten women came from families in which the mothers were subtly controlling and the fathers were a figurehead of authority. Ostensibly, fathers were dominant and mothers were supportive, passive, and acquiescent to fathers' authority. On closer examination, fathers' "benign tyranny" (as one women described it) was subtly delimited by mothers' control. Fathers often alternated between being bombastic and silent; mothers treated them as being childish and unable to cope. By implication, mothers were the competent ones who, by subtle approval or disapproval, cause the fathers ultimately to follow the others' wishes while proclaiming them their own. These marriages were stable, as was fathers' employment, during the women's childhood years.

Outwardly, these families presented a united front of stability and normality. The women often initially reported unambivalently positive feelings towards their parents, seeing their relationship as "ideal, perfect" because "they never argued." However, these "ideal" families produced female offspring who, as adults, were not only involved with a violent alcohol abuser but also showed evidence of serious emotional disorder (psychosis, drug abuse, kleptomania, etc.). Two male offspring had committed suicide in adolescence.

> In Mrs. A.'s ostensibly close and mutually supportive family, Mrs. A. had become pregnant while in high school; her boyfriend panicked and disappeared, her parents never showed any curiosity about her physical condition, and she received no prenatal care: "They all thought I was just getting fat." Her parents were informed of her pregnancy over the telephone by a hospital nurse just prior to her delivery. Initially, they seemed surprised and delighted; nevertheless, they were slightly delayed arriving at the hospital because her father insisted on first shopping for baby clothes.

ROLE RELATIONSHIPS. The mothers' protectiveness towards men extended to their sons, towards whom they were uncritically overprotective. Mothers frequently expressed disappointment that their daughters were not boys, and thus withheld approval. Some daughters reacted by becoming good, obedient girls who spent much time at home and thus developed few peer relationships. Others compensated by becoming "the apple of father's eye," an alignment that further distanced them from their mothers. The fathers, nevertheless, often asserted their authority, albeit at mothers' request, by disciplining the children. Thus, the daughters were often punished (sometimes severely) by their fathers, the person to whom they felt closest. Fathers became both punishers and advocates; they both administered punishment and bargained with the mothers for lesser punishments.

> As a child, Mrs. A. had often been banished to her room for minor transgressions. Father was the only family member who would "sneak" into her room and talk with her, reporting on the progress of negotiations with mother for her release. It was during these times that she felt closest to him.

Brothers were usually only reprimanded mildly for the same things for which these women had been punished.

CONTINUITY OF RELATIONSHIPS. These parents' relationships remained intact while the children were in the home, but became troubled when the women, who had served as an emotional buffer, left the home. The parents resolved this either by divorcing after twenty or more years of marriage (in three cases) or becoming overly involved in their children's lives (seven cases). As will be discussed later, the parents in these latter cases played a subtle but influential role in the couples' violent episodes. These women currently had difficulty separating from their parents, and needed to maintain unambivalently positive feelings about their families.

CONJUGAL ADJUSTMENT. The remaining material on this group of women describes recent factors in their lives at the time of study. At the point of referral to the clinic, nine of the ten women had been married to the current spouse for an average of eight years; two had been previously married, and one was being sued for divorce by her husband of ten years. All but three women had completed high school, and four had some college education. Seven of them worked, but were still somewhat financially dependent on their husbands.

Six men and their partners were referred to the clinic by the legal justice system. Four men and three of their partners were self-referred, seeking help after a nearly fatal violent episode. Seven of the women agreed to participate in treatment.

MATE SELECTION. These marriages usually occurred at the initiative of the women, often for reasons other than "love" (*e.g.,* convenience, mutual assistance, or a desire to align themselves with a man who seemed respected by others, decisive, and having direction in life). The women were unaware of any drinking or legal problems in their spouses when they married. They seem to have been motivated to marry someone whom they did not know very well in order to escape the parental home.

ATTITUDES TOWARDS THE MEN.   Initially, the women were sympathetic toward what they labeled as the men's "Jekyll-Hyde" personality, describing them as good husbands and fathers, flawed only by unpredictable, occasional alcohol-induced violence. One woman stated, "If he stopped drinking, he'd be perfect in my eyes."

TYPES OF VIOLENCE.   The six court referrals resulted from such charges as drunk driving and disturbing the peace, malicious mischief, assault on a police officer, and assault with a deadly weapon. As none of the women had pressed charges against their husbands, the legal difficulties usually resulted from a neighbor calling the police during the couple's violent argument and the men belligerently resisting the police. These incidents, and those motivating the four self-referred couples, followed violent behavior associated with alcohol use and directed mainly toward the women.

> Mr. G. had been depressed and drinking heavily for several months. One evening a discussion of Mr. G.'s unemployment escalated into an argument while he was cleaning his rifle. The rifle "accidentally" discharged, barely missing Mrs. G. but blasting a large hole in the front door. Neighbors called the police, whom Mr. G. briefly threatened with his rifle before surrendering. Both Mr. and Mrs. G. were angered and astonished when police pressed charges. Mrs. G. refused to press charges because she "only wanted to get rid of the gun," not her husband.

RESPONSES TO VIOLENCE.   These women rarely called for outside assistance, and never brought legal charges against the men. Rather, they played down the seriousness of the episode after it occurred, protecting and defending the men who had assaulted them. They inappropriately denied their very real physical jeopardy and their fear of the violence, despite obvious personal injury (broken bones, bullet wounds, bruises, etc.) and physical damage (holes in the wall, torn clothing, battered cars, dead animals, etc.). This denial seemed to be their way of defending against their own anxiety and concern that verbalizing or showing fear would further antagonize the men.

Five women were targets of moderate assault or verbal assault. These women forgave verbal denigration. They prided themselves on maintaining their composure during the outbursts, and on their saint-like ability to live with the abuse.

Five women were the targets of severe physical aggression; all "stood toe-to-toe" (as one described it) and fought it out with the patients. They repeatedly sought out the patients at the local bar to "protect" them from the violent consequences of their drinking, and yet were later shocked when the reaction to the rescue attempt was hostility, not gratitude.

After episodes of violence, the women often left the home, either to seek the support of their parents or to go to a motel. Their mothers often reinforced the attitude that men were creatures who needed to be controlled, and fathers were again cast in the role of advocate. If in a motel, even though the women feared their husbands learning their whereabouts, they often called home and had lengthy long-distance discussions. One wife continued to do her husband's grocery shopping and laundry while she and her daughter were holed up in a motel ("I never could really leave him because we mean too much to each other.").

MEANING OF VIOLENCE IN THE RELATIONSHIP.   These couples often stated that they felt closer following an episode of violence. They joined in denying their individual contributions to the episodes, and instead projected responsibility onto outside agencies such as the police or the probation system, quickly preoccupying themselves with how to avoid legal entanglements rather than how to avoid similar incidents in the future. The anger and fear experienced by the women during the episode usually disappeared when the remorseful and contrite men wanted to reconcile.

Certain family role conflicts seemed to trigger violent outbursts. When the women strove to become good mothers, which often meant becoming overprotective, the husbands frequently felt excluded from the children or became overly strict in compensation for the mother's perceived "spoiling," thus putting the children in the middle in a struggle for allegiance. Violence was also sparked by the men's failure to live up to the projected image that the partners had of them. The women saw themselves as "encouraging" the men to be more adequate; the men heard this as criticism of their already shaky adequacy and self-esteem. Unable to express their hostility directly, they started drinking and attacked the women, who represented all the critical controlling figures in their past. Similarly, violence also occurred when the women unknowingly recreated an earlier conflictual experience for the patients.

> Mr. A. felt abandoned almost from birth by his alcoholic parents, who always left him in the care of others, often strangers. One evening, when Mr. A. returned home from work, Mrs. A. was not present as usual, and he did not know her whereabouts. He became increasingly agitated, went out drinking, and later returned to have a physical fight with Mrs. A.; he threw her two cats and her clothing over the apartment balcony, and tore up the house. During the melee, Mr. A. broke her arm and she broke his nose.

In all these cases, the women acted not only on their own needs but also on ambivalent messages from the men. For example, one man consistently beat his wife after she followed him to the bar. But he once let slip that he thought his father's death could have been averted if only his mother had loved his own father enough to seek him out and bring him home from the bar.

STABILITY OF RELATIONSHIP   Despite occasional separations, these couples would usually reunite, with divorce occurring only at the men's initiative. As one extremely verbally demeaning man told his wife, "I married you because you'll put up with me. Why should I go through the hassle of getting divorced only to marry somebody else just like you?"

PARALLELS TO CHILDHOOD.   There are many parallels between their childhood and the current life these women had created or chosen for themselves. Their mothers were controlling of bombastic but ineffectual fathers; they married men who often need rescuing. Their fathers inappropriately, severely punished them; their husbands now serve that function. When they were children, their mothers drove a wedge between them and their fathers; now they drive a wedge between their husbands and children. Their parents' relationships stayed stable in spite of chronic unhappiness; so do their own marriages. Their parents united to present a good "face" to the community, while these women and their husbands blame community agencies for their difficulties; in both generations, there is a sharp difference between what goes on inside the home and in public.

*Submissive Mother/Dictatorial Father*

Six women were from families in which the mother was submissive to a dictatorial father. Father's long hours on the job, heavy drinking and numerous highly-touted romances resulted in prolonged absences and desertions from the family. Marital separations and reconciliations were common. When fathers were home, they tended to be verbally and physically abusive to their wives. The mothers were dependent, unassertive women, often unable to protect themselves or their children from fathers' demeaning aggressive onslaughts. The mothers themselves were often daughters of violent, abusive fathers.

The aggression of fathers toward mothers was much more open in those families than in the preceding group. Consequently, in this group, the women's ability to be openly critical about their parents was much greater.

ROLE RELATIONSHIPS.    When father drank heavily, the children either participated in verbal and physical battles between the parents or they received excessive, unsolicited affection from the fathers. When sober, fathers were irritable, harsh, and intolerant of weakness or imperfection in others, being particularly critical of mothers' deficiencies as wives, mothers, and housekeepers. In either case, they often punished arbitrarily and excessively. Mothers tried unsuccessfully, to "carry on" and "keep the peace at all costs," passively tolerating fathers' comings and going. They compensated for their marital rejection by becoming their daughters' "pals." Mothers often became so overwhelmed and defeated that they were unable to give to anyone, and major child care and household responsibility fell to the daughters at an early age.

> Mrs. W., a 43-year-old woman in her third marriage, initially refused to discuss her childhood because it made her "sad and furious." Mrs. W. was the only product of her mother's first marriage to a violent alcoholic. Her stepfather drank heavily when not working twelve hours a day in a factory, and he physically abused Mrs. W. and her mother. She always resented her parents for making her drop out of grammar school to care for her eight siblings, and for arranging for her first marriage, at age fourteen, to a violent, alcoholic man seven years her senior. After seven years of marriage, Mrs. W. took her three children and left her first husband; she struggled to emigrate to the United States, learn the language, get a high school diploma, and train as a beautician.

To avoid the fathers' wrath towards women, several women identified with their fathers and became self-described "tomboys."

> Mrs. C., an attractive 24-year-old bartender, used to accompany father on long truck hauls, and grew up "surrounded by men." She never got along with girls who were "jealous of my good looks." In adolescence, father was "super possessive, wanted me for himself," and never allowed her to date.

This typically oversexualized relationship with the fathers during adolescence was most pronounced when the parents were separated. Mothers would then view the daughters (their "pal") as competitors for fathers' attentions, and simultaneously encourage the daughters to defy the fathers' authority and the fathers to punish the daughters for the defiance.

CONTINUITY OF RELATIONSHIPS.    These parents' relationships were not likely to dissolve after the children left the home, despite ample opportunity and provocation for both spouses. Half of the women totally rejected their parental families, having no contact with them. Other partners were caught in a hostile-dependent relationship with their parental family, and their parents, similar to those described in the first group, remained overly involved with them and played an active role in the violent episodes.

CONJUGAL ADJUSTMENT.    Of the six women in this group, five were married to, although only three were living with, husbands in marriages averaging 6.2 years. This was the first marriage for all but one woman, who was in her third marriage. All but one had completed high school; four were steadily employed self-supporters, and two were supported by public assistance. The three living with husbands participated in the treatment program.

Of the men, five were self-referred or came from mental health agencies; one was referred by his probation officer. Four had extensive legal and psychiatric histories (resulting in many documented episodes of assaultive behavior); two had had no such previous troubles.

MATE SELECTION.    These women often chose their husbands impersonally. One married her childhood sweetheart right after high school graduation "because everyone expected me to and there was nothing else to do." Another married her husband, whom she had known for two weeks, after they were arrested for passing counterfeit bills; she hoped the marriage would prevent their having to testify against one another. Others married to forestall the loneliness of old age. One woman's brother reminded her at age 40, after two failed marriages, that she "wasn't getting any younger."

Unlike the previous group, all of these women knew before marriage that the men drank heavily. Half had seen the men's violent behavior prior to marriage, and the others had been targets of such behavior. Because all of these women had violent, alcohol-abusing fathers, it cannot be said that they naively entered the relationship unaware of the consequences. It seems more than coincidental that they chose men similar to their own fathers, with whom they also had a disturbed relationship.

ATTITUDE TOWARDS THE MEN.   These women did not describe the patients as having "Jekyll-Hyde" personalities; their men would not be perfect if they just stopped drinking. The women rarely described their mates' violence in terms of a sudden, unexpected rage, as did the first group, but rather seemed to view it as part of life.

TYPES OF VIOLENCE.   The violence in these relationships differed only in that it was also directed toward other persons (drinking buddies, relatives, police, etc.) as well as those women. The men themselves differed in that they expressed little, if any, remorse over the injury they inflicted on either the women or others. The violent behavior, often tinged with a sadistic quality, appeared compatible with the men's self-image; they often were hypermasculine types who felt justified in "keeping women in their place."

> During a group meeting, Mr. J. unexpectedly announced that he intended to stop drinking. Both he and Mrs. J. were concerned that drinking might lead to a violent encounter and harm their soon-to-be-born child. When asked by the group why it was all right to beat his wife but not his child, Mr. J. offhandedly stated, "Oh, she can take care of herself." Mrs. J. giggled and nodded in agreement.

RESPONSES TO VIOLENCE.   All of these women were targets of severe physical abuse. They are like the previous group in that they rarely called in the police for protection. However, they differ in that they often sheltered the men from the legal consequences of their violent behavior and also illegally harboured them from prosecution for crimes (violent and nonviolent) directed towards others.

These women initially denied fearing the patients. They often stated that they are able to "talk the men down," rely on female wiles to subdue them, or use their own abilities to defend themselves. This may have partially resulted from their having coped with their fathers' wrath by becoming a seductress or a tomboy or both. In actuality, these women were often severely assaulted, and "saved in the nick of time" by a friend who was strangely able to subdue the men when no one else could.

> Mrs. W.'s husband became increasingly paranoid during weekly drinking binges. He often mumbled threats to kill his ex-wife during drunken tirades to which he forced Mrs. W. to listen. Eventually, Mr. W. began to mistake Mrs. W. for his ex-wife. During one such episode, he threatened her with a knife, saying, "It will be the end of us soon," and cut the telephone wires to prevent Mrs. W. from calling for help. He was disarmed by a friend who happened to drop by. Mrs. W. initially stated she was not afraid. ("I can handle him.")

Despite initial denials, the women eventually expressed appropriate fears of being killed or maimed by the men. They seemed to be immobilized in the relationships by both their neurotic needs to stay and their realistic fears of the men's retribution if they did leave.

The women's parents often play a significant role in the episodes of violence. Women used their parents' homes as havens following violent episodes or as a not-so-secret hiding place for the men's weapons. (Two women were attacked with their own guns, which they later hid at their parents' home). The parents, however, were not likely to provide protection. Mothers often became involved in physical battles with their daughters' husbands, while fathers frequently became allies, business associates, or drinking partners of their sons-in-law. One man's father-in-law actually made the initial contact with the clinic on behalf of his son-in-law, not out of concern for his daughter, but rather because he was employed by the man and feared that the failing business was due to his mismanagement.

MEANING OF VIOLENCE IN THE RELATIONSHIP. These women became preoccupied with the men's violent behavior, much as their parental families were with that of their fathers. The couples' behavior during the violent episodes usually mobilized numerous people in their environment (friends, relatives, bystanders, police, etc.), making the much neglected men feel the center of attention and in control. Through their violence, the men reasserted their shaky dominance over the women. One woman, smiling proudly, told how it once took seven policemen to subdue her husband during an altercation. This type of unconscious pride in the men's aggression unwittingly bolstered their low self-esteem and reinforced the reoccurrence of violence.

If children were present in this type of relationship, they too were likely to become targets of the patients' abuse. Unlike the previously described women, these women were not likely to attempt to compensate for their problematic relationships with their own mothers by spoiling their children or becoming "perfect" mothers. Rather, they were more likely to be modeled after their mothers, and be unable to protect either themselves or their children from the patients' abuses.

STABILITY OF RELATIONSHIP.    As in the women's parental families, separations and reconciliations were common. (Only one woman in this group actually followed through on divorce; the precipitating factor, however, was not 22 years of severe abuse but the husband's more recent bizarre sexual behavior.) These relationships were characterized by mistrust and suspicious mutual accusations of infidelity. Threats of infidelity were common; however, in contrast to the partners' parental families, they were infrequently acted on.

PARALLELS TO CHILDHOOD.    In addition to those already mentioned, there are other similarities between these women's early and adult lives. Like their mothers, they married men who they knew had violent, alcohol-abusing propensities similar to their fathers'. Their lives seemed structured around the men's violent episodes and comings and goings, much as their parental family was preoccupied with their fathers' violence and absences. Tumultuous separations and reconciliation were common. In addition, these women were often blatantly indiscrete concerning their sexual involvements with other men. Their indiscretions resulted in abusive retaliation by their jilted spouses, not unlike the punishment meted out by their fathers when they learned of the women's sexual activity during adolescence. Further, although these women were financially self-sufficient, they were like their mothers in their inability to terminate the relationship.

### Disturbed Mother/Multiple Fathers

Six women came from families with chronically emotionally disturbed mothers who had numerous mates. These men were heavy drinkers who abused both the mothers and their daughters. The families moved often, as the mothers impulsively left their mates, frequently to return to their own mothers. Children were neglected and separated, being relegated to the care of their grandmothers or strangers. Mothers related to their daughters by being either affectionately smothering, intrusive, and overly close, or by being withdrawn, angry, and rejecting.

ROLE RELATIONSHIPS. The daughters repressed anger and anxiety about their tenuous environment for fear of triggering further rejection and abandonment. Instead, they tried, in vain, to win mothers' fidelity by making themselves good, indispensible daughters. At an early age, they assumed the mothers' household and child care responsibility, and functioned as the mothers' counselor and confidant. One woman proudly stated that, by age ten, she was mother's "right hand man;" she was doing all household chores, grocery shopping, and caring for two small sisters.

Unfortunately, these women were overburdened at home as children and so mobile that they too had little opportunity for forming peer relationships. They felt like "outsiders" at school, and usually dropped out before completing high school. Despite attempts to please their mothers, they were both scapegoated for the transgressions of other siblings and physically abused by both their mothers and mothers' male friends. They frequently admitted to false accusations to stop a beating.

These women also harbored unexpressed resentment toward their mothers for separating them from their natural fathers and for distancing them from their stepfathers. They often developed idealized fantasies of their "good fathers," and silently defended their memory of their fathers against their mothers' denigration.

> Mrs. E. said she had always resented her mother for leaving her father, especially after learning from an old family friend, at age sixteen, that it was her mother's promiscuity, not father's, that prompted the separation. She also resented her mother for not allowing her stepfather to be close to her after an episode of incest when she was seven years old. She was totally unaware of her triumphant smile in relating how, at age 22, after seven years of marriage, she impulsively left her husband and eloped with her mother's third husband.

As children these women often witnessed the mothers' sexual promiscuity and were also victims of incest on the part of their fathers or stepfathers. Mothers overstimulated early sexual interest but severely punished early sexual activity by their daughters.

As a result of this upbringing, the women had either provoked their mothers' rejection or currently maintained a distant although hostile-dependent relationship with them.

CURRENT ADJUSTMENT. These six women had, among them, a history of six divorces from, and numerous common-law relationships with, violent alcohol abusers. Four of the couples were married, although three lived separately. Two couples had common-law relationships. Relationships lasted an average of six years, and were marked by multiple separations and much promiscuity. Thus, like their mothers, these women had a history of similar relationships prior to, or concurrent with, their marraige to a violence-prone alcohol abuser. Generally, although these women were dissatisfied with their men, they were not motivated to change the relationship. They begrudgingly completed the evaluation phase of the program, and only one entered treatment.

Generally, these women were less educated than those in the other groups (only one had completed high school). All had married by age eighteen. However, none of the women was financially dependent on her mate; five women worked full time, and one couple was supported by public assistance.

All of the men had been referred to the clinic by the legal justice system. All had histories that abounded with psychiatric disturbances, multiple marriages, job instability, and legal troubles resulting from assaultive behavior and alcohol abuse.

MATE SELECTION. These women usually formed quick, intense, dependent relationships with their men. They described an "undefinable mysterious attraction" to the men, which both attracted them to and kept them in the relationships. In some cases, this "mysterious attraction" seemed related to the women's never-ending search for the fantasied fathers by whom they felt abandoned.

> Mrs. E. married, at age fifteen, a man seven years older than she because he was the best friend of a man on whom she had a crush. She left him after seven years because he had become an alcoholic and transvestite. She impulsively eloped with her mother's third husband. This physically abusive alcoholic man abandoned her after three years when he jumped bail to avoid an embezzlement charge. Within a few

weeks she met her current partner, a 40-year-old unemployed accountant. He had just dropped out of a residential treatment program for alcoholics, where he had been referred by the court in lieu of jail for assaulting his third wife. After knowing each other for six weeks, they became engaged to be married. Mrs. E. stated that, during an outing with him, she thought to herself, "This is what it would be like if I had a father."

All of these women chose men they knew to be violence-prone alcohol abusers, and by whom they had been physically abused. They seemed to align themselves with inadequate, dependent men for whom they could provide financial security and a haven from the consequences of their action. In so doing, they made themselves indispensable to the patients, just as they made themselves indispensable to their mothers. For women with very low self-esteem and a history of rejection by significant others, becoming indispensable seemed their only safeguard against abandonment. Their indispensability and self-sacrificing also seemed to be a defense against their unmet dependency needs, which they sacrificed as children when they inappropriately assumed too much responsibility at too early an age.

ATTITUDE TOWARDS THE MEN.   These women usually derogated their men, terming them "irresponsible," "self-centered," and "mentally screwed up." They described in detail the men's violence, inability to hold a job, failure to provide financially, and chronic indebtedness. Interestingly enough, the women presented these observations factually, blandly, and uncritically. Little anger or disappointment came through. In contrast to the previously discussed partners, these women simply accepted the men's shortcomings. All drew a complete blank when asked to describe the men's "good points."

TYPES OF VIOLENCE.   All these women had been targets of severe physical abuse by numerous men. Like the other women, none had pressed legal charges against the men. In addition to their violence towards the women and towards others, many of the men had also attempted suicide.

RESPONSES TO VIOLENCE.   These women's responses differed from the others in several ways. They rarely helped harbor the men from legal authorities. Their parental families were not involved in the episodes. The women did not deny their fear of the man's violence. However, their descriptions of the episodes and verbalizations of fears were accompanied by inappropriately bland affects and occasional smiles. Their bland acceptance of the abusive behavior was coupled with their passive acceptance of the men's self-destructive behavior. As one women sighed, "If he wants to die, what can I do about it?"

The violent episodes were not followed by a feeling of closeness, nor by a banding together in a mutually reinforced denial. Instead, a period of separation followed, during which the men apologetically pressed for reconciliation. Despite the women's ambivalence about the men's return, their fears of loneliness ultimately exceeded their fears of closeness. They resisted for a time, but eventually allowed the men to return, especially if they reached the point of being able to function without the women's indispensable assistance.

> Mrs. E.'s engagement was characterized by tumultuous separations and reconciliations. At one point, she broke off the engagement completely, returning his letters and obtaining a new and unlisted phone number. She inadvertently encountered him in a grocery store; he ignored her. When she got home, she phoned him to "thank him sincerely for ignoring me." The call reestablished the relationship.

MEANING OF VIOLENCE IN THE RELATIONSHIP.    Becoming indispensable was problematic for these women because it resulted in an overly close, dependent relationship which neither they nor their mates could tolerate. One woman described her relationships as being like a "yo-yo," in that she "liked to be close at a distance." Violence thus served as a distancing mechanism, as well as a source of some excitement in the relationship.

Violent episodes were sometimes sparked by the women's threat of separation or confessions of sexual infidelities. The men (who had histories of profound maternal rejection and previous unsuccessfuly relationships) felt rejected, and responded violently. Other times, the women were unable to immediately gratify the men's insatiable, infantile needs, and the men went into a rage.

STABILITY OF RELATIONSHIP.    These women blandly related a history of violent encounters with men—ranging from their own fathers and their mothers' other husbands and boyfriends. Their relationships with these particular men were stormy and characterized by frequent separations and reconciliations. Some women's passivity outweighed their impulsive wish to separate. As one woman stated, her husband "stayed with me because he needs someone to take care of him . . . he knows I'll always be there because I never leave." These women all had no insight into the repetitive nature of their behavior and, not being too disturbed by the violence, had little need to question their role in its occurrence.

PARALLELS TO CHILDHOOD.    As in the previous groups, there are parallels between these women's early and adult lives. Like their mothers, they have difficulty maintaining consistent relationships with any other person. They relate to their own children much as their mothers related to them, alternately smothering or neglectful. Just as they learned to forestall their mothers' abandonment by functioning as "little adults," they maintain their relationships with men by encouraging dependency. They knowingly choose a series of inadequate, abusive men—strikingly similar to the multitude of abusive men who passed through their early years. Having been raised in an environment in which they both witnessed and received physical abuse, they had come to expect physical abuse as inherent in male-female relationships and were not disturbed by its occurrence.

## DISCUSSION

The main parameters on which the partners' childhoods and current lives have been described are outlined in Table 1.

RATING OF VIOLENT INTERACTIONS.    Episodes of violent dyscontrol associated with alcohol use on the men's part, and of which the women were the chief targets, were rated for a period of two years preceding referral to the clinic (or for the length of the relationship, if less than two years). Physical assault on the women was rated as either "severe," i.e., seriously life threatening (attacked with a weapon, beaten resulting in internal injuries and broken bones, thrown from a car, choked, etc.), or "moderate," i.e., not necessarily life threatening (threatened with a weapon, slapped, hair pulled, punched, etc.); destruction of property almost always accompanied physical assault. Verbal assault encompassed denigrating sarcasm, degrading comments, name calling, etc. Seventeen of the 22 women were the targets of severe physical aggression. Three women were targets of moderate physical aggression. Two women were targets of verbal assaults only.

## Table 1 Summary of Salient Characteristics of Women From Three Types of Background

| Characteristic | Subtly controlling mother/figure-head father (N = 10) | Submissive mother/dictatorial father (N = 6) | Disturbed mother/multiple fathers (N = 6) |
|---|---|---|---|
| **PARENTAL FAMILY** | | | |
| Parental marriage | Stable | Frequent separations and reconciliations | Mothers had multiple mates |
| Parents' roles: | | | |
| Mother (homemaker) | "Perfect" mother | Overwhelmed | Neglected |
| Father (work) | Stable | Overworked | Unstable, unpredictable |
| Alcohol abuse: | | | |
| Mother | None | None | Little |
| Father | None | Much | Much |
| Parental violence | None between parents; father punished daughter severely | Father abused mother frequently, children occasionally | Fathers abused mothers and daughters; mothers abused daughters |
| Women's view of parents | "Perfect" family, unable to separate | Critical but unable to separate | Hostile, rejecting |
| Women's Education | High school or college | Primarily high school | Most did not complete high school |
| **CONJUGAL RELATIONSHIP** | | | |
| Current relationship | Stable | Frequent separation, reconcilation | Frequent change of partner |
| Aware before marriage of husband's: | | | |
| Alcoholism | No | Yes | Yes |
| Violence | No | Yes | Yes |
| Husband's prior psychiatric & legal history | None | Slight | Extensive |
| Reason for marrying | Escape parents | Situational, unrelated to man | "Mystical" attachment |
| Attitude to husband | "Perfect" except for violence | Hostile, critical | Denigrating |
| Response to husband after violence | Mutual denial of physical jeopardy | Denies fear, shelters him from law | Accepts as expected |
| Economic dependence on husband | Moderate | Slight | None |
| Type of violence: | | | |
| Severe physical | 5 | 6 | 6 |
| Moderate physical | 3 | 0 | 0 |
| Verbal only | 2 | 0 | 0 |

EARLY AND ADULT LIFE PARALLELS. As suggested above and illustrated in Table 1, the conditions of childhood are continued into the present. The tendency to be involved with a violent man who drinks is part of the psychic economy of each of the women, no matter what kind of family she comes from. If she is from a Subtly Controlling Mother/Figurehead Father family, she finds a "perfect" man whose violence makes her superior and allows her to feel needed as she rescues him from his legal troubles. If she is from a Submissive Mother/Dictatorial Father family, she couples with a man who is abusive towards her, but who provides a focus for her otherwise directionless life. If she comes from a Disturbed Mother/Multiple Fathers family, she forms an almost mystical attachment to relative strangers who never turn out to be the long-sought, idealized father she never knew well.

PARTICIPATION IN THERAPY. Not only did the stability of the childhood family predict to some degree the nature of current conjugal relationships, it also predicted entrance into therapy. Of the ten women in the first group, seven entered therapy in our program; of the six women in the second group, three entered therapy; and of the six women in the last group, characterized by chaos and lack of trust between mother and daughter, only one entered therapy offered by the female social worker.

TRAITS COMMON TO ALL COUPLES. In spite of their differences, these couples did share some common traits. In all cases, the men were identified by both partners as being the ones with "the problem." The women had no insight into how the marital roles they modeled and the specific roles they had played in their families of origin were influencing their current behavior. They were completely unaware of any contribution they may have made in escalating angry interactions into violent interactions.

In most cases, the women were the ones who would recall and describe in detail the violent episodes. The men were often "blacked out" in regard to the event. Interestingly enough, the women rarely challenged the validity of the men's blackouts, and the men never questioned the credibility of the women's reports. In addition, when describing the episodes, some women did report anger, disappointment, or fear, but none expressed shock or indignation that they had been battered by the men.

In almost all cases, the couples were socially isolated, having few, if any, close relationships. Neither the men nor the women could tolerate the other forming friendships, their reactions ranging from heightened suspiciousness to paranoid mistrust. Even relationships with members of the same sex were suspect. Women feared the men's male friends would encourage infidelity. The men feared the women's female friends would encourage them to leave. Because of this often extreme social isolation, the women became depressed and increasingly dependent on the men. Thus, terminating the relationship became all the more difficult.

SIGNIFICANCE OF THE FINDINGS. The violence that occurred between these couples cannot be simplistically explained away by either psychological theories of sadomaschistic behavior or social theories of male dominance-female submission. Certainly the women were not the reason the men became violent; the men had equally complex familial and psychological histories and, most often, a propensity to violence prior to coupling with the women. However, although not the cause, the manner in which the women often unwittingly interacted with the men during certain vulnerable times did help ignite the violence.

The findings have implications for the treatment of these battered women. If a woman is unwilling or unable to terminate an abusive relationship, conscious awareness and alteration of her behavior during angry encounters may serve as a method of self-protection. Similarly, a woman who wishes to terminate her relationship must have an understanding of how her early life influences her current behavior. This insight, combined with supportive concrete services (housing, money, employment, etc.), is essential in preventing her from reestablishing the abusive relationship or moving on to similar relationships.

*Chapter 8*

# CHILD MALTREATMENT AND MATERIAL DEPRIVATION AMONG AFDC-RECIPIENT FAMILIES

## Isabel Wolock
## Bernard Horowitz

### INTRODUCTION

The primary objective of this study was to examine the role in child abuse and neglect of a number of factors asserted in the literature to be associated with the maltreatment of children within an AFDC-recipient population.[1] Our principal reason for focusing on AFDC-recipient families was to begin to explore the factors, interacting with poverty, which may result in child maltreatment. Another major reason for focusing on public assistance recipients is that almost all reported child abuse and neglect situations come into the public agency network at one point or another. Since these public agencies consistently report that the bulk of their protective-service clientele is poor,[2] it is necessary to know more about the factors that result in child maltreatment among the poor.

Although the overwhelming majority of poor families do not abuse or neglect their children, studies generally show poor families to be disproportionately identified in reported incidents of abuse and neglect. As part of a nationwide study of reported abuse cases, Gil,[3] found that nearly half (48.4 percent) of them earned less than $5,000 per year per family and that nearly 60 percent of the families had received aid from public assistance agencies during or prior to the study year. Boehm[4] found that the preponderance of families referred for neglect came from the lower socioeconomic strata of the community. Giovannoni and Billingsley,[5] in a comparison of neglectful with nonneglectful parents, both from low-income groups, found a much higher incidence of extreme poverty among the neglectful parents. Other studies have reported a lack of material resources, such as inadequate housing, household, and personal goods, among abusing families.[6] Giovannoni and Billingsley do not infer "that poverty is an invariant concomitant of neglect. Rather, the implication is that poverty exposes parents to the increased likelihood of additional stresses that may have deleterious effects upon their capacities to care adequately for their children."[7] We share their interpretation of the empirical data. This view represented the basic perspective for the research, although one which cannot be tested within the limited socioeconomic stratum surveyed.

We assume that, within the narrow socioeconomic stratum of our AFDC sample, material level of living is a central factor affecting a family's capacity to provide adequate child care. Thus, even within a welfare population, differences exist in quality of housing, household items available, consumption levels for food and clothing, short-term economic difficulties, and handling of the extremely limited available resources. We expected to find that the families who maltreat their children experience even greater difficulties in these areas than other AFDC-recipient families.

The resources of the larger community are expected to have a major impact upon the ability of the family to cope at a subsistence income level. The quality of the neighborhood (the extent of neighborliness, safety, and socioeconomic characteristics), the resources provided by the community, and the degree of communication with family and friends can either exacerbate or help counteract difficulties in child rearing. To the extent that this environment is harmful, we predicted a greater likelihood of child maltreatment.

Within the family itself a number of factors, including number and spacing of children and parent's child-rearing knowledge, attitudes, and practices, are expected to make these parents more susceptible to maltreating their children. Parents living in poverty with many children to care for and close in age to one another are likely to find child rearing a greater burden. Families who favor harsher discipline, are unrealistic about what can be expected of children at particular ages, who derive little satisfaction from child care, who participate in activities with their children less frequently, and who encounter more serious difficulties in such areas as toilet training and feeding are more likely to maltreat their children.

We also assume that the parent's own family background has a pervasive effect over time on the quality of care parents are able to provide their children. Thus, parents who were materially and socially deprived and who were abused and neglected themselves as children would be more likely to maltreat their own children.

It is further anticipated that the quality of child care will be associated with attitudes toward the larger societal environment. The maltreating group may feel more alienated and may also have lower expectations for themselves and for their children. Thus, we anticipate that parents who maltreat their children will show greater anomie and have lower educational expectations for them.

Finally, it is expected that, when parental problems such as alcohol and heroin abuse, mental and physical illness, and physical abuse occur in a context of material deprivation, they will substantially increase the likelihood of child maltreatment.

## METHODOLOGY

In order to explore the relationship of these factors and child maltreatment in a welfare population, the Bureau of Research, Planning and Program Development of the New Jersey Division of Youth and Family Services (DYFS) and the Research Center of the Rutgers Graduate School of Social Work jointly undertook a study of AFDC-recipient families in the ten northern counties of the state. The same interview schedule was administered to AFDC families who were identified as having abused or neglected their children and to families not so identified.

The group of families in which abuse and neglect were identified was drawn from a complete listing of all 1,700 northern New Jersey families known to DYFS for some reason related to child abuse or neglect that had at least one child born on or after January 1, 1964, for whom they were receiving AFDC in April 1976. The case records for these families were screened to see whether they met our operational definitions of child maltreatment.

Child abuse was defined as the physical assault on and/or nonaccidental injury of a child. Neglect was defined as the failure to provide necessities for the child that might or had resulted in damage to the physical, emotional, or intellectual development and well-being of the child. It included the lack of the provision of physical necessities and supervision and/or a severe lack of a basic level of affection and attention. The readers used a pretested manual which made explicit a number of the procedures to be used to determine whether or not a family should be included in the study. Readers had a set of anchoring examples available to assist them in making judgments. The operational definitions of child abuse and neglect used for the purposes of this study are not necessarily identical with legal or agency definitions, though the overlap is substantial. The researchers attempted to include only those instances where standards of child care were clearly reported and were substantially below that considered acceptable by the community. However, our use of the terms *child abuse* and *neglect* is not restricted to cases where abuse or neglect was legally determined. Many of the most serious cases of child abuse and neglect are not part of this study, since frequently all children in a family are removed in such situations. Nevertheless, the cases selected for the maltreating group clearly represent the types of child abuse or neglect known to public child-welfare agencies.

Out of the 552 families screened into the study in the maltreating group, we were able to obtain interviews for 380 (69 percent). These included families indicating neglect only ($N$=246), neglect and abuse ($N$=106), and abuse only ($N$=28). A representative comparison group was selected by drawing a random sample of families receiving AFDC in April 1976 with at least one child born on or after January 1, 1964, who resided in the same northern counties of the state as the abusing and neglecting families and who were not identified in DYFS records as maltreating their children ($N$=191). We were able to complete interviews with 75 percent of these families. The interviewers were not informed of the purposes of the study, nor were they told anything about the families besides the fact that they were receiving public assistance. Interviews were conducted only after receiving the voluntary signed consent of the respondents. Each respondent was paid twenty dollars for her time and trouble.

### RESULTS

*Study Sample*

All but eleven respondents were women; the average age was thirty-two. Sixty-one percent were black, 29 percent white, and 10 percent Hispanic. About seven out of ten respondents did not complete high school; the median number of years of schooling was 10.3. Slightly more than six out of ten were born in New Jersey. Sixty-one percent were Protestants, and 29 percent were Catholics. Nearly nine out of ten respondents had worked at some time, almost all at low-prestige jobs; only 11 percent earned $140 or more per week on their last job. For most of these factors the comparison and maltreatment groups were essentially similar. The maltreatment group had less schooling (9.7 vs. 10.5 mean years; $t = -3.53$; df $= 246$; P $< .001$), and a higher proportion were born in New Jersey (64 percent vs. 48 percent; $\chi^2 = 11.7$; df $= 1$; $P < .01$). As Table 1 shows, the proportion of blacks was nearly the same, while proportionately more whites and fewer Hispanics were represented in the maltreating sample.

Overall, the families in the sample reported a high degree of deprivation. For almost two out of three families, the welfare check runs out within the first two weeks of the month. Slightly more than one out of ten respondents said someone in the family had gone hungry for a day or more in the month prior to the interview because there was not enough food in the house.

About two out of three families lived in homes with more than one person per room. For more than one out of four, interviewers rated the state of the room in which the interview took place as being in poor repair. A third of the families had seen rats in their home, 14 percent had been without heat for most of the last winter, and 18 percent had been evicted at some time.

A substantial proportion of all the respondents perceived their neighborhood as crime ridden (41 percent), dangerous at night (42 percent), and run down (40 percent), and 36 percent felt that people

Table 1   Ethnicity of Maltreating and
Comparison Groups

| Ethnicity | Maltreating | | Comparison | |
| --- | --- | --- | --- | --- |
| | % | N | % | N |
| White | 31 | 119 | 22 | 31 |
| Black | 60 | 228 | 63 | 89 |
| Hispanic | 9 | 31 | 15 | 21 |
| Total | 100 | 378 | 100 | 141 |

NOTE: There are 380 families in the maltreating group and 144 families in the comparison group for Tables 1–8. Where the number of cases is less than these amounts it is due to missing information for the cross-tabulated variable: $\chi^2 = 7.93$: df $= 2$; $P < .05$.

in the neighborhood do not help each other out when there is trouble.

The families were socially isolated. That is, almost one in four had had no contact with relatives living outside the household in the two weeks prior to the interview, almost one in five saw no friends during the same period, and a quarter did not get out of the house more than once or twice in the week prior to the interview.

A substantial proportion of the parents reported having grown up under adverse circumstances. About a third felt they did not have happy childhoods. Almost half were not raised by both their natural parents, and 18 percent spent more than six months out of the home they were raised in. Twenty percent of their families had been on welfare during at least some part of their childhood. Sixteen percent said they went hungry a good number of times, and slightly more than a fourth did not have decent clothes to wear most of the time.

About a third said they were badly beaten as young children, and 17 percent were beaten often or very often. Nearly three out of ten felt neglected, and one out of four indicated that someone in their home was a heavy drinker.

## Group Comparisons

PARENT'S OWN CHILDHOOD.    As shown in Table 2, in accordance with our expectations, there were a number of ways in which the childhood experiences of the maltreating-group parents were even more adverse than those of the parents in the comparison group.[8] They were less likely to have been raised by both parents and more likely to indicate they did not have decent clothes to wear, to say they had been neglected, and to report having been badly beaten often as a young child.

An index comprised of a wide range of items concerning the parent's own background showed that the childhoods of maltreating respondents were more stressful than those of comparison ones.

MATERIAL LEVEL OF LIVING.    Many of our expectations that maltreating families encounter even more severe material deprivation than comparison ones were supported. As shown in Table 3, maltreating families are more likely to occupy small, crowded homes without a shower, and their children are more likely to share a bed. Interviewers were more apt to describe the rooms of maltreating-group families as being in poor or very poor repair. In addition, proportionately

Table 2   Parent's Own Childhood for Maltreating and
Comparison Groups

| | Maltreating | | Comparison | | | | |
|---|---|---|---|---|---|---|---|
| Childhood experience | % | N | % | N | $\chi^2$ | df | P |
| Not raised by both parents | 51 | 193 | 39 | 56 | 5.34 | 1 | <.05 |
| Did not have decent clothes to wear | 29 | 109 | 18 | 26 | 6.69 | 1 | <.01 |
| Felt neglected as child | 29 | 111 | 21 | 30 | 4.56 | 1 | <.05 |
| Were beaten hard and often as young child | 20 | 75 | 6 | 9 | 13.29 | 1 | <.001 |
| Scored most deprived on childhood index | 33 | 118 | 18 | 24 | 10.64 | 1 | <.01 |

Table 3   Material Conditions for Maltreating and
Comparison Groups

| | Maltreating | | Comparison | | | | |
|---|---|---|---|---|---|---|---|
| Material condition | % | N | % | N | $\chi^2$ | df | P |
| Crowding | 33 | 124 | 20 | 29 | 7.58 | 1 | <.01 |
| Shared child's sleeping spot | 66 | 250 | 45 | 65 | 19.19 | 1 | <.01 |
| No shower in home | 49 | 185 | 37 | 53 | 5.47 | 1 | <.02 |
| Interviewer's observation of state of repair of room as poor or very poor | 28 | 108 | 18 | 26 | 5.36 | 1 | <.05 |
| Going hungry for a day or more | 14 | 54 | 7 | 10 | 4.49 | 1 | <.05 |

more maltreating-group families state that in the month prior to the interview someone had gone hungry for a day or more because there was not enough food in the house.

A comparison of major consumer items possessed by the two groups (Table 4) showed that maltreating families were less likely to have a telephone, an air conditioner, and a color television. The difference between the two groups was particularly pronounced in the percentage that had a telephone, a standard item in most American households.

From a large pool of items on families' material circumstances, we selected a set of twelve which represent key areas of current material living conditions: quality of housing, the possession of

Table 4   Possession of Major Consumer Items for
Maltreating and Comparison Groups

| Consumer item | Maltreating % | N | Comparison % | N | $\chi^2$ | df | P |
|---|---|---|---|---|---|---|---|
| Telephone | 47 | 177 | 69 | 100 | 21 | 1 | <.001 |
| Washing machine | 44 | 168 | 46 | 65 | ... | ... | NS |
| Air conditioner | 12 | 47 | 26 | 38 | 14 | 1 | <.001 |
| Color TV | 27 | 101 | 37 | 53 | 5 | 1 | <.05 |
| Car | 15 | 58 | 15 | 21 | ... | ... | NS |

Table 5   Material Level of Living Index for
Maltreating and Comparison Groups

| Material level of living index | Maltreatment % | N | Comparison % | N |
|---|---|---|---|---|
| Lowest (score of 25 or less) | 33 | 122 | 14 | 20 |
| Medium (26–28) | 32 | 120 | 34 | 48 |
| Highest (29–35) | 35 | 128 | 52 | 73 |
| Total | 100 | 370 | 100 | 141 |

NOTE: $\chi^2 = 21$; df = 2; $P < .001$.

household and other material goods, and consumption patterns for food and clothing. On this index, as Table 5 shows, the maltreating families were living at a significantly lower level than the comparison ones.

COMMUNITY ENVIRONMENT.   Our findings on the quality of neighborhood and extent of social participation support our expectation that there is a relationship between the characteristics of the larger community and the quality of child rearing that is provided. As shown in Table 6, the respondents in the maltreating group were significantly more negative about two aspects of their neighborhood: the condition of housing and neighborliness. On the remaining items, although the differences were not statistically significant, the maltreating parents viewed their neighborhood more negatively. Consistent with these findings, an index combining the eight neighborhood items showed the maltreating group to be significantly more negative than the comparison group (see Table 7).

In addition to the relationship found between quality of child care and the neighborhood, the maltreating group was observed to have fewer contacts with friends, relatives, and organized groups outside their households. An index of social isolation, measuring the extent of these contacts, indicated that the maltreating group was more isolated than the comparison group. Means were 12.3 for the maltreating group, versus 13.3 for the comparison group ($t = 2.56$; df $= 511$; $P < .05$).

INTRAFAMILIAL FACTORS.    We found, as expected, that larger and more closely spaced families were much more prevalent among maltreating families. The mean number of children was 3.9 in the maltreating families and 2.7 in the comparison families ($t=6.74$; df$=316$; $P<.0001$). In the maltreating families the mean age difference among children was 2.38 years, versus 2.98 in comparison ones ($t = 3.18$; df $= 144$; $P < .01$).

We failed to find the expected differences between the two groups on a number of measures of child-rearing knowledge, attitudes, and practices. The maltreating and comparison parents were, on the whole, similar in their attitudes toward discipline, expectations concerning the ages at which children reach certain developmental levels, beliefs about why children misbehave, and the extent to which they participate in various activities with their children.

We did find, however, that maltreating families had somewhat less favorable attitudes toward their children. They expressed more negative feelings about their children, described them in more negative terms, and indicated that they enjoyed taking care of them less.

ATTITUDES TOWARD THE LARGER SOCIAL ENVIRONMENT.    Attitudes toward the larger social environment did not seem to be related to child maltreatment. Both groups of families showed similar high levels of alienation as measured by Srole's Anomie Scale. Also, maltreating and comparison groups were basically similar in educational expectations for their children.

PARENTAL PROBLEMS.    Though there were some statistically significant relationships between parental problems and child maltreatment, parental problems were not as important as we had expected. An index based on the respondents' consumption of alcohol showed essentially similar patterns for the maltreating and comparison parents. However, though only a minority of respondents reported that someone living in their family had used heroin, the proportion of maltreating families reporting this is significantly greater than that in the comparison group (15 percent vs. 6 percent;

## Table 6 Neighborhood Perceptions for Maltreating and Comparison Groups

| Statement | Response | Maltreating group % | Maltreating group N | Comparison group % | Comparison group N | $x^2$ | df | P |
|-----------|----------|---|---|---|---|---|---|---|
| There is a lot of crime in the neighborhood | True | 43 | 163 | 36 | 52 | . . . | . . . | N.S. |
| There are mostly people on welfare in the neighborhood | True | 52 | 198 | 44 | 63 | . . . | . . . | N.S. |
| The people in the neighborhood have good jobs | False | 31 | 118 | 24 | 35 | . . . | . . . | N.S. |
| There are a lot of drugs used in the neighborhood | True | 38 | 143 | 34 | 49 | . . . | . . . | N.S. |
| Most of the houses are pretty run down | True | 43 | 163 | 33 | 47 | 4.57 | 1 | < .05 |
| People in the neighborhood help each other out when there is trouble | False | 38 | 146 | 28 | 40 | 5.15 | 1 | < .05 |
| It is dangerous in this neighborhood at night | True | 44 | 168 | 35 | 51 | . . . | . . . | N.S. |
| It is dangerous in this neighborhood in the daytime | True | 22 | 84 | 16 | 23 | . . . | . . . | N.S. |

## Table 7 Perception of Neighborhood Index for Maltreating and Comparison Groups

| Perception of neighborhood | Maltreating % | Maltreating N | Comparison % | Comparison N |
|---|---|---|---|---|
| Negative | 32 | 118 | 20 | 28 |
| | 34 | 127 | 33 | 46 |
| Positive | 34 | 127 | 47 | 65 |
| Total | 100 | 372 | 100 | 139 |

NOTE: $x^2 = 9.07$; df = 2; $P = .01$.

122

$\chi^2 = 5.64$; df = 1; $P<.02$). The types and number of physical illnesses reported by the two groups were approximately similar. On an index of emotional well-being, comprised of items inquiring into current emotions (e.g., being bored, depressed, restless, pleased, lonely, or interested), maltreating parents showed greater current emotional stress. The mean score was 44.51 for the maltreating ones, versus 46.94 for the comparison group ($t = -2.48$; df = 260; $P < .05$). We inquired into another major parental problem currently receiving considerable attention: whether the respondents had ever lived with anyone who beat them as adults. Thirty percent of the maltreating parents said yes, versus 19 percent of the comparison group ($\chi^2 = 5.59$; df = 1; $P<.02$).

MULTIVARIATE ANALYSIS. Using a stepwise discriminant analysis for the total sample, we looked at the combined effect of a number of factors we found to be associated with being in the maltreating or comparison groups: (1) number of children in the household, (2) material level of living index score, (3) quality of respondents' childhood index score, (4) perception of neighborhood index score, (5) social isolation index score, (6) number of years of schooling of respondent, and (7) emotional well-being index score. As shown in Table 8, four variables met the criteria for inclusion in the equation differentiating the groups. The respondents' number of children emerged as the most important variable, followed, in order, by quality of respondents' childhood, material level of living, and social isolation.

The perception of one's neighborhood, number of years of schooling, and emotional well-being did not have sufficient discriminatory power to remain in the equation. The canonical correlation for the four variables remaining in the equation was .319, which suggests a moderate ability of these combined variables to differentiate between the maltreating and comparison groups for the sample as a whole.

## Types of Maltreatment

As shown in Table 9, the predominant type of maltreatment is neglect, with inappropriate supervision and inadequate provision of food, clothing, and shelter most frequently recorded in the case records of maltreating families.

Table 8    Maltreating/Comparison Group
Discriminant Function Analysis

A.  *Classification of variables**

| Variables | Discriminant function coefficients | F-ratio |
|---|---|---|
| Included: | | |
| Number of children | .623 | 29.78 |
| Quality of respondent's childhood index | −.422 | 12.13 |
| Material level of living index | −.352 | 6.89 |
| Social isolation index | −.148 | 1.00 |
| Excluded: | | |
| Respondent's education | . . . | .53 |
| Emotional well-being index | . . . | .35 |
| Neighborhood | . . . | .07 |

B.  *Predicted and actual group membership†*

| Actual group | N | Predicted group membership % | |
|---|---|---|---|
| | | Maltreating | Comparison |
| Maltreating | 328 | 60.7 | 39.3 |
| | | (199) | (129) |
| Comparison | 128 | 29.7 | 70.3 |
| | | (38) | (90) |

*Eigenvalue = .11; canonical correlation = .319.
†% of "grouped" cases correctly classified = 63.38.

## DISCUSSION

Our results show a consistent pattern of a world of great poverty for welfare families, one in which they and the communities in which they live are without many of the things most Americans regard as essential for a minimal standard of living. The maltreating parents have more children, encountered greater material, physical, and social deprivation when they were growing up, are currently living in even more difficult material circumstances, and are more socially isolated than other welfare families. In short, these families are the poorest of the poor.

The findings seem to support a social contextual explanation of child maltreatment. A key background factor, the deprived circumstances under which the parent herself grew up, limits her capacity

Table 9    Types of Maltreatment for the Families
in the Maltreating Group

| Type of maltreatment | % of families | N |
|---|---|---|
| Neglect: | | |
| Lack of/inappropriate physical supervision (e.g., leaving child alone, leaving with inappropriate sitter) | 66 | 242 |
| Failure to provide adequate food, clothing, shelter | 59 | 217 |
| Failure to provide emotional support/ excessive harassment | 37 | 134 |
| Failure to attend to medical/dental needs | 32 | 117 |
| Lack of attention to schooling needs | 31 | 113 |
| Abuse | 37 | 137 |

SOURCE: DYFS case record review.
NOTE: The DYFS case records were reviewed for 465 of the 552 families screened into the maltreating group. An analysis of these data is currently under way. Case record review data were not available for fourteen families screened into the maltreating group; $N = 366$.

to deal with the current extremely stressful situation of a large family, extreme poverty, and few social supports. In the urban central city areas of northern New Jersey it is extremely difficult to find adequate low-cost housing for large welfare families who are receiving flat grant payments that do not reflect the cost of their housing. At best, caring for a large number of children can be a difficult enterprise. For the mother who lives in extreme poverty and carries all the family responsibilities, living in substandard and overcrowded housing without adequate support from relatives and friends, the tasks of child care can become overwhelming. It is difficult to get out of the house and tend to essential tasks, such as visits to doctors, dentists, and schools, as well as to maintain social relations on a firm basis. There are few opportunities to get relief from the combined demands of household maintenance and child care.

Focusing on the four major factors which emerge from our discriminant function analysis, we find that many of our expectations are confirmed, though some are at variance with other empirically based studies in the field.

## Number of Children in Family

The number of children in the family emerged as the most important factor in the discriminant analysis. Large family size has also been found by other family researchers to be characteristic of maltreating parents.[9] In the maltreating families children tended to be born in close succession; this finding is supported by Elmer's research.[10]

## Parent's Own Childhood

The importance of parents' own family background is widely mentioned throughout the literature. Parke and Collmer[11] review some of the basic studies; other more recent findings are presented by Polansky et al.[12] and Kotelchuck.[13] Jayaratne[14] questions the empirical status of the widely accepted conclusion that lack of adequate parenting as a child results in an inability to provide adequate parenting to one's own child. A major methodological problem in the available studies, according to Jayaratne, is the lack of a normative comparison group. The present study incorporates a comparison group and shows that the child-maltreating parents had more difficult childhoods. These parents were less likely to have been raised by both their parents, more likely to say that they did not have decent clothes and had felt neglected, and less likely to indicate that their childhoods were happy. What is more, proportionately more maltreating parents recalled having been beaten hard and often. Thus, in contrast to Jayaratne's conclusion, there is some consistent evidence that the parent's childhood is a factor in child maltreatment. At the same time, it cannot be demonstrated that childhood factors are a major determinant of maltreatment, since a large majority of both groups report adequate care in areas into which we inquired.

Focusing, for example, on the classic assertion in the child-abuse literature that children who are maltreated will maltreat their children in turn, we found, as Table 2 shows, a statistically significant 14 percent difference between the groups. However, we must not overlook the fact that both groups overwhelmingly reported never having been badly beaten as young children (comparison group, 75 percent, vs. maltreating group, 65 percent). Therefore, while useful for furthering our understanding of child maltreatment, knowledge of the physical abuse suffered by a parent in childhood, as well as knowledge of the conditions under which a parent was raised, is insufficient by itself to predict if one will be an abusive parent.

## Material Level of Living

Though our study was restricted to an extremely narrow stratum representing the bottom of the U.S. socioeconomic status pyramid, we found that our measure of material level of living differentiated between families which did and did not maltreat their children. We feel that if there had been a broader spectrum of social classes represented in our study the modest relationship we found would have been considerably strengthened and would have assumed even more importance in explaining child maltreatment from a social situational perspective.

The relationship between material level of living and child maltreatment may be explained in alternative ways. Some claim that other familial difficulties such as illness, addiction, personal problems, and mismanagement of resources are the reasons for both child maltreatment and low material level of living. While the data do not definitely answer this question, we believe that our findings support the assertion of the centrality of material level of living in the complex set of factors that result in child maltreatment. Thus far, our analysis shows either no or small direct relationships between most of the familial difficulties cited above and child abuse and neglect. For example, there were no significant differences between maltreating and comparison groups on reported rates of physical illness and alcohol use. While there was a difference on emotional well-being, it was not a strong relationship when analyzed in cross-tabulation and not strong enough in a discriminant function analysis to remain a significant factor when combined with other variables such as number of children, quality of parents' childhood, and material level of living. While we did not deal extensively with the management of income, in two areas (extent of family indebtedness and the length of time the monthly welfare check lasted) both groups showed essentially similar patterns.

Recently, Ilfeld,[15] in a survey done in a Chicago area of 2,299 community residents, found a strong relationship between low income and psychiatric symptomatology. The basic relationship remained even when controlling for demographic characteristics, personality variables, and social setting factors. This finding, in a sample with a far greater socioeconomic range, supports the assertion that material level of living is one of the primary determinants of coping behavior.

The earlier mainstream literature in child abuse and neglect, as represented, for example, in Parke and Collmer's 1975 review, argues that child abuse is probably an equally serious problem in all social classes. In support of this argument, they cite the many reports of child abuse in both middle- and upper-class families.[16] While no one with a knowledge of the literature could deny that child maltreatment occurs in all social classes, the more important question is the extent to which it occurs and the distribution of types and severity of maltreatment among various socioeconomic groups. Gil's survey, one of the more comprehensive early studies in the field, collected available national data indicating that child abuse is much more likely to occur and is more severe among lower-income families.[17] More recently, Kotelchuck, Pelton, Polansky and colleagues, Garbarino and Crouter, and Gelles have provided data supporting a view of child maltreatment that considers poverty a crucial factor.[18]

### Social Isolation

Our finding that social isolation is an important factor has also been found in other studies, despite the somewhat different methods used to measure it.[19]

The literature suggests that social isolation may be related to the availability of child care from family and friends. Our findings on one-parent AFDC-recipient families do not support this, since the vast bulk of both maltreating and comparison families have no child-care help of this type on a regular basis. Rather, it is our view that participation in a social network offers a family entrée into a system of interpersonal material and emotional exchanges. As Carol Stack notes, many urban welfare families which suffer the endemic economic crisis constantly faced by such families develop patterns of exchange for funds, goods, services, and favors.[20] These social networks also serve as sources of relief at times of emotional crisis and provide a social outlet for lonely, cooped-up, or harassed women.

### Nonconfirmed Assertions

We have thus far concentrated on discussing those assertions that have received more than a slight measure of support in our study. Other factors the literature suggests are associated with maltreatment failed to receive support from our data. A number of measures of child-developmental expectations and child-rearing knowledge, attitudes, and practices showed maltreating and comparison families to be essentially similar. While this finding is contrary to earlier exploratory studies,[21] a recent study by Kotelchuck, with a carefully drawn comparison group, also did not find many child-rearing factors to be associated with child maltreatment.[22]

Both maltreating and comparison groups held similar attitudes toward the larger social environment. They expressed high educational expectations for their children, while showing much alienation. Such attitudes are commonly found in studies of poverty populations.[23] The maltreating group, while statistically slightly more likely to show current emotional stress, did not show the extensive emotional difficulties much of the literature asserts are a major distinguishing characteristic of abusive parents.[24]

## Explanatory Power of the Multivariate Analysis

Combining a number of factors resulted in modest success (canonical correlation $= .319$) in differentiating the maltreating- and comparison-group families. The limited ability of these variables to explain child maltreatment may be due to (1) the extremely narrow socioeconomic range of the population studied, (2) the crudity of the measures, and (3) the difficulty in developing measures of relevant factors and gathering data on many important variables. It may be that these research-implementation problems obscure the true interrelationships among the variables. The argument gains some support from the recent findings of Kotelchuck and Garbarino and Crouter, which like this study document the critical importance of the social context of child maltreatment.[25] The cumulative evidence presented by these studies indicates that, as one moves from intrapersonal to environmental and social factors, the researcher's ability to explain child maltreatment increases.

## Types of Child Maltreatment

Though the literature emphasizes that there are important distinctions that must be made between child abuse and neglect, our findings for an AFDC population served by a public child-welfare agency disagree. As noted earlier, the bulk of our sample involved neglect; as noted in Table 9, the main types were inappropriate supervision and inadequate provision of food, clothing, and shelter. These types of maltreatment are more frequently found among the poor, who live in more vulnerable environments with fewer resources.

Where abuse occurred, in almost all cases it was combined with neglectful behavior. Out of a total of 380 maltreating families only twenty-eight showed no evidence of neglect. The two maltreating groups, neglect only and neglect and abuse, were quite similar to one another on nearly all the factors measured.

The most striking finding about the twenty-eight abuse-only respondents is that they tended to live in better circumstances and in many ways exhibited characteristics and attitudes which were more like those of the parents in the comparison group. The abuse-only group was similar to the other maltreating groups in degree of social isolation and in the quality of their own childhood. Additonal analyses have not yet been able to explain these anomalous findings for the abuse-only group.

The profile of child maltreatment which emerges from our study of low-income families supervised by a public child-welfare agency is typical of most identified child abuse and neglect in the United States. It is quite different from the descriptions of the public problem given by medical researchers who unleashed a great flurry of public concern with child abuse in the 1960s.[26] Medical definition of the problem has emphasized physical abuse, diverted attention from the far wider prevalence of neglect, suggested that the problem is primarily class free, and, as Stephen Antler argues, "has exaggerated the tendency to view child abuse as a disease, a phenomenon upon whose cure treatment must focus. The disease model places further stress upon the physical aspects of child abuse while locating the cause of the disease in the personality of the abusive parent."[27]

The implications of these data are far reaching. Many major child-welfare problems in our society are the consequence of families being forced to live on a subsistence-level income inadequate for rearing a healthy and well-functioning child. A vast amount of literature shows poverty to be associated with a disproportionately high incidence of physical illness, infant mortality, mental illness, poor school achievement, and other social problems.[28] As noted in the report of a national task force concerned with the welfare of families and children, the weight of the evidence from recent studies points to the conclusion that the relationship between poverty and social problems is due to a lack of adequate resources, rather than to a set of characteristics which result both in poverty and in inadequate parenting. As stated in the report: "There is increasing evidence that many of the differences between the poor and non-poor would disappear if the poor had more money and other material resources."[29]

In the light of this evidence, we believe that there should be a fundamental realignment of public priorities aimed at attacking the social, economic, and political bases of maintaining a large proportion of the nation's young families at the subsistence level. A national coalition is needed to press for those much-discussed societal changes which will have greatest impact on families living in poverty —guaranteed employment, guaranteed income, and a national system of universal health care.

In addition the public child-welfare system must also be modified so that it is more responsive to the concrete and tangible needs of the families it was established to serve, and substantially increased resources must be made available for child abuse and neglect prevention and service programs.

## NOTES

Funded by the National Center on Child Abuse and Neglect, Administration for Children, Youth, and Families, Department of Health, Education, and Welfare (grant no. 90-C-418).

1. A more comprehensive report of methodology and findings of this study is available in Isabel Wolock and Berny Horowitz, "Factors Relating to Levels of Child Care among Families Receiving Public Assistance in New Jersey," vols. 1 and 2. Volume 2 contains data-collection instruments (appendices G and H), a full description of the structure of the indices (appendix D), and operational definitions of child abuse and neglect (appendix B). Available as ERIC documents ED 144336 and ED 148094, June 30, 1977, from: Document Reproduction Service, P.O. Box 190, Arlington, Virginia 22210.

2. David G. Gil, *Violence against Children: Physical Child Abuse in the United States* (Cambridge, Mass.: Harvard University Press, 1970).

3. Ibid.

4. Bernice Boehm, "The Community and the Social Agency Define Neglect," *Child Welfare* 43 (November 1964): 453–64.

5. Jean Giovannoni and Andrew Billingsley, "Child Neglect among the Poor: A Study of Parental Adequacy in Families of Three Ethnic Groups," *Child Welfare* 49 (April 1970): 196–204.

6. Claire Hancock, *Children and Neglect: Hazardous Home Conditions* (Washington, D.C.: Government Printing Office, 1963); Rose Massing, "Neglected Children: A Challenge to the Community," *Social Work* 3 (April 1958):

30–36; Alfred J. Kahn, *Planning Community Services for Children in Trouble* (New York: Columbia University Press, 1963).

7. Giovannoni and Billingsley.

8. Special methodological difficulties emerge concerning the ability of adult respondents to recall childhood experiences and circumstances. It is extremely difficult to obtain independent substantiation of reliability and validity of measures based upon respondents' recollection of the distant past. However, we believe that the questions we asked about the respondents' childhoods were sufficiently concrete and salient for us to have reasonable confidence in the information they provided. It may be argued that the picture of the maltreating respondent's background is negatively biased by the poor psychological state and more deprived social and economic condition of the maltreatment group. However, this a priori assumption about the direction of possible bias has no more empirical support than would an a priori assumption that living under more deprived conditions would cause respondents to remember their childhood as more adequate than it actually was.

9. Leontine Young, *Wednesday's Children: A Study of Child Neglect and Abuse* (New York: McGraw-Hill Book Co., 1964); Elizabeth Elmer, *Children in Jeopardy: A Study of Abused Minors and Their Families* (Pittsburgh: University of Pittsburgh Press, 1967); Gil; Alfred Kadushin, *Child Welfare Services* (New York: Macmillan Co., 1974).

10. Elmer, p. 77.

11. Ross D. Parke and Candace Whitmer Collmer, "Child Abuse: An Interdisciplinary Analysis," in *Review of Child Development Research, Volume 5,* ed. E. Mavis Hetherington (Chicago: University of Chicago Press, 1975).

12. Norman Polansky, Mary Ann Chalmers, Elizabeth Buttenwieser, and David P. Williams, "The Isolation of the Neglectful Family," mimeographed (Athens: University of Georgia, April 1978).

13. Milton Kotelchuck, "Child Abuse: Prediction and Misclassification," mimeographed (Boston: Family Development Study, Children's Hospital Medical Center, June 28, 1977).

14. Srinika Jayaratne, "Child Abusers as Parents and Children: A Review," *Social Work* 22 (January 1977): 5–9.

15. Frederick W. Ilfeld, Jr., "Money and Psychiatric Symptomatology" (paper presented at the American Psychiatric Association Annual Meeting, Toronto, May 1977).

16. Parke and Collmer, p. 525.

17. Gil.

18. Kotelchuck. Leroy Pelton, "Child Abuse and Neglect: the Myth of Classlessness," *American Journal of Orthopsychiatry* 48 (October 1978): 608–17; "Child Abuse and Neglect and Protective Intervention in Mercer County, New Jersey: A Parent Interview and Case Record Study," mimeographed (Trenton: New Jersey Division of Youth and Family Services, Bureau of Research, November

1977); "Some Problems of Knowledge: Regarding Child Abuse and Neglect" (paper presented at Conference on Child Welfare Policy, Howard University, Washington, D.C., March 1978). Norman Polansky, Carolyn Hally, and Nancy F. Polansky, *Profile of Neglect: A Survey of the State of Knowledge of Child Neglect,* Public Services Administration Papers, no. 76-23037 (Washington, D.C.: U.S. Department of Health, Education, and Welfare, Social Rehabilitation Service, 1975). Polansky et al., "The Isolation of the Neglectful Family." James Garbarino and Ann Crouter, "Defining the Community Context for Parent-Child Relations: The Correlates of Child Maltreatment," *Child Development* 49 (September 1978): 604-16. Richard J. Gelles, "Child Abuse as Psychopathology: A Sociological Critique and Reformulation," *American Journal of Orthopsychiatry* 43 (July 1973): 611–21.

19.  Garbarino and Crouter; Polansky et al., "The Isolation of the Neglectful Family"; Kotelchuck.

20.  Carol Stack, *All Our Kin: Strategies for Survival in a Black Community* (New York: Harper & Row, 1974).

21.  Young (n. 9 above); B. Korsch, J. Christian, E. Gozzi, and P. Carlson, "Infant Care and Punishment: A Pilot Study," *American Journal of Public Health* 55 (December 1965): 1880–88; Elmer (n. 9 above); S. Wasserman, "The Abused Parent of the Abused Child." *Children* 14, no. 5 (1967): 175-79: R. Gladston, "Observations on Children Who Have Been Physically Abused and Their Parents," *American Journal of Psychiatry* 122 (October 1965): 440-43; Brandt Steele and Carl Pollock, "A Psychiatric Study of Parents Who Abuse Infants and Small Children," in *The Battered Child,* ed. R. E. Helfer and C. H. Keme (Chicago: University of Chicago Press, 1968); Gil.

22.  Kotelchuck.

23.  See, e.g., the review of the literature on Srole's Anomie Scale presented in *Measures of Social Psychological Attitudes,* ed. John P. Robinson and Phillip R. Shaver, rev. ed. (Ann Arbor, Mich.: Survey Research Center Institute for Social Research, 1973), p. 257; also, on educational aspirations, see Elizabeth Douvan and Martin Gold, "Modal Patterns in American Adolescence," in *Review of Child Development Research, Volume 2,* ed. Lois W. Hoffman and Martin L. Hoffman (New York: Russel Sage Foundation, 1966), p. 469.

24.  Ray E. Helfer and C. Henry Kempe, eds., *The Battered Child,* 2d ed. (Chicago: University of Chicago Press, 1974); J. J. Spinetta and D. Rigler, "The Child-abusing Parent: A Psychological Review," *Psychological Bulletin* 77, no. 4 (1972): 296–304.

25.  Kotelchuck; Garbarino and Crouter.

26.  Stephen Antler, "The Rediscovery of Child Abuse: Perspectives on an Emerging Social Priority" (paper presented at the 22d Annual Meeting of the Council on Social Work Education, Philadelphia, February 29-March 3, 1976); S. Pfohl, "The 'Discovery' of Child Abuse," *Social Problems* 24, no. 3 (February 1977): 310-23.

27.  Ibid., p. 11.

28. For a review of these studies, see Elizabeth Elmer, *Fragile Families, Troubled Children: The Aftermath of Infant Trauma* (Pittsburgh: University of Pittsburgh Press, 1977), pp. 109 ff.; also see John Kosa and Irving Kenneth Zola, eds., *Poverty and Health: A Sociological Analysis,* rev. ed. (Cambridge, Mass.: Harvard University Press, 1975).

29. Advisory Committee on Child Development, Assembly of Behavioral and Social Sciences, National Research Council, *Toward a National Policy for Children and Families* (Washington, D.C.: National Academy of Sciences, 1976), p. 48.

*Chapter 9*

# HELPLESSNESS AND HOPELESSNESS AMONG THE INSTITUTIONALIZED AGED

## An Experiment

## Susan Mercer
## Rosalie A. Kane

Admission to a nursing home often represents a sharp decrease in the control that a person has over his or her own life. The decision to enter the facility may have been out of the older person's hands, and, once admitted, the resident often has no choice over the routines and activities of daily life. Professionals offering services to residents of nursing homes must examine the impact of institutionalization and find ways of minimizing or counteracting its negative effects.

One useful and feasible way to blunt the impact of institutionalization is to allow the aged person to be given choices and maintain control even within the nursing home environment. The study reported on in this article was an experiment to determine the effects that increased control and choice can have on levels of hopelessness, amounts of physical activity, and psychosocial functioning among residents in a nursing home. The changes in these three dependent variables were then compared with those shown by residents in a control group who were not given the opportunity for increased control and choice.

### NURSING HOME ENVIRONMENT

Nursing homes have become a last way station, a repository for many of the nation's elderly. The nursing home's role as the ultimate solution for a variety of residual social and health problems can be attributed to many causes, ranging from the infusion of funds under Medicare and Medicaid to changes in family structure over the last decades. Despite the current movement emphasizing the importance of community services, the nursing home is deeply entrenched in this country's system of caring for the aged.

Long-term care facilities have been roundly criticized. One writer considers care of the aged in the United States as "one of the fastest growing branches of organized crime."[1] Moss, the former chairman of the Long-Term Care Committee of the U.S. Senate, conceded that the average citizen perceives the nursing home as "a human junkyard, a prison . . . a kind of purgatory, halfway between society and the cemetery."[2] According to Nader, nursing home residents are "an aggregation of poverty, sickness, loneliness, and powerlessness."[3] Less inflammatory and more germane to the present study is the somber statement that nursing home care is often oriented toward the least competent person in the residence.[4] If this is true, then nursing home personnel may perceive normal, competent behavior as atypical and inappropriate.

Although extreme examples of neglect and fraud in nursing homes exist, the broadest area of negligence has been in the psychosocial aspects of care.[5] Shoestring budgets, insufficient and untrained staff, and a scarcity of professional personnel have been blamed for the lack of individualization and stimulation in the nursing home environment. There is evidence, however, that even lush facilities and extensive programming will not compensate for the devastating psychological effects that individuals incur when they realize that they no longer have control over the decisions that affect their lives.

The need to surrender responsibility for the direction of one's personal life produces some of the most negative effects that the institution has on the individual. For the aged person, admission to a nursing home is a dramatic departure from life in the community. The range of personal choice is restricted in even the most basic activities—meals, bedtime, rising time, dressing or not dressing, frequency and timing of baths, being with others or being alone, medical examinations, use of alcoholic beverages, choice of roommate, and a host of other details. A recent survey of nursing homes in Florida showed that most homes offered no choice in these matters.[6] In another detailed study of life in nursing homes it was discovered that the home provided few supports for the development of sustained relationships or the exercise of self-determination. The tendency on the part of residents was simply to submit to the routine. The researcher concluded that "frustration, helplessness, hopelessness, and powerlessness prevail."[7] Engle has called this apathy the "giving-up, given-up complex" and suggests that it plays a major part in residents' vulnerability to illness.[8]

## LEARNED HELPLESSNESS

The concept that most individuals wish to have control over their personal environment is central to many theoretical positions. Institutionalization for the aged represents an abrupt loss of personal control or, to use de Charms's words, a loss of the sense of "personal causation."[9] The opposite of personal causation is helplessness and hopelessness.

Seligman has formulated a concept of helplessness that has profound implications for services in nursing homes.[10] According to his theory, learned helplessness is the belief that one's actions have no influence on or relationship to the outcomes of events or experiences. The syndrome of learned helplessness is characterized by depression, motivational deficiencies, and even cognitive deficits, which ultimately render individuals incapable of distinguishing when their actions have an influence on events. Learned helplessness is manifested in ways that are similar to those of reactive depression, as in, for example, its sharp reduction of levels of activity. More ominous, however, is its presence among nursing home residents where it increases mortality among its victims.

Although Seligman's original experiments were performed with laboratory animals, validation of the concept comes from observations of the elderly. One study of persons on a nursing home waiting list, which unfortunately failed to control for health factors, showed a higher mortality rate among those who perceived that they had no choice in making the application than among those who believed that the decision had been theirs.[11]

The behavior of aged persons in institutions has been linked to how passive the residents believe that the setting requires them to be.[12] One experiment showed that a volunteer's regular visits to nursing home patients were most beneficial when the patient was permitted to control and predict the timing of the visits.[13] Similarly, it has been demonstrated that simple interventions designed to increase the sense of control and choice among nursing home residents led to increased levels of activity among members of one group. No comparable increase in activity was found, however, in a control group that received equal attention from a benevolent staff but was given no opportunity to make choices.[14] Langer proposes that the illusion of control can be as beneficial as actual control in eliminating the effects of learned helplessness and perhaps in reducing mortality.[15]

## HOPELESSNESS

As defined by Beck, hopelessness is characterized by a negative outlook toward the future. A depressive affect is secondary to the negative cognitions and perceptions.[16] Proponents of this theory believe that potential suicide is more accurately predicted by the extent of hopelessness than by manifestations of depression.[17] Although the word "hopelessness" continually appears in descriptions of nursing home residents, Beck's twenty-point Hopelessness Scale has never been standardized with the elderly. Therefore, there are no age norms with which to compare hopelessness among the institutionalized aged and that of comparably aged persons living in the community.

There is a similarity between Beck's position on depression and that of Seligman. The negative cognitions noted by Beck might be expected of individuals who had lost control over their environment and were reduced to a helpless state. Conversely, persons who perceive themselves as being in control of their environment would be more likely to enjoy confident and optimistic expectations about the future than would those who felt helpless. Helplessness and hopelessness are parallel concepts; both have been used anecdotally to describe the elderly in institutions and both are investigated in this study.

## METHOD OF STUDY

A quasi-experimental design was used to test the hypothesis that nursing home residents who were exposed to an experimental intervention that was designed to increase choice and control would show less hopelessness, a higher level of activity, and a better level of psychosocial functioning than would members of a control group.

Table 1    Comparison of Experimental and Control Nursing Homes

| Variables | Experimental home | Control home |
|---|---|---|
| Characteristics of home | | |
| Bed capacity | 197 | 167 |
| Nursing staff | 43 people, 3 nurses | 61 people, 4 nurses |
| Social service staff | Social work designee | Social work designee |
| | Activities director | Activities director |
| | Consultant (monthly) | Consultant (monthly) |
| Characteristics of residents | | |
| Female residents[a] | 81 | 68 |
| White residents[a] | 100 | 87 |
| Private pay residents[a] | 32 | 26 |
| Admissions requirements | Space available | Space available |
| | Level of care needed | Level of care needed |
| | Physician's orders | Physician's orders |
| | 1 month's pay in advance | 1 month's pay in advance |

[a] Figures presented in percentages.

The sample groups were selected from among the residents of two proprietary nursing homes in the vicinity of Little Rock, Arkansas. Because the intervention was designed to change the milieu for all nursing home residents, not just those in the sample, individuals in Home A were used in the experimental group and those in Home B made up the control group.

As Table 1 shows, the two facilities were comparable with respect to size, admissions policies, and the ratio of private patients to those whose care is covered by third-party payments. In addition, accommodations in both homes were similar; the majority of patients were in double rooms and the more alert patients were separated in different wings of the nursing home from those who were more infirm. Both homes housed a high proportion of white women, but there were more men and more blacks in the control home, which was also somewhat smaller and enjoyed a higher ratio of nursing staff to patients. The sample group included all residents of the two homes who were at least 60 years old, were receiving either a minimum or intermediate level of care, were ambulatory, and were able to communicate. In each home a committee comprising an administrator, a nurse, a social worker, and a senior researcher selected those residents whom they considered eligible. Only three eligible individuals refused to take part in the study, and the final sample consisted of forty residents from Home A and a control group of thirty-five residents from Home B.

## DATA COLLECTION

The senior author interviewed each subject, administering the following instruments: (1) a Background Questionnaire to elicit demographic variables and attitudes toward life in the nursing home, (2) the Activity Instrument, and (3) the Beck Hopelessness Scale.[18] In addition, three or more staff members who were unaware of the hypothesis of the study filled out a Behavioral Scale, used to assess various aspects of psychosocial functioning.[19]

Immediately after the pretest measures had been completed, members of Group A were offered a five-week experimental intervention plan. The plan had the following five separate parts:

1.  The administrator of the nursing home delivered a message to the residents as a group, indicating a desire to have them take responsibility for themselves, itemizing possibilities for decision-making that existed for them in the home, and encouraging residents to contribute ideas or complaints.
2.  One week later, the message was reinforced by the same administrator who went from room to room, seeing the residents individually.
3.  At this time, patients were given the opportunity to care for a plant and were allowed to select one from an array on a cart.
4.  Five days later, those who had chosen a plant were shown how it could be repotted and were given a choice of times when they could get the necessary supplies.
5.  Patients were invited to participate in the newly established resident council, their ideas were solicited for the agenda of the first meeting, and 3½ weeks after the interventions began, residents were notified of the first meeting.

In each case, a record was kept of the subjects' choices. With the exception of attention paid to members of the control group while baseline data was being collected, no particular intervention was directed toward these patients.[20]

All subjects were retested on the Activity Instrument and the Hopelessness Scale, and staff members made a second set of ratings on the Behavioral Scale. Three subjects in each group were not available for the posttest because of illness or injury, which meant that the final numbers included thirty-seven persons in the experimental group and thirty-two in the control group. Although analysis of variance showed no significant differences between the two groups on the pretest scores, an analysis of covariance was nevertheless performed to provide a conservative measure of the extent of difference in change between the experimental and control groups.

## INSTRUMENTS

The Hopelessness Scale is a twenty-item true-false scale, on which higher scores connote greater hopelessness. In field tests with other populations, the instrument has been shown to be reliable, providing correlation with both clinical ratings of hopelessness and other measurements of depression and hopelessness. The scale has also proved to be sensitive to changes in hopelessness over a period of time. However, as has been stated, the test has not been standardized with a population of elderly people.

The Activity Instrument consisted of patients' self-reports that indicated levels of activity for seventeen different items, each of which was reported on a five-point scale of increasing frequency. Of these, four items were discarded from the analysis because it was realized that patients did not have true control over the activity. The remaining thirteen items were totaled to produce an overall score. Passive activities such as reading, watching television, and letter-writing were included as well as activities that were more active or social.

The Behavioral Scale is a sixteen-item instrument used by the staff for rating the residents on such behaviors as eating and sleeping patterns and indexes of depression, hostility, suspiciousness, disorientation, social withdrawal, social participation, and independence, all of which reflect psychosocial adjustment. These categories were rated on a scale of 1 to 4, with behavioral anchorpoints provided for the raters. A total score was calculated by adding the scores on individual items.

The morning nurse, the nurse on the night shift, and the social service worker served as independent raters in each home. Their first rating was performed immediately before the experimental intervention and a second one was made five weeks later. The administrator in Home A also completed the ratings, but in Home B—the control —the administrator had been hired too recently to be sufficiently familiar with the residents.

## FINDINGS

All subjects were ambulatory, mentally intact, and over age 60. In terms of race, all were white. The majority of them had come to the nursing home directly from their own homes. There were no differences between the groups with regard to perceived reason for admission (in all cases, a combination of illness and the need for a caretaker were cited), occupational history, and visiting patterns of family and friends. The large majority of subjects in both groups indicated a desire for greater control over such aspects of their lives as kinds of food eaten and daily activities. Most of them understood that residence in a nursing home meant giving up someting of value —particularly privacy, personal responsibility, friendships, and social and religious activities.

The differences between the two groups are depicted in Table 2. The control group contained more men and more residents who were divorced or who had never married. In addition, members of the control group had lived in the nursing home longer. The mean age of the residents and their level of education was slightly lower

Table 2   Comparison of Subjects in Experimental and Control Groups

| Variables | Subjects in home A (N = 40) | Subjects in home B (N = 35) |
| --- | --- | --- |
| Age[a] | 79.9 | 76.9 |
| Age range | 62–94 | 60–93 |
| Sex | | |
| Female | 39 | 21 |
| Male | 1 | 14 |
| Marital status | | |
| Widowed | 34 | 20 |
| Married | 2 | 0 |
| Single | 0 | 8 |
| Divorced or separated | 4 | 7 |
| Number of surviving children[a] | 2.5 | 1.4 |
| Number of surviving siblings[a] | 3 | 1.6 |
| Years of education[a] | 10.1 | 7.8 |
| Choice perceived in admission | | |
| None | 17 | 28 |
| Some | 12 | 7 |
| Complete | 11 | 0 |

[a] Figures represent means.

for the control group. Perhaps the most significant difference was that members of the control group felt they had had less choice in entering the nursing home than did the experimental subjects. Few residents in either group—but more in the experimental group—had visited the facility prior to admission.

Pretest scores on the three dependent variables were similar for the two groups. Although the groups were assessed as being roughly comparable, initial differences have been taken into account in interpreting the findings.

## Participation

As was previously described, the experimental intervention was comprised of five parts. Phase 1 consisted of a message delivered to a group of twenty-five residents (68 percent of the experimental group), which emphasized self-responsibility and the need to make choices. Phase 2 consisted of the same message—this time delivered personally—which was received by 100 percent of the group. At this time, the entire group received the chance to choose a plant and thirty-three individuals (90 percent) decided to do so. A smaller group of twenty-six residents (70 percent) took advantage of the opportunity to repot the plant. And, finally, twenty-eight people (76 percent) decided to attend the first meeting of the resident council.

## Hopelessness

As Table 3 indicates, the two groups showed no significant difference in their scores on the Hopelessness Scale that was administered prior to the experimental intervention. Five weeks later, however, the experimental group showed a significant reduction in hopelessness in comparison with the control group ($F=10.58$; $p<.01$). Thus, the first hypothesis to be investigated was supported.

As was mentioned, there was an attrition of three subjects in each group because of illness or injury, and these subjects were dropped from the analysis reported in Table 3. It should be noted, however, that on the pretest all six of these individuals scored well above the group mean, which indicated a high degree of hopelessness. Although the numbers are too small to be used to draw firm conclusions, this finding supports the literature suggesting that a high level of hopelessness sustained over a period of time can contribute to a greater susceptibility to injury and illness.

Table 3   Differences in Mean Scores of Experimental and Control
Groups between Pretest and Posttest on Hopelessness Scale,
Activity Instrument, and Behavioral Ratings

| | Group A | | | Group B | | |
|---|---|---|---|---|---|---|
| Instrument | Pretest score | Posttest score | Mean change | Pretest score | Posttest score | Mean change |
| Hopelessness Scale[a] | 10.21 | 7.43 | −2.78 | 9.62 | 9.28 | −.34 |
| Activity Instrument[b] | 29.86 | 44.32 | 14.46 | 29.21 | 33.88 | 4.67 |
| Behavioral Scale[c] | | | | | | |
| Rating of day nurse | 50.63 | 51.27 | .64 | 46.45 | 42.28 | −4.17 |
| Rating of night nurse | 51.10 | 53.35 | 1.95 | 51.85 | 49.25 | −2.60 |
| Rating of social worker | 45.68 | 50.67 | 4.99 | 48.03 | 45.44 | −2.59 |

[a] Score of 20 = maximum hopelessness; analysis of covariance test showed difference in change significant at $p < .01$.
[b] Score of 65 = maximum activity; analysis of covariance test showed difference in change significant at $p < .001$.
[c] Score of 64 = maximum; analysis of covariance test showed difference in change significant at $p < .001$.

## Activity

Table 3 shows the mean scores for the two groups on the pre- and posttest for the activity instrument. Again, analysis of covariance showed a significant increase in overall activity for the experimental group in comparison with the control ($F = 80.48$; $p < .001$).

Because the activity score was a composite of thirteen different activities, a separate analysis was undertaken to examine change in each of the separate variables that made up the activity score. Table 4 shows that the mean level of activity increased for the experimental group in all the designated activities. More change was reported for active items, such as personal housekeeping, walking, and visiting other residents, than for passive ones. In contrast, the control group reported a decrease in the mean score for six of the activities, although these decreases were not stastically significant. When analysis of covariance was conducted for the individual items, there was a statistically significant difference in the degree of change between the experimental and the control group for each item except listening to the radio. Thus the hypothesis was confirmed that at the end of the experiment Group A would be significantly more active than Group B.

In addition, a correlation was found between positive change on the Hopelessness Scale and an increase in the level of activity ($r = .62$; $p < .001$). Thus those subjects in bothe groups who tended to decrease in hopelessness showed an increase in activity. Although

Table 4   Differences in Mean Scores of Experimental and Control
Groups between Pretest and Posttest Reports of Activity Levels

| Activity | Group A | | | Group B | | |
|---|---|---|---|---|---|---|
| | Pretest score[a] | Posttest score | Mean change | Pretest score[a] | Posttest score | Mean change |
| Watching television[b] | 3.65 | 3.87 | .22 | 3.5 | 3.3 | −.19 |
| Listening to radio | 1.65 | 2.00 | .35 | 2.59 | 2.38 | −.21 |
| Reading[c] | 3.35 | 3.89 | .54 | 2.93 | 2.84 | −.09 |
| Letter-writing[c] | 1.89 | 2.24 | .35 | 1.31 | 1.34 | .03 |
| Sewing[c] | 1.46 | 1.76 | .30 | 1.38 | 1.25 | −.13 |
| Playing games[c] | 1.22 | 1.81 | .59 | 1.75 | 1.81 | .06 |
| Housekeeping[c] | 2.24 | 3.81 | 1.57 | 2.19 | 2.69 | .50 |
| Visiting other residents[c] | 2.86 | 4.27 | 1.41 | 2.56 | 2.46 | −.09 |
| Visiting out of home[c] | 1.73 | 2.24 | .51 | 1.72 | 1.56 | −.16 |
| Receiving visitors[c] | 2.62 | 2.92 | .30 | 2.34 | 2.50 | .16 |
| Walking[c] | 1.86 | 2.70 | .84 | 2.09 | 2.16 | .06 |
| Using lobby[c] | 2.70 | 4.19 | 1.49 | 3.13 | 3.47 | .34 |
| Telephoning (initiating use)[c] | 2.59 | 3.13 | .54 | 1.72 | 1.88 | .16 |

[a] Possible score for each item was 5.
[b] Analysis of covariance significant at $p < .01$.
[c] Analysis of covariance significant at $p < .001$.

this finding cannot imply a particular temporal sequence of causal relationship, it does suggest a substantial correlation between hope and activity.

## Behavioral Scale

As with the other measures, there were no significant differences between the staff ratings of the two groups during the pretest. Table 3 reports the changes in staff ratings according to the individual rater; all reported positive changes in functioning for the experimental group. Similarly, all raters for the control group perceived a diminishment of functioning in the group as a whole. Analysis of covariance showed a significant difference in staff ratings between experimental and control groups, which confirmed the third hypothesis.

Although all raters perceived positive change in the experimental group, the social worker rated the improvement more highly than did the other raters. This discrepancy may be due to a greater sensitivity to psychological changes; alternatively, the nurses might have been more accurate because they had more opportunity to observe all the residents regularly. It is possible, too, that the social worker had a greater investment in obtaining positive results from the study.

However, this likelihood is minimized because the investigator spent an equal time in each home. In addition, because the staff were not briefed about the purpose of the study, any bias on the part of the worker should have been shown in the control groups as well. The important finding is that all three raters, each with a different role and perspective, perceived that the experimental group had improved and the control group had deteriorated during the five-week period of the experimental plan.

The administrator in the experimental home also rated the residents, but because her counterpart in the control home could not fulfill this task, these are not reported in Table 3. Of all raters, the administrator was most likely to have been influenced by the experiment, because it was she who gave the original message on self-responsibility. Her ratings, which must be interpreted cautiously, supported the trend, with a $t$-test showing a significant difference at the .05 level.

## Limitations

Because the experimental design required intact groups, the researchers were not able to make a random assignment of individual patients to experimental and control groups. It is possible that initial differences between groups, such as length of residence and perceived choice about admission, influenced the outcome. However, the nursing home constituting the control home was somewhat smaller and better staffed, a difference that might favor that group. Future studies should control for length of institutionalization.

In addition, one cannot know whether the behavioral changes that were reported resulted directly from the changes in choice and control, from the resident being treated with greater respect and concern, or from a general Hawthorne effect secondary to the study. Nor does the study indicate which single component of the experimental package accounted for the greater impact. Finally, it is acknowledged that further study is needed to determine whether the effects of the intervention are sustained over time. A follow-up study is currently being planned to address this matter.

## WAYS OF INCREASING CONTROL

After an initial reluctance, social workers have enthusiastically entered the nursing home arena and are currently in the process of setting forth guidelines for social work practice in long-term care settings.[21] Such guidelines are necessary because, when Medicare reimbursement was first established, too many social workers who were inadequately prepared became consultants to nursing homes. In addition, the potentially devastating effects of perceived helplessness and hopelessness among nursing home residents suggest a number of implications for the social worker's role.

The relatively simply intervention, which involved a staff member emphasizing the importance of self-responsibility, was associated with statistically significant change on all the variables measured. Because of this, the importance of offering choice to nursing home residents has obvious implications for staff members. Social workers can help develop programs and policies within nursing homes that will increase the degree of control, choice, and predictability available to residents. In addition, it seems important that such programs are contingent on an individualized assessment of the residents of the home to insure that the control and choice being offered correspond to what the residents themselves value. In the present study, the use of plants in the experimental design was appropriate because the residents were from rural environments and had indicated that they missed the gardening they were accustomed to. With their professional penchant for individualization, social workers would do well to expend their energy in determining what is important to each individual rather than focusing exclusively on the residents' problems.

In the questionnaire dealing with their background, respondents indicated that they wanted more control over a number of areas. Control over the selection and even the preparation of food, for example, was a paramount concern for many residents, especially women. Another important issue was privacy. Concrete suggestions included the provision of some space—even a drawer—that could be locked and controlled by the individual resident and the requirement that all staff and residents knock before entering a person's room. Such ideas can be implemented by the nursing home with minimal expense and may be more important than personnel realize. Similarly, a shop on the premises, which could be run by the residents or by volunteers, would give the resident an opportunity to make small personal purchases themselves instead of depending on family members. Furthermore, it is important that the privilege of being given choices begin as soon as possible during the preadmission procedures, so that residents are offered preadmission visits, a choice in time of admission, and some input into the decision about room, roommate, and furnishings. The staff social worker or social work consultant might assist in planning preadmission and orientation policies.

## DISCUSSION OF OUTCOMES

Although, as a whole, the experimental group improved on all outcome measurements, there were individual subjects in the group whose hopelessness increased markedly. It appeared that those in the experimental group whose hope had declined had been in the home for the longest period of time and tended not to accept the choices offered during the experiment. Although the numbers are too small for extensive interpretation, these findings suggest that there may be an optimum time for making a concerted effort at intervention and, furthermore, that the beliefs and behavior associated with helplessness and hopelessness become difficult to alter or reverse.

The substantial correlation between low levels of activity and hopelessness represents a provocative but not definitive association. Although there is evidence that reduced activity can result from the loss of perceived control and the learned helplessness that ensues, there is also independent corroboration that the opportunity for activity in itself elevates morale and life satisfaction.[22] Some authorities maintain that exercise has a beneficial effect on depression, anxiety, and tension.[23]

For those elderly persons participating in the study, as with most nursing home residents in the United States, opportunities for physical activity and recreation are limited and physical therapy to improve functional capabilities is almost nonexistent.[24] Therefore, programs of activity should not be neglected in nursing homes and, furthermore, such programs should be planned to offer a range of choice to the participants. If activities are compulsory and routinized, novel and interesting programming alone seem insufficient in relieving the pervasive sense of helplessness.

The impressive accumulation of research suggesting the positive effects of enhanced control and choice with the institutionalized aged needs to be systematically organized and explained to such legislative bodies as state health departments that generally license nursing homes. Such an approach could give impetus to needed change. Too frequently, licensing bodies place emphasis on adequacy of food, nursing care, and physical facilities, but ignore conditions which may be psychically debilitating for the nursing home resident. Loss of perceived control is a life-threatening condition, equally as deplorable as a lack of fire extinguishers.

In addition to direct service, administrative planning, and legislative lobbying, the social worker has another method of enhancing control among residents. Staff training at all levels is a prerequisite for meaningful and lasting changes. And, because of turnover in personnel, such training must be ongoing. It is probable that nursing home personnel are not even conscious of the extent to which many small areas of choice and control are being taken away from residents. As one respondent said, "I used to clean up my room every day, but I quit when an aide said I was putting her out of work."

## CONCLUSIONS

Before remedial action can be taken, social workers must be made aware of the effects of learned helplessness. However, the concepts of that syndrome have not yet entered the mainstream of social work thought.[25] The research base for understanding helplessness, hopelessness, control, and choice should be incorporated into the social work curriculum at both the bachelor's and master's levels. Social workers will find this compatible because such concepts provide an empirical base for the profession cherished values of client self-determination and individualization.

The phenomenon of learned helplessness is relevant to other populations, such as patients hospitalized with chronic physical or mental illness, rehabilitation patients, and juvenile and adult offenders. Everyone experiencing a loss of control and a loss of the sense of personal causation is vulnerable to the syndrome of learned helplessness. However, the institutionalized aged are particularly at risk because the losses incurred are rarely temporary but become part of a permanent life-style.

The social worker who is painfully aware of the enormous residue of unmet needs may find practice in nursing homes discouraging. Paradoxically, a focus on helplessness might be a helpful tactic. The study reported here supports previous work, suggesting that although it is prevalent in nursing homes, hopelessness is not a hopeless problem.

## NOTES AND REFERENCES

1. Alexander Comfort, "Age Prejudice in America," *Social Policy,* 7 (November–December 1976), pp. 3–9.

2. Frank Moss, "It's Hell to be Old in the U.S.," *Arkansas Gazette,* July 17, 1977.

3. Claire Townsend, *Old Age, The Last Segregation: The Report on Nursing Homes,* "Ralph Nader Study Group Reports" (New York: Grossman Publishers, 1971).

4. J. Posner, "Notes on the Negative Implications of Being Competent in a Home for the Aged," *International Journal of Aging and Human Development,* 5 (Fall 1974), pp. 357–364.

5. Elaine Brody and Stanley Brody, "Decade of Decision for the Elderly," *Social Work,* 19 (September 1974), pp. 544–554.

6. Michael Austin and Jordan Kosberg, "Nursing Home Decision-Makers and the Social Service Needs of Residents," *Social Work in Health Care,* 1 (Summer 1976), pp. 447–456.

7. Joseph D. Halbfinger, "The Aged in Institutions." Unpublished Ph.D. Dissertation, Case Western Reserve University, 1976.

8. George Engle, "A Life Setting Conducive to Illness . . . The Giving-up, Given-up Complex," *Bulletin of the Menninger Clinic,* 32 (November 1968), pp. 355–365.

9. Richard de Charms, *Personal Causation* (New York: Academic Press, 1968). *See also* H. H. Kelley, *Attribution in Social Interaction* (New York: General Learning Press, 1971); and Camille B. Wortman, "Some Determinants of Perceived Control," *Journal of Personality and Social Psychology,* 31 (February 1975), pp. 282–294.

10. Martin Seligman, *Helplessness: On Depression, Development and Death* (San Francisco: W. H. Freeman & Co., 1975).

11. N. Ferrari, "Institutionalization and Attitude Change in an Aged Population." Unpublished Ph.D. Dissertation, Case Western Reserve University, 1962.

12. Richard Schulz and D. Aderman, "Effects of Residential Change on the Temporal Distance of Death of Terminal Cancer Patients," *Omega: Journal of Death and Dying* 4 (Summer 1973), pp. 157–162; and Richard Schulz and Gail Brenner, "Relocation of the Aged," *Journal of Gerontology,* 32 (May 1977), pp. 323–333.

13. Richard Schulz, "Effects of Control and Predictability on the Physical and Psychological Well-being of the Institutionalized Aged," *Journal of Personality and Social Psychology,* 33 (May 1976), pp. 563–573.

14. Ellen Langer and Judith Rodin, "The Effects of Choice and Enhanced Personal Responsibility for the Aged," *Journal of Personality and Social Psychology,* 34 (August 1976), pp. 191–198.

15.  Ellen Langer, "The Illusion of Control," *Journal of Personality and Social Psychology,* 32 (August 1975), pp. 311–328.

16.  Aaron T. Beck et al., "The Measurement of Pessimism: The Hopelessness Scale," *Journal of Consulting and Clinical Psychology,* 42 (December 1974), pp. 861–865.

17.  Maria Kovacs, Aaron T. Beck, and Arlene Weissman, "The Use of Suicidal Motives in the Psychotherapy of Attempted Suicides," *American Journal of Psychotherapy,* 29 (July 1975), pp. 363–368.

18.  The Activity Instrument is adapted from instruments in Langer and Rodin, op. cit., and Schulz, op. cit. The Hopelessness Scale is found in Beck et al., op. cit.

19.  The Behavioral Scale is modified from one found in Robert Kane, Ginette Pepper, and Lou Ann Jorgensen, "Can Nursing Home Care Be Cost Effective?" *Journal of the American Geriatrics Society,* 22 (June 1974), pp. 265–272.

20.  A complete account of methodology as well as results can be found in Susan Mercer, "Helplessness and Hopelessness in the Institutionalized Aged: A Field Experiment on the Impact of Increased Control and Choice." Unpublished Ph.D. dissertation, University of Utah School of Social Work, 1978.

21.  Jordan Kosberg, "The Nursing Home: A Social Work Paradox," *Social Work,* 18 (March 1973), pp. 104–110; Elaine Brody, ed., *A Social Work Guide to Long-Term Care Facilities* (Rockville, Md.: National Institute of Mental Health, 1974); and Rose Dobroff, ed., *Social Work Consultation in Long-Term Care Facilities* (Washington, D.C.: U.S. Department of Commerce, 1978).

22.  *See* S. H. May, "Purposeful Mass Activity: A Provocative Experiment with the Aged," *Geriatrics,* 21 (October 1966), pp. 193–200; Marian MacDonald and Audrey Butler, "Reversal of Helplessness: Producing Walking Behavior in Nursing Home Wheel Chair Residents Using Behavior Modification Procedures," *Journal of Gerontology,* 29 (January 1973), pp. 97–101; and M. Rodstein, "Challenging Residents to Assume Maximal Responsibility in Homes for the Aged," *Journal of the American Geriatrics Society,* 23 (July 1975), pp. 317–321.

23.  Richard Stuart, *Act Thin, Stay Thin* (New York: W. W. Norton & Co., 1968); and James F. Fixx, *The Complete Book of Running* (New York: Random House, 1977).

24.  *See* Ruth Knee, "The Long-Term Care Facility," in Dobroff, op. cit.; and Austin and Kosberg, op. cit., for documentation of this point.

25.  *See* Carol Hooker, "Learned Helplessness," *Social Work,* 21 (May 1976), pp. 194–199; Mary Van Hook, "Female Clients, Female Counselors: Combatting Learned Helplessness," *Social Work,* 24 (January 1979), pp. 63–65; and Carolyn A. Smith and Christopher J. Smith, "Learned Helplessness and Preparedness in Discharged Mental Patients," *Social Work Research and Abstracts,* 14 (Summer 1978), pp. 21–27.

Chapter 10

# DISCUSSION OF THE SELECTED STUDIES

## Henry Wechsler

Three studies have been included in this section to represent types of research designs frequently employed in social work research.

### HANKS AND ROSENBAUM: BATTERED WOMEN: A STUDY OF WOMEN WHO LIVE WITH VIOLENT ALCOHOL-ABUSING MEN

Hanks and Rosenbaum's study of physically abused women offers an example of exploratory research. They interviewed 22 women who "lived with violence-prone alcohol-abusing men and who were physically abused by them" concerning the relationship the women had with their men, and the prior relationships the women had with their parents. Hanks and Rosenbaum developed a typology of the families of origin of these women: subtly controlling mother/figurehead father; submissive mother/dictatorial father; disturbed mother/multiple fathers. They described the characteristics and relationships of the women within each of the three groups.

Since only a very small group of women who came to an alcohol and violence clinic was studied, the findings cannot be generalized to all battered women. Furthermore, the study did not include a control or comparison group. Thus it is not possible to determine the extent to which the battered women differed from other women of the same cultural and social background in terms of their personal characteristics. This exploratory study, however, does provide a number of interesting hypotheses concerning subtypes of battered women—hypotheses to be tested in larger scale studies with appropriate control or comparison groups. Types of control groups that can be used in studies stemming from this exploratory research might involve the use of nonabused wives of alcoholic men coming to the clinic, or of married women who reside in the same neighborhood.

## WOLOCK AND HOROWITZ: CHILD MALTREATMENT AND MATERIAL DEPRIVATION AMONG AFDC-RECIPIENT FAMILIES

Wolock and Horowitz's study of child maltreatment among AFDC-recipient families is a descriptive study that seeks to determine which factors interacting with poverty may result in child maltreatment. Wolock and Horowitz found that a number of previous studies had showed "poor families to be disproportionately identified in reported incidents of abuse and neglect." They selected a sample of 552 families from a listing of 1,700 families who were receiving AFDC and whose case records indicated possible child abuse or neglect. A comparison group of 191 families was selected at random from a listing of AFDC families residing in the same counties whose records did not indicate maltreatment of their children. The use of such a comparison group, matched in terms of several characteristics to the study sample, is a common technique in human services research.

Interviews were obtained with nearly three-quarters of the families in each sample. The study found that the families in which maltreatment of children was present tended to be more materially deprived than the comparison families. A number of differences between the two groups was found both in terms of current poverty and material deprivation and in terms of the parents' own childhood environment. In addition to examining differences between the two groups with respect to each of a number of specific variables, Wolock and Horowitz used multivariate statistical analysis to look at the combined effect of a number of factors. On the basis of these variables, they were able to accurately classify two-thirds of the cases in the maltreating and comparison groups.

## MERCER AND KANE: HELPLESSNESS AND HOPELESSNESS AMONG THE INSTITUTIONALIZED AGED: AN EXPERIMENT

Mercer and Kane used a quasi-experimental research design to test the hypothesis that nursing home residents who were given increased control over their own activities would show less hopelessness, a higher activity level, and improved psychosocial functioning than would a control group of other nursing home residents. This study represents one of the limited number of instances in which the researcher can introduce a social intervention—increased possibilities for decision making and personal control.

The study met most of the requirements for an experimental design—pretest and posttest measures—and an intervention controlled by the experimenter and applied to the experimental group but not the control group. As is often the case, however, it was not feasible to randomly assign nursing home residents to either the control or experimental group. Instead, Mercer and Kane used two similar nursing homes, applying the intervention to all residents in one, and using residents in the other as controls. Pretest data indicated no differences between patients in the two nursing homes on the dependent variable: the Hopelessness, Activity, and Behavioral scales. There were some differences, however, in certain patient characteristics such as sex and length of stay in the nursing homes. Such differences arise more frequently in studies in which random assignment of experimental subjects is not possible than in true experimental designs. Analysis of covariance was used as an additional statistical control.

Mercer and Kane indicate a possible limitation of the quasi-experimental design: posttest differences may reflect differences between the two homes other than the introduction of the experimental intervention in one home. The initial differences between the groups may have influenced the outcome. In addition, any study that uses a broad intervention program may produce results that cannot be attributed to any specific segment of the intervention. For example, it is not possible to determine whether the beneficial changes in the intervention group are due to "changes in choice and control, from the resident being treated with greater respect and concern, or from a general Hawthorne effect secondary to the study."

## Articles Reprinted

Hanks, S. E., & Rosenbaum, C. P. Battered women: A study of women who live with violent alcohol-abusing men. *Amer. J. Orthopsychiat.,* 1977, *47*(2), 291–306.

Mercer, S., & Kane, R. A. Helplessness and hopelessness among the institutionalized aged: An experiment. *Health and Social Work,* 1979, *4*(1), 91–116.

Wolock, I., & Horowitz, B. Child maltreatment and material deprivation among AFDC-recipient families. *Social Service Review,* 1979, *53*(2), 175–194.

Part III

# DATA GATHERING

*Chapter 11*


# SOURCES AND STRATEGIES FOR DATA COLLECTION

## Donald D. Dobbin


The function of research in human services, as elsewhere, is to add
to the available knowledge. To achieve this we must refine, reorder,
or otherwise manipulate what is known, or bring together disparate
bits of information, facts, figures, and numbers in such a fashion that
the knowledge base is extended, refined, or clarified.

The assembling of information for research purposes may be
distinguished from the more general collecting of impressions and
observations by the nature of research itself. Data gathering is a tool
for research; it has no intrinsic value in itself. It is a means, a vehicle,
in the attempt to define, describe, explain, and shed light on a felt
need, an issue, or problem of concern. It is a disciplined, systematic
endeavor to examine specified phenomena in an objective, measur-
able manner. Embodied in the formulation of the problem and elaborated in the research design are the crucial elements or variables that
point to the appropriate data fields for investigation, and specify
which items of data are relevant to a given study. It is in these earlier
aspects of the research process that the role of data gathering has its
genesis, and finds its orientation and frame of reference.

The common task in all forms of data collection in research is
measurement. This point is made convincingly by Kerlinger in relation to securing data through interviews, "The interview, in other

words, is a psychological and sociological measuring instrument" (Kerlinger, 1973).

As measurement, data collection must address the issues of reliability and validity. Reliability involves stability, consistency, predictability. Will two interviewers obtain the same responses from a subject? Will two observers make the same observations of a situation? Will the same subject provide the same response when asked the same question again? A data collection technique must have high reliability in order to be useful. Validity means that an instrument measures what it is supposed to measure. Does an index of family functioning actually measure family functioning? Do subjects give honest answers to a questionnaire constructed to measure life-style?

Reliability may be assessed by having two different interviewers or observers collect data. Through applying the "interrater" method, the extent of agreement between the two produces a measure of reliability. Another method, called "test-retest," relies on repeated administration of the interview or questionnaire to the subject. The degree of similarity of responses on the two occasions then measures reliability. If exact repetition is impractical or impossible, two similar instruments may be used to determine reliability. Selltiz (1976) has a very complete discussion of methods of assessing validity and reliability.

Validity is more difficult to establish. There are several different approaches. On the simplest level are two forms of validation that examine the measure in question to determine a priori whether it is measuring what it is supposed to measure. "Face validity" asks whether a measure, on the face of it, is measuring the kind of behavior that it claims to measure. "Content validity" asks whether a measure includes a wide enough cross-sampling of the kinds of behaviors that it seeks to measure.

"Concurrent" or "predictive validity" relies on a single criterion in the validation of a measure. For example, do people who have a high score on a neuroticism scale visit a psychiatrist more often than people who have a low score? Will people who have a high score on compliance with medical treatment visit physicians' offices more frequently in the next three months than people who have low scores? The use of predictive validation requires that there be a sound criterion available against which a particular measure may be examined.

"Construct validity" is more complicated and demanding since no single measure is used. On the basis of the meaning of a particular measure, relationships are predicted with other measures. These are then tested to determine the validity of the measure in question.

For the purpose of clarifying the data-gathering process, we will now discuss the matter of data sources and the various strategies for tapping these sources.

## DATA SOURCES

Two general sources of data may be readily identified. One is the data on hand, data in a variety of places, already collected and presumably available to the researcher. These existing collections of data are sometimes referred to as secondary data sources. They will be discussed here simply as "available data sources" (Kerlinger, 1973, Selltiz, 1976). The second general source of data may be thought of as the actual phenomenon under study. The point is that if data are collected from their original source as a part of the research undertaking, they are usually referred to as original data (Jenkins, 1975).

### Available Data Sources

Social work research in the human services draws upon a wide range of information and observation. Much of the material used in the process of conducting a study may be drawn from existing data files. Rapidly expanding computer technology has made it possible to abstract, store, and manipulate large quantities of valuable data economically. This has led to the development of extensive automated data banks in many fields of human service: for example, in mental health, public welfare, and corrections, and also in related fields essential to research, such as demography and economics. Perhaps the data source of this type most widely used by social scientists, policy makers, and planners is the United States Bureau of the Census. From the tapes and publications made available by the Bureau, it is possible to abstract valuable data for research purposes. The data files developed by the Bureau of the Census provide denominator data, against which other data files may be examined. This is a common practice of researchers when relating vital events, health status, mental health conditions, and the incidence of crime to general population characteristics.

The Division of Biometry and Epidemiology, Public Health

Service, D.H.E.W., has been in the vanguard in the development of concepts and constructs for new technologies in the use of Census and other available data sources to serve research purposes. Social area analysis and community analysis models have advanced significantly because of these developments. The programs of the Bureau of the Census reflected in *Social Indicators, 1976* is also oriented to the use of secondary data sources in applied as well as basic research (U.S. Department of Commerce, 1976).

The United States Bureau of the Census is but one of the many available data sources maintained by the government. A wide range of useful information is collected and stored periodically by local, state, and federal government agencies. Large amounts of data are also available in the record systems of other human service organizations. These data (case records, clinical files, minutes of meetings, bookkeeping accounts, and so on), which are collected and maintained for organizational and administrative purposes, are often useful in research undertakings. In fact, they frequently provide the linkage or port of entry for the collection of original data by identifying a particular study group.

Confronted with the reality of these extensive existing data sources, it is incumbent upon the researcher to justify the use of time, effort, and materials in collecting original data. Such endeavors are frequently quite costly. They can hardly be defended on the grounds that available data will not do unless this can be proved. Significant contributions have been made to the field by researchers who have used existing records; it may hence be argued that with constantly improving record systems, and concomitant methodologic advances in the use of data, the available data remain a fertile field.

## Original Data Sources

The very purpose of research, to contribute to knowledge, to answer questions, almost implies that original data collected anew to help to answer the research questions will be needed. It seems evident that the data requirements of the current emphasis on such matters as accountability, program evaluation, and hypothesis testing in research cannot be met through established data sources. Any record system designed to cover such a multipurpose function would soon fall of its own weight.

The articles reproduced in this book provide a variety of examples of the use of original data sources. In a particular study the appropriate source may be individuals, families, groups, or communities; or it may be an agency, an organization, groups of organizations, or individual practitioner level service providers. In many research efforts numerous sources are used for the gathering of original data.

Exploratory studies focus heavily on ways of collecting new data relevant to the subject of the research. Descriptive studies frequently use concepts drawn from the social and behavioral sciences, such as social class, family structure, social functioning, and self-concept. In order to classify or categorize phenomena on the basis of these formulations, original data in experimental designs is self-evident.

In practice, the nature of the research problem, the level of the study, and the design to be used tend to indicate which sources of original data are relevant.

## STRATEGIES FOR DATA COLLECTION

In adding to what is known, the researcher must first be aware of the existing knowledge base. In this sense, all research may be said to be based on former research. In formulating the research problem (as discussed in Part I), the practitioner is responsible for using what is known, the available data sources, as a frame of reference. Some very useful state of the art reports have been produced in recent years (see, for example, Maas, 1966, 1971, and 1979).

Particular strategies for gathering research data include the abstraction of data from secondary sources (for which prepared schedules or formats are sometimes used), observation, and techniques such as interviews, questionnaires, and a variety of test and measurement instruments. The strategy to be employed, especially where human subjects are involved, is limited by requirements of ethical conduct on the part of the researcher in respect of the rights, interests, and well being of the subjects involved (Selltiz, 1976).

Observation is widely used and is frequently the central data-gathering strategy in exploratory studies. In the Wodarski (1977) study reprinted in Part III, the researchers were nonparticipant observers using an observer checklist to tabulate the incidence of the three different types of behavior. The Fraiberg (1970) study reprinted in Parts I and V concentrates on direct observation and the use of a camera to capture data. The development of video technology and techniques in recent years has added new dimensions to this aspect of data gathering, and is employed in the Shulman (1978) research discussed later.

The number of observers, the roles they are to play, the focus of their concern, and the means they use to record observation, vary with the nature of the research task. A number of different observational methods are described in Selltiz, 1976. One advantage in using observation as an unobtrusive approach to data collection is that it helps the researcher avoid contaminating responses through overt interaction with the data source (Webb et al., 1966).

Much of the data essential to social research cannot be collected through observation; for these situations other strategies have been developed for the gathering of data. Through the use of interviews and questionnaires, information is collected on phenomena such as peoples' attitudes, feelings, and past experiences. This approach is based on the person's own statements or written responses to inquiries. Such self-reports are widely used in social research. The possible pitfalls involved in these strategies center on the validity and reliability of the self-reports. For example, what evidence is there that a respondent is reporting truthfully? Do the same words mean the same things to different people? Would the respondent have replied differently to a different interviewer? Other such questions are numerous. In order to collect pertinent data, a great deal of attention must be paid to the construction of the research instruments and to their administration (Selltiz, 1976, Chaps. 9 and 10, Appendix B).

Questionnaires filled out by the subjects themselves have the advantage of lower cost and easier administration, particularly in large samples. They are also more standardized in the presentation of questions than interviews administered by many different interviewers. Questionnaires have generally been considered to yield lower response rates than personal interviews, but this need not be the case when adequate follow-up techniques are employed.

Personal interviews, on the other hand, permit more follow-up of the questions and more in-depth probing of emotions and feelings. Questionnaires may influence responses through the way questions are asked. When data are collected through personal interviews, the presence of the interviewer and the verbal or nonverbal cues he or she provides to the respondent may influence responses. A nod, facial expression, or gesture may reinforce certain responses while discouraging others. Personal characteristics of the interviewer, such as race, age, sex, or attire have also been found to be important influences on interview responses.

Telephone interviews are a technique for data gathering. This approach combines the anonymity of mail questionnaires with the personal interview's advantage of following up and explaining questions.

Tests and measurements, drawn largely from the field of psychology, provide another method of collecting useful data. The strategy is to collect data through indirect approaches such as projective techniques. The underlying assumption is that through well-developed techniques, the necessary data can be collected to define, describe, quantify, and qualify such illusive phenomena as feelings, beliefs, attitudes, personal orientations, and basic characteristics.

Familiar approaches used include the Rorschach, Thematic Apperception Test, and Self-Concept scales. Indirect methods rely heavily on "proxy" variables. They draw data on responses to issues and situations that reflect or are assumed to stand for what the researcher is attempting to measure.

The three research reports that follow were selected because they exemplify a number of data-gathering activities. They reflect the decisions made in selecting data sources and the strategies used to gather data. Within this context, the function of data gathering as a tool in research is highlighted.

## REFERENCES

Kerlinger, F. N. *Foundations of behavioral research,* 2nd ed. New York: Holt, Rinehart and Winston, 1973.

Maas, H. S., (Ed.). *Five fields of social service: Reviews of research.* New York: National Association of Social Workers, 1966.

Maas, H. S., (Ed.). *Research in the social services: A five-year review.* New York: National Association of Social Workers, 1971.

Maas, H. S. (Ed.). *Social service research: Reviews of studies.* New York: National Association of Social Workers, 1979.

Jenkins, S. (Ed.): *Collecting Data by Questionnaire and Interview.* In Polansky, N. A. (Ed.) Social work research. Chicago: University of Chicago Press, 1975, pp. 131–153.

Selltiz, C., Wrightsman, L. S., & Cook, S. W. *Research methods in social relations.* 3rd Ed. New York: Holt, Rinehart and Winston, 1976.

Webb, E. J., Campbell, D. T., Schwartz, R. D., & Sochrest, L. *Unobtrusive measures: Nonreactive research in the social sciences.* Chicago: Rand McNally, 1966.

U.S. Department of Commerce. *Social indicators,* 1976. Washington D.C.: U.S. Government Printing Office, 1977.

*Chapter 12*

# ANTISOCIAL AND PROSOCIAL CHILDREN AT A COMMUNITY CENTER

**John S. Wodarski**
**Stephen J. Pedi**

The usual mechanisms that provide antisocial children with therapeutic services, such as juvenile courts and child guidance clinics, have not had significant success in changing the behavior of the clients they serve.[1] In recent years, innovations such as halfway houses and group homes have been implemented to reduce antisocial behavior exhibited by deviant children. Even with these innovations, however, many dysfunctional delivery patterns exist that pose serious problems for the provision of services to such clients. For instance, antisocial children are usually grouped together for the purpose of treatment. Consequently, the probability of their finding deviant role models to emulate is increased. In addition, the segregation of antisocial children leads to the perpetuation of the label, with attendant dysfunctional consequences for self-definition, future behavioral opportunities, and subsequent behavior. Finally, even if the behavior of antisocial children changes within the context of treatment, the generalization of these behaviors to other contexts seems to be hindered.[2]

The authors contend that establishing programs in the community, rather than segregating antisocial children, will alleviate many of these dysfunctional aspects of previous treatment programs.[3] However, virtually no rigorous empirical assessment of community-based programs exists in the literature. The investigation reported in this article represents one facet of a five-year project to conduct such an evaluation of a community-based treatment program for antisocial children. This particular aspect of the project was conducted over a three-year period to determine if 40 children classified as antisocial could be integrated into regular groups of prosocial children at a community center. Measures used to determine whether the children were integrated were behavior ratings carried out by observers and self-inventories that were filled out by the children and group leaders.

Previously reported aspects of the five-year study have reviewed the integration of antisocial children into a residential summer camp.[4] This report, focusing an integration at a community center, is another effort at comparing the antisocial behavior of children characterized by the society as being antisocial with those characterized as prosocial when they are brought together in an open setting. In addition, it attempts to assess the degree of consistency between the various self-rating scales and the behavioral observations of the nonparticipant observers.

The site for the study was a community agency that provides a recreational and educational services for 16,000 enrolled members and for the community. The physical plant includes two modern buildings, a 100-acre day camp, and a 400-acre residential camp. Each year the professional group work staff of the agency organizes approximately 200 clubs and classes for children ranging in age from 6 to 18 years.

## SUBJECTS

The subjects were 40 boys ranging in age from 8 to 16 years. About 10 percent of them also participated in the studies at the summer camp. These boys were defined as antisocial according to various diagnostic measures and by members of the professional therapeutic community, including teachers, counselors, psychologists, psychiatrists, and social workers. During the three years of the program, these children were referred to the community center from various agencies, including a special school district, mental health centers, juvenile courts, and residential children's homes. To help professionals refer children, the investigators devised a checklist illustrating the types of behaviors that a child should exhibit to be considered for referral. The behaviors denoted on the checklist were analogous to those listed on the observational scale used in the research and to those reported on the self-inventories that were completed by the child and their counselors. The majority of professionals expressed the belief that if therapeutic intervention did not substantially change the behavior of these children, the children would ultimately be referred to training schools.

Each year the children referred to the project were divided by age and placed by random selection in either a group composed solely of other antisocial children or a group of prosocial children (the children designated as prosocial had no official records of delinquency). Only one antisocial subject was placed in each mixed group, except in a few instances where there were scheduling conflicts. In addition, other groups at the community center composed solely of prosocial children were compared to the antisocial and mixed groups. Table 1 provides data according to each year about the number and placement of the subjects. Approximately 20 percent of the children dropped out of the program each year during the baseline period—the first eight weeks—owing to factors such as scheduling and transportation difficulties and illnesses.

The groups met at the community center for a two-hour period once a week to engage in various physical activities such as basketball, hockey, swimming, and nature hikes and to discuss topics of mutual interest, such as difficulties with school, parents, drugs, sex, and girls. The groups met for an average of 21.5 times, with a range of 14 to 28 meetings. Attendance at these meetings averaged five members, with a range of four to seven members. Every precaution was taken to avoid undue stigmatization of the referred children. They were treated as regular members, were given regular membership cards, and were encouraged to participate in other activities offered at the center. In addition, efforts were made in the training

Table 1   Distribution of Children in Groups ($N$ = 961)

| Year of study | Children in antisocial groups | Children in mixed groups | | Children in prosocial groups |
| --- | --- | --- | --- | --- |
| | | Antisocial children | Prosocial children | |
| I | 47 | 14 | 124 | 139 |
| II | 114 | 16 | 153 | 110 |
| III | 90 | 10 | 89 | 55 |
| Total | 251 | 40 | 366 | 304 |

of group counselors to insure that relatively similar expectations would be held for all children in the program, including the referred children.

All groups leaders were randomly assigned to one of three group treatment methods and subsequently trained in the method.[5] The various treatments used—social learning, traditional, and group-centered—did not lead to significant differences in facilitating the integration of the children. The group leaders were categorized into two groups, trained and untrained. Trained therapists were first- and second-year male students from two accredited graduate schools of social work. The untrained therapists were regularly employed male recreational leaders at the agency and were undergraduate students who, with only one exception, majored in the social sciences. They were assigned to groups on a random basis; however no significant differences in facilitating the integration of the children occurred between trained and untrained group leaders.

## BEHAVIORAL OBSERVATION

A nonparticipant observation technique was devised to measure the frequency of prosocial, nonsocial, and antisocial behavior exhibited by the children. With the exception of the authors' use of this technique in the summer camp studies, this procedure has seldom been implemented in open settings such as community centers. An observer was placed in each group and was instructed to remain as unobtrusive as possible and to avoid social interactions with the group. When he was introduced to the group, the children were informed that the observer would not interfere in any way with the group, that all information obtained would be confidential and would be reviewed only by the research team, and that they could help the observer do his job by ignoring him as much as possible.

Observations of one child at a time were made in a fixed order every ten seconds until all the children had been observed. The procedure was repeated for the duration of the group meeting. In each instance, the first behavioral act observed for a child was rated as prosocial, nonsocial, or antisocial. To minimize bias owing to the observers' expectations, they were not informed of the hypothesized changes for each experimental condition or for any particular subject.

An observer checklist, which yielded highly reliable data, was used to tabulate the incidences of prosocial, nonsocial, and antisocial behavior observed. The impartial observers were trained by means of videotapes illustrating the small-group behavior of similar children, including numerous illustrations of antisocial behavior. Different tapes illustrating children interacting in various types of situations, such as discussing difficulties with school, parents, drugs, sex, and girls, painting, playing ball, building a campfire, and so forth were used in each session to prevent the observers from rating a child solely on the basis of previous acquaintance with the videotape. Training was considered complete when each observer could reliably agree on behavioral coding with one of the investigators and other observers at a level of .90 or above.

To insure consistent agreement among the observers, reliability checks were performed approximately every two weeks for the duration of the study. During reliability sessions, the observers simultaneously rated the interaction of children on videotapes chosen randomly from a pool of 25, again to prevent familiarity with the tapes from interfering with the ratings. The following formula yielded a ratio of interobserver and investigator-observer agreement in scoring a particular behavior for each ten-second interval:

$$\frac{\text{Number of agreements}}{\text{Number of agreements}+\text{Number of disagreements}}$$

The mean of these reliability ratios was 92.25, with a range of 84 to 99. No observer was allowed to collect data unless his reliability was consistently above .90.

The central importance of the recording scheme is its capacity to tabulate antisocial behaviors systematically and clearly according to a time sampling format and, consequently, to calculate relatively accurate frequencies of antisocial, prosocial, and nonsocial behavior per unit time for each child. This format permits an approximation of the proportion of total behavior observed for each child that is either antisocial, prosocial, or nonsocial in nature.

## CATEGORIES OF BEHAVIOR

The following were the categories and definitions on the checklist used by the independent observers to rate the children's activities:

*Antisocial behavior* is defined as any behavior exhibited by a group member that disrupts, hurts, or annoys other members or that otherwise prevents them from participating in the group's tasks or activities. Antisocial *motor behaviors* include those that disrupt, hurt, or annoy others as a result of the child's running, jumping, moving furniture, and so forth. Antisocial *physical contacts* include those that disrupt, hurt, or annoy others as a result of the child's biting, kicking, shoving, pinching, slapping, and so forth. Antisocial *verbalizations* include name-calling, crying, screaming, disruptive whistling, and similar behaviors. Antisocial *object interference* refers to such actions as destroying or hiding others' belongings or slamming toys against walls. *Distracting behaviors* include not sitting in one's chair, luring others away from group activities, and similar actions.

No effort was made to differentiate qualitatively the extent to which each particular behavior could be classified as antisocial in nature. In all probability any effort to weight differentially antisocial behaviors would be doomed to failure at this stage of knowledge development.

*Prosocial behavior* is any behavior exhibited by a group member that helps the group move toward completion of a task or that otherwise exemplifies constructive participation in the group's activities. Illustrative prosocial behaviors are a child helping another, demonstrating skills, providing others with materials or objects necessary for participation, asking the group leader to help someone who is experiencing difficulty, requesting others to engage in the group's activities, positively reinforcing others' participation in a task, seeking relevant information, stopping others from arguing, and attending to instructions necessary for participation.

Not all behavior can be categorized solely as prosocial or antisocial. In many instances children temporarily withdraw from group activity without either helping or disrupting others. For the present study, *non-social behavior* is defined as any behavior exhibited by a group member that is not directly related to the group's ongoing activity. Such behavior is neither directed toward helping the group move toward completion of a task nor toward disrupting, hurting, or annoying others participating in the group's activities. Illustrations include staring out of a window or into space, laying one's head on a piece of furniture, and playing or remaining alone while others are engaged in a group activity.

## STATISTICAL ANALYSIS

Behavioral observations were secured for each year of the project. For the last two years, all children completed a self-inventory. The inventory was administered at the end of the baseline period (Test 1)—eight weeks after the beginning of the program—and four weeks before the program terminated (Test 2). Approximately four months elapsed between the test periods. The "Child's Checklist" inventory was designed to measure the average incidences of prosocial, nonsocial, and antisocial behavior that a child estimated he exhibited during an average week. At the same time a similar inventory, titled "Counselor's Checklist," was administered to the children's group counselors.

The analysis of convariance technique was executed on the self-inventories and the checklists of children's observed behaviors to adjust for initial differences in scores that were significantly different and to control for significant variables that could be postulated to account for the results, such as age, therapist style, dropouts, and so forth. The analysis was performed by the NYBMUL computer program.[6] This statistical technique provided an analysis whereby the experimental treatments could be evaluated through analysis of change scores between two points in time with adjustments made for initial group differences at the start.

In the following sections only $F$ scores that were significant will be presented. The testing procedure consisted of initially evaluating general factors such as treatment methods. If the $F$ scores were significantly different, additional analyses specifically assessed which level of the factor was significantly different from the other. To obtain these data the appropriate comparisons were executed. These isolated those levels of a factor, contrasted against other factor levels, that were significantly different. For instance, to evaluate the levels of the types of treatment factor, each of the three types of treatment was contrasted with one another—social learning was contrasted with traditional, traditional with group-centered control, X and social learning with group-centered. When relevant, this testing procedure was executed on all variables throughout the analysis.

Behavioral data are reported here only for the second- and third-year cohorts of the study. First-year findings were analogous.

## Results

### Behavioral Observations

The results of the nonparticipant observations of the children's behavior are presented in Table 2. Intragroup subject comparisons were executed on this data in which each subject was composed with every other child in his mixed group for the three years of the project. These statistical analyses, provided by the analysis of variance computer program, consisted of 366 tests of significance and indicated that each antisocial child's behavior for all three behavioral categories fell within the general range established by his prosocial peers. Statistical tests on intergroup comparisons of child categories likewise yielded no significant differences between categories of children on antisocial or nonsocial behavior for the last two years of the

Table 2   Mean Percentage of Children's Prosocial, Nonsocial, and Antisocial Behavior as Recorded by Nonparticipant Observer

| | Type of behavior | | | |
| | Year II | | Year III | |
| Classification of child | During baseline | After baseline | During baseline | After baseline |
|---|---|---|---|---|
| Prosocial | | | | |
| Antisocial in Antisocial Groups | 90 | 91 | 93 | 95 |
| Antisocial in Mixed Groups | 93 | 91 | 92 | 95 |
| Prosocial in Mixed Groups | 94 | 95 | 92 | 95 |
| Prosocial in Prosocial Groups | 91 | 90 | 90 | 97 |
| Nonsocial | | | | |
| Antisocial in Antisocial Groups | 5 | 3 | 3 | 2 |
| Antisocial in Mixed Groups | 2 | 2 | 5 | 1 |
| Prosocial in Mixed Groups | 2 | 1 | 2 | 1 |
| Prosocial in Prosocial Groups | 3 | 3 | 3 | 1 |
| Antisocial | | | | |
| Antisocial in Antisocial Groups | 5 | 5 | 5 | 3 |
| Antisocial in Mixed Groups | 5 | 7 | 3 | 4 |
| Prosocial in Mixed Groups | 4 | 4 | 7 | 4 |
| Prosocial in Prosocial Groups | 6 | 7 | 7 | 2 |

[a] The baseline period was set as the first eight weeks of the program. Observations during the after-baseline period were continued up to the end of the program (approximately five months).

project or for prosocial behavior for the second year. For the third year, the prosocial children in unmixed groups exhibited significantly more prosocial behavior in the after-baseline period than children in the other three categories.

## Child's Checklist

The data from the Child's Checklist inventories are presented in Table 3. Antisocial children in mixed groups significantly increased their self-estimates of prosocial behavior over time during both years, as compared to the changes in all other groups of children. Moreover, they viewed themselves in a more prosocial manner than did their antisocial peers in the antisocial groups, and the increment in self-estimates of prosocial behavior was greater than for such peers.

On nonsocial behavior, the estimates of the children were similar in all categories and the significant differences that did occur were not consistent from year to year. Estimates of antisocial behavior by

Table 3    Mean Percentage of Children's Prosocial, Nonsocial, and Antisocial Behavior Estimated on Child's Checklists

| | Type of behavior | | | |
|---|---|---|---|---|
| | Year II | | Year III | |
| Classification of child | Test 1[a] | Test 2 | Test 1 | Test 2 |
| Prosocial | | | | |
| Antisocial in Antisocial Groups | 53 | 51 | 55 | 57 |
| Antisocial in Mixed Groups | 66 | 77 | 58 | 70 |
| Prosocial in Mixed Groups | 58 | 58 | 70 | 71 |
| Prosocial in Prosocial Groups | 48 | 56 | 66 | 64 |
| Nonsocial | | | | |
| Antisocial in Antisocial Groups | 11 | 7 | 9 | 8 |
| Antisocial in Mixed Groups | 3 | 1 | 8 | 5 |
| Prosocial in Mixed Groups | 4 | 6 | 5 | 5 |
| Prosocial in Prosocial Groups | 9 | 8 | 4 | 6 |
| Antisocial | | | | |
| Antisocial in Antisocial Groups | 36 | 43 | 36 | 33 |
| Antisocial in Mixed Groups | 31 | 22 | 34 | 25 |
| Prosocial in Mixed Groups | 38 | 37 | 24 | 24 |
| Prosocial in Prosocial Groups | 44 | 37 | 30 | 30 |

[a] Test 1 was administered eight weeks after the program began, at the end of the baseline period. Test 2 was given four weeks before the end of the program (approximately four months after Test 1).

antisocial children in segregated groups significantly increased over time in the second year when compared to the change in the estimates of all other groups—in which estimates of antisocial behavior decreased. Antisocial children in mixed groups had a significant decrease in their estimates of antisocial behavior as compared to all other groups for both years of the study.

The prosocial children in mixed groups showed little change in their estimates of prosocial, nonsocial, and antisocial behavior for either year. The prosocial children in unmixed groups increased their estimates of prosocial behavior for the second year. However, the prosocial children in mixed groups estimated larger proportions of prosocial behavior on each test than their cohorts in the solely prosocial groups. Clearly, prosocial children in mixed groups viewed themselves no worse than prosocial peers in prosocial groups.

## Counselor's Checklist

It is evident from Table 4 that group leaders estimated similar incidences of prosocial, nonsocial, and antisocial behavior on the Counselor's Checklist for antisocial children in both mixed and unmixed groups and also for prosocial children in mixed and unmixed groups. No significant differences were found between any categories of children in the estimated incidence of prosocial behavior for either year. For both years of the study the leaders estimated that antisocial children in homogeneous or mixed groups would exhibit more nonsocial behavior than prosocial children in mixed or unmixed groups. On Test 2 in the second year, leaders estimated that antisocial children would exhibit a higher frequency of antisocial behavior than prosocial children in mixed or unmixed groups. For the third year of the investigation, leaders estimated higher frequencies of antisocial behavior for the antisocial children in segregated groups than any of the other three categories of children.

## Effects on Children

It is apparent from these data that children classified by various mental health professionals as antisocial can be incorporated into an open community setting with minimal difficulties. As indicated in the discussion of the results, intragroup comparisons, in which each antisocial child in a group was compared with every other group member on prosocial, nonsocial, and antisocial behavior as rated by

Table 4    Mean Percentage of Children's Prosocial, Nonsocial, and
Antisocial Behavior Estimated on Counselor's Checklists

|  | Type of behavior | | | |
|  | Year II | | Year III | |
| Classification of child | Test 1[a] | Test 2 | Test 1 | Test 2 |
| Prosocial | | | | |
| Antisocial in Antisocial Groups | 51 | 52 | 56 | 52 |
| Antisocial in Mixed Groups | 55 | 43 | 51 | 65 |
| Prosocial in Mixed Groups | 69 | 69 | 66 | 63 |
| Prosocial in Prosocial Groups | 69 | 69 | 70 | 73 |
| Nonsocial | | | | |
| Antisocial in Antisocial Groups | 11 | 9 | 11 | 10 |
| Antisocial in Mixed Groups | 6 | 12 | 34 | 8 |
| Prosocial in Mixed Groups | 4 | 5 | 8 | 7 |
| Prosocial in Prosocial Groups | 5 | 4 | 5 | 4 |
| Antisocial | | | | |
| Antisocial in Antisocial Groups | 38 | 39 | 33 | 38 |
| Antisocial in Mixed Groups | 39 | 44 | 15 | 28 |
| Prosocial in Mixed Groups | 27 | 26 | 26 | 30 |
| Prosocial in Prosocial Groups | 27 | 27 | 26 | 23 |

[a]Test 1 was administered eight weeks after the program began, at the end of the baseline period. Test 2 was given four weeks before the end of the program (approximately four months after Test 1).

the outside observer, yielded few significant differences. The so-called antisocial children in both mixed and unmixed groups exhibited similar behavior to the prosocial children in both types of groups. However, on the second set of self-inventories in both years of the project, the antisocial children in mixed groups perceived themselves to be less antisocial and more prosocial as compared to changes perceived by children in the other categories. In contrast, for both years of the project the group leaders increased their estimates over the year of the incidences of antisocial behavior they perceived in the same antisocial children. Apparently, the antisocial children in mixed groups believed they were changing for the better, whereas their group leaders believed they were becoming worse.

The data suggest that in order to achieve therapeutic changes among antisocial children, a bona fide therapeutic program must be implemented. Although mere integration into prosocial peer groups produces no negative consequences for antisocial children, neither does it produce positive change. On the other hand, there were no significant negative effects on prosocial children exposed to antisocial peers as compared with unexposed prosocial peers, whether in terms of observers' behavioral ratings, group leaders' estimates, or their own self-judgment. These data provide a preliminary empirical rationale for the programs a number of states have already established that place antisocial children in agencies such as group homes, university dormitories, and so forth, rather than in traditional institutions.[7]

The professionals involved in youth service during the study believed that the integration of antisocial and prosocial children in the community based program represented a positive experience for all the children. However, their evaluation differed somewhat from those of group leaders who participated in the similar project at summer camp, where certain aspects of the project were evaluated negatively. The prime issue concerning the camp leaders was the number of antisocial children that could be accommodated. Apparently the large community center could readily assimilate 10 to 16 antisocial children into groups each year, whereas the camp could not. At the community center the antisocial children were less visible because of the greater numbers of children who participated in group activities.

It is difficult to assess the merits of these subjective evaluations since the behavioral data seem to indicate that the antisocial children did not exhibit any significant deviant behavior either at camp or at the community center. It is possible, however, that the deviant acts that disturbed staff at camp occurred at times when behavioral observation was not possible, such as during the night, during the waking process, and so forth. Informal observations by the observers indicated that they considered the behavioral data to be highly representative of the children's behavior at other times when formal observations were not being made. However, important differences between community-based programs involving children at a center for two hours a week, as opposed to a five-week camping situation, cannot be ignored.

## AGREEMENT OF RATINGS

One of the purposes of this study was to assess the degree of agreement between inventories completed by the children and their group leaders and between the self-inventories and the behavioral observations. It is interesting to note that both the antisocial children in segregated groups and their group leaders perceived them to be more antisocial and less prosocial than the three other groups of children, although this did not correspond with the behavioral data.

During the third year, the observers completed the Counselor's Checklist at the same time as the group leaders, and their estimates were closer to the behavioral data. However, they too estimated more nonsocial and antisocial behavior and a lesser incidence of prosocial behavior in all groups of children than the behavioral data revealed. This discrepancy was greater for the two categories of antisocial children.

This finding may have implications for how professionals make judgments. The observers were trained according to time sampling procedures to secure the behavioral data, and the more systematic observation of the children led to more systematic assessment on their part. The leaders, on the other hand, were not trained in such systematic data collection but made their estimates on the basis of infrequent observations and on the basis of "critical" behaviors. For instance, when a child exhibited an extremely antisocial behavior, this might have been given more weight in estimating what behaviors a child would exhibit during the week. More adequate training of professionals to make clinical assessments, especially in a community setting such as this one, might insure that they have a more accurate impression of the behaviors children are exhibiting.[8] Such a process may prevent inaccurate labeling from occurring and reduce the chances of counselors creating expectancies that lead to self-fulfilling prophecies. Accurate observation would also provide consistent data on which programs can be evaluated.

Even though many social work researchers and other behavioral scientists have called for use of multimeasurement evaluation when therapeutic interventions are assessed, this research points out the difficulties involved in using these procedures for the evaluation of program effectiveness. It seems that when multicriterion measurement is utilized, change may occur on one operationalized variable and not others, but the changes do not necessarily correspond to one another. For example, a child may change his perception of the incidence of various antisocial behaviors, or a leader may change his perception of various behaviors exhibited by the child, yet in each case the behaviors observed by an outsider remain the same. This indicates a need for a sharpening of measurement devices at various levels in terms of how the measures relate conceptually to each other.

## Defining Behavior

Such a process should attempt to define an adequate reference point for the definition of antisocial behavior. Is it the behavior that a majority of society calls antisocial, the behavior of the child's peer group, or some other social entity? Antisocial behavior is a relative phenomenon and is dependent on who defines it, the social setting in which such behavior occurs, and the measurement processes used to secure the data. Similar difficulties are encountered in trying to operationalize such concepts as predelinquent, deviant, asocial, agressive, and illegal behavior, concepts that have been used in corresponding investigations.

The children in the study exhibited very low frequencies of antisocial behavior at the community center (as they did at the summer camp); however, referrers believed that the incidence of such behavior was substantial. Several reasons could account for this: (1) They were labeled accurately—the children were really antisocial according to the labelers' points of reference—but for some undetermined reason antisocial behaviors were not elicited in the research context. (2) The children at one time exhibited a significant incidence of antisocial behavior; however, they did not exhibit these behaviors consistently, and therefore do not deserve the label. (3) They were antisocial in other contexts but did not want to give up the opportunity of going to the community center. The center was a potent reinforcer for them; therefore, they behaved well because they were afraid that if they acted out, the activities the center provided would not be available to them. All of these reasons are plausible.

Experience with this program leads the authors to believe that direct measurement of behavior, with specific delineation of target behaviors, is necessary for adequate referrals to a treatment program.[9] As one deviates from direct measurement, the amount of error that can take place increases. Moreover, the data suggest that it may be necessary for professionals to periodically reassess their judgments of children. The diagnostic category "antisocial" may be assigned to a child on the basis of a low-frequency behavior, such as running away, defying authority, fighting, theft, or assault. The practitioner may generalize these characteristics to the child's behavior in other contexts, without systematically assessing whether or not such behaviors actually occur in those contexts.

Further research is needed on the following issues and problems:

1. The effects of including antisocial children in a community center or camp on cognitive and affective as well as behavioral variables, both for prosocial and antisocial children.
2. The maximum number of children that can be incorporated into such community settings.
3. Whether staff training programs can facilitate the incorporation of antisocial children into such groups.
4. The development of inventories that provide more consistent, reliable data on antisocial behavior.

Only when these questions are answered can social workers begin to offer services to antisocial children on a more rational basis.

## NOTES AND REFERENCES

1. Lamar T. Empey and Steven G. Lubeck, *The Silverlake Experiment* (Chicago: Aldine Publishing Co., 1971); Empey and Maynard L. Erickson, *The Provo Experiment* (Lexington, Mass.: D. C. Heath & Co., 1972); Charles H. Shireman et al., "Findings from Experiments in Treatment in the Correctional Institution," *Social Service Review,* 46 (March 1972), pp. 38–59; Rosemary C. Sarri and Elaine Selo, "Evaluation Process and Outcome in Juvenile Corrections: Musings on a Grim Tale," in Park O. Davidson, Frank W. Clark, and Leo A. Hamerlynck, eds., *Evaluation of Behavioral Programs in Community, Residential, and School Settings* (Champaign, Ill.: Research Press, 1974); and Steven P. Segal, "Research on the Outcome of Social Work Therapeutic Interventions: A Review of the Literature," *Journal of Health and Social Behavior,* 13 (1972), pp. 3–17.

2. Ronald A. Feldman, et al., "Treating Delinquents in Traditional Agencies," *Social Work,* 17 (September 1972), pp. 71–78; Feldman et al., "Delinquency Theories, Group Composition, Treatment Locus, and a Service-Research Model for 'Traditional' Community Agencies," *Journal of Sociology and Social Welfare,* 1 (Fall 1973), pp. 59–74; Feldman et al., "Prosocial and Antisocial Boys Together," *Social Work,* 18 (September 1973), pp. 26–36; John S. Wodarski, Ronald A. Feldman, and Stephen J. Pedi, "Labeling by Self and Others: The Comparison of Behavior Among Anti-Social and Pro-Social Children in an Open Community Agency," *Journal of Criminal Justice and Behavior,* 2 (September 1975), pp. 258–275; Wodarski, Feldman, and Pedi, "The Comparison of Anti-Social and Pro-Social Children on Multi-Criterion Measures at Summer Camp," *Journal of Abnormal Child Psychology,* 3 (March 1975), pp. 255–273; and Wodarski, Feldman, and Pedi, "The Comparison of Pro-Social and Anti-Social Children on Multi-Criterion Measures at Summer Camp: A Three-Year Study," *Social Service Review,* 50 (June 1976) pp. 256–272.

3.  For a detailed discussion, *see* Feldman et al., "Treating Delinquents in Traditional Agencies;" Feldman et al., "Delinquency Theories, Group Composition, Treatment Locus, and a Service-Research Model for 'Traditional' Community Agencies;" and Ronald A. Feldman and John S. Wodarski, *Contemporary Approaches to Group Treatment* (San Francisco: Josey-Bass, 1975), chap. 1.

4.  Feldman et al., "Prosocial and Antisocial Boys Together;" Wodarski, Feldman, and Pedi, "The Comparison of Pro-Social and Anti-Social Children on Multi-Criterion Measures at Summer Camp;" and Wodarski, Feldman, and Pedi, "The Comparison of Pro-Social and Anti-Social Children on Multi-Criterion Measures at Summer Camp: A Three-Year Study."

5.  For an elaboration of these methods, *see* Feldman and Wodarski, *Contemporary Approaches to Group Treatment.*

6.  Jeremy D. Finn, *NYBMUL* (Buffalo, N.Y.: Computing Center Press, 1969).

7.  Yitzhak Bakal, *Closing Correctional Institutions* (Lexington, Mass.: D. C. Heath & Co., 1973).

8.  For a discussion of this issue, *see* Wallace J. Gingerich, Ronald A. Feldman, and John S. Wodarski, "Accuracy in Assessment: Does Training Help?" *Social Work,* 21 (January 1976), pp. 40–48.

9.  Ronald A. Feldman, John S. Wodarski, and Mortimer Goodman, "Interagency Referrals and the Establishment of a Community Based Treatment Program," *Journal of Community Psychology,* 4 (February 1976), pp. 269–274.

*Chapter 13*

# CONTRACT NEGOTIATION IN THE INITIAL STAGE OF CASEWORK SERVICE

## Sonya L. Rhodes

An examination of the contracting process is increasingly important in light of a growing body of literature that suggests that a focused goal-oriented service maximizes treatment gains within a shorter period of time. Research findings emphasize that ambiguities about the contract and its unsystematic application as a principle of practice may account for a consistently high percentage of unplanned client withdrawal from treatment. Reporting on their research, both Shyne[1] and Stark[2] argue that client discontinuance seems to be related to an absence of communication concerning the reciprocal expectations of clients and workers. Faulty communication can lead to confusion and mutual frustrations which prevent workers and clients from being able to work successfully. Mayer and Timms,[3] stressing the client as a consumer of social services, present convincing data that highlight the profound discrepancies in worker and client perspectives that preclude a joint effort.

Related to the need for a clearer conception of the contracting process are developments in contemporary casework practice and the emergence of new models of casework treatment. Research on planned short-term treatment indicates that an important variable in successful intervention is focused treatment with specific limited goals.[4] In addition to the brief service model of treatment, considerable current attention is given to a task-oriented model which is being evolved by Reid and Epstein.[5] In this model there is a concerted attempt to target a problem area and engage the client in a series of tasks related to it. The viability of the task-oriented model depends on the agreement between the worker and the client on the problem area as this provides the matrix for interventions. In the behavioral-modification model,[6] the contract is an explicit agreement between worker and client on what is to be worked on. Furthermore, the interrelationship in philosophy and practice between contracting as it exists in family systems and the ecological models[7] emphasizes the compatibility of the integral ideas in a variety of perspectives. Thus the emphasis on mutuality with efforts to maximize client participation and involvement as the pivotal dimension to service is thematic in contemporary approaches. However, even a cursory review of the practice literature discloses ambiguities in definition and inconsistencies in practice with respect to the contracting process. The need for a systematic approach to beginnings which would be applicable to a variety of emerging models provided the impetus for this study.

It is my purpose to report on research which systematically examined the initial stage of casework service with respect to the contracting process. This was accomplished through questionnaires addressed to workers and their clients and the acquisition of audiotape recordings of actual interviews between these same individuals. I was interested in identifying and examining the dimensions of the contract[8] from both the workers' and clients' perspectives, measuring status of the contract for caseworker-client pairs engaged in service, and specifying the nature and extent of verbal participation which characterizes contract negotiation.

## RESEARCH QUESTIONS AND STRATEGY

Initial casework contacts were examined in ongoing general practice. The casework service employed in this research reflected an eclectic practice, and caseworkers were not advised or instructed in contracting procedures. Though the caseworkers were not following any contracting model, the research design reflected the assumption that contracting procedures are operative in general casework practice. The research intended, however, to ascertain to what extent contracting processes were implicit in practice and which dimensions

of contract negotiation contributed to variation among paired caseworkers and clients.

Research questions pertaining to contract negotiation included
the following: To what extent do workers and their clients agree on
problem focus and expectations of each other after three in-service
contacts? What is the status of the contract in actual ongoing treatment cases after three interviews? How do these contract scores vary
among worker-client sample pairs? What aspects of the contract are
vulnerable to disagreement between workers and clients? Which
dimensions of the contract reflect consensus on issues pertaining to
contract negotiation? Which areas reflect a noticeable lack of consensus between pairs?

Client and Worker Questionnaires were devised as instruments
to measure the status of the contract. These instruments were designed by the researcher to reflect the formal definition of the contract as "an explicit agreement between the worker and the client on
the work presently engaged in and their expectations of themselves
and each other in relation to the work." The three sections of the
Client and Worker Questionnaires were devoted to measuring the
extent to which each worker-client pair agreed on (1) the work
presently engaged in (problem focus), (2) the part the client expects
to play in working (expectations of client role), and (3) the part the
worker expects to play in working (expectations of worker role).[9]
The extent of the agreement between client and worker pairs on the
three dimensions of the contract (problem, expectations of client
role, expectations of worker role) constituted contract subscores and
a total score which reflected the status of the contract.

A second thrust of the research was to identify and code specific
content relating to contract negotiation within the first three sessions
of contact. Interest in verbal activity with respect to the contracting
process necessitated the development of a coding instrument for
audiotapes of treatment interviews which would define units of participation. Verbal contracting activity of the workers and clients
which was coded included questions or comments reflecting the
client's reasons for associating with the agency, explorations of the
agency's function and discrepancies between agency service and
client's expectations, and discussions about worker and/or client
roles.[10] Research questions focused on how participation in the contracting process was distributed within the worker-client pair, who
took major responsibility for contracting, and how workers and
clients paced themselves over the three interviews (did workers initi-

ate contracting activity, did clients follow workers' leads, was contracting evenly spaced over three interviews, etc.?).

## CHARACTERISTICS OF THE STUDY SAMPLE

The study was undertaken under the sponsorship of the Veterans Administration, and an outpatient medical and psychiatric facility was chosen as the setting for this study. The study sample included fifteen worker-client pairs; both members of each pair submitted questionnaires; each pair also submitted three forty-five-minute tape recordings of their first three interviews. The sample of social workers for this study included almost the total professional staff drawn from the three social work services (mental hygiene, medical, posthospitalization). The workers were a relatively homogeneous group by virtue of their eclectic orientation, professional experience of considerable length and breadth, and familiarity with social work concepts relating to the contracting process.

Because of the audio equipment used in the study, clients diagnosed as paranoid schizophrenics were not included as subjects for fear of exacerbating their symptoms. Vietnam and World War II veterans dominated the client sample; clients were predominantly lower-to-middle class and evenly distributed in terms of employment status among employed, unemployed or retired/student situations.

The cases assigned to workers after a brief intake procedure covered a wide range of presenting problems such as a request for job counseling and/or placement, personality adjustment problems, depression, marital conflicts, social and psychological problems related to physical illness, reentry into the community due to psychiatric hospitalization, etc. In order to be eligible for the study, the patient needed to be initiating a new contact at the clinic; he could thus be a former clinic patient but not an ongoing case that was being transferred to a new worker. Thus reapplication for social service was seen to represent a continuous thread of agency availability to the range of the veteran's needs, while at the same time each renewed contact presents the opportunity for a newly explored focus and partialized goals to emerge. All study clients were screened for one interview prior to being assigned to a worker, in order to eliminate those clients who required only a very brief and/or concrete service which would prevent the three-session sequence required for inclusion in this study.

## STATUS OF THE CONTRACT: CLIENT AND WORKER QUESTIONNAIRES

The formal definition of the contract as "an explicit agreement between the worker and the client on the work they are presently engaged in and their expectations of themselves and each other" is operationalized in sections I, II, and III of the Client and Worker Questionnaires. Section I relates to that part of the formal definition which describes the contract as "an explicit agreement between the worker and the client on the work they are presently engaged in" and includes the following dimensions (which are translated into questions): expectations of the agreement between worker and client; flexibility of the agreement; realistic focus; agreed-upon focus; focus related to client's motivation; focus related to client's perception of his needs; focus consistent with agency service; client involvement in the work; and expectations relating to attendance, duration of service, and involvement of family members. The same question appears on the worker's and the client's questionnaires, except that the question is phrased so that each respondent in the worker-client pair answers for himself. No question is devised to anticipate someone else's response. Scoring is consistent with our definition, in that the criteria for contracting relates to the extent of *agreement* between the worker-client pair; one point is given for each agreed-upon response, and no credit is given for disagreement. An optimum score on section I of the questionnaire is +18; the lowest score is 0. Each worker-client pair has a score on this section.

Section II is designed to gather information on the extent of agreement between the worker-client pair on the *client role.* Thus there are thirty-six "yes" and "no" items which deal with the worker's and the client's expectations of the client in relation to the work they are doing together. All questions were considered neutral, in the sense that credit (½ point) is given for each question that reflects agreement between the worker-client pair, regardless of whether agreement is in the "yes" or "no" column.

Section III is similar to section II, except that this section is developed to gather information on the extent of agreement between the worker-client pair on the *worker role.* Thus there are thirty-six "yes" and "no" questions which deal with the worker's and the client's expectations of the worker in relation to the work they are doing together. Again, all questions are considered neutral, in the sense that credit (½ point) is given for each question that reflects agreement between the worker-client pair, regardless of whether agreement is in the "yes" or "no" column.

The rationale for this design is that the questions in sections II and III reflect a wide range of worker and client behaviors in the interviewing situation. Moreover, expectations listed cover a range of theoretical preferences from the psychosocial to the problem solving to the existential approaches, as well as idiosyncratic and stylistic differences among workers and cultural differences among clients. Optimum subscores on each of these sections is +18, and the range of scores is 0 to +18.

The three sections of the questionnaire that assess the status of the contract thus described make it clear that contracting subscores in addition to a total (or status of contract) score are available: one subscore reflects extent of agreement on the work presently engaged in; another subscore reflects extent of agreement between the client's expectations of himself and the worker's expectation of the client in relation to the work; and a third subscore reflects the extent of agreement between the client's expectations of the worker and the worker's expectations of himself in relation to the work. One might find that clients and workers are in closer agreement and thus clearer about their expectations of the client role than they are about the worker's responsibility or vice versa. Each subscore is given equal weight in accordance with our definition; an advantage of the instrument is that one can make comparisons of the three subscores and define the area of the contracting process which is underdeveloped as well as determine the overall status of the contract.

## Summary of Research Findings Pertaining to Contract Status

Contract status scores among the fifteen worker-client pairs varied from a low score of 23.5 to a high score of 39.5. Theoretically optimal low and optimal high scores range from 0 to 54. The mean contract score was 34.166. Contract scores achieved in each of the three sections of the questionnaire were correlated with each other in order to determine their interrelationship. Statistically significant correlations were found between section I (problem) and section III (expectations of worker role) ($r = .517$, $P < .05$) and between section II (expectations of client role) and section III ($r = 0497$, $P < .05$). However, a positive correlation was not found between section I and section II, indicating that a delineation of a problem focus and expectations of client role are not related and thus remain independent of one another. On the other hand, section III is related on a statistically significant basis to delineation of focus and client role. This finding suggests that the worker's ability to convey what his tasks are in relation to offering help to the client reverberates into other essential aspects of contract negotiation and may be pivotal to the contracting process. However, it also suggests that the client's needs and tasks are underdeveloped aspects of contract negotiation and do not appear to develop in relation to one another. An interpretation of these findings suggests that contract negotiation might benefit from an approach which maximizes the interplay between client-identified needs and clarity of client tasks in the treatment process so that these facets of contract negotiation could be interrelated.

## Problem Focus as a Dimension of Contracting

The data were analyzed for each section of the contracting questionnaires with respect to those issues that appeared to be vulnerable to worker-client disagreement. Table 1 ranks the items in section I of the questionnaire in which there was a high percentage of disagreement within pairs. Studying these tabulations, we can ask in what areas relating to problem focus worker-client pairs fail to come to an understanding. The table is organized by ranking these items in terms of percentage of worker-client pairs who did not achieve agreement on the items and then showing the way these mismatched pairs disagreed in terms of "yes" and "no" responses for workers and clients.

Following the computations in Table 1 suggests that it might be worthwhile and time saving for workers to take responsibility for initiating and clarifying potential areas of misunderstanding, confusion, and ambiguity between themselves and their clients with respect to the following dimensions of the problem focus:

1. *Guaranteed improvement.*—This item asks for a "yes" or "no" response from each worker and client on whether the worker is "guaranteeing improvement or changes in those areas that you've agreed to focus on." Thirteen out of fifteen pairs (or 87 percent) of the study sample were mismatched on this item. More clients than workers answered affirmatively. Therefore at least one partner in 87

Table 1   Items from Section I of Questionnaires Ranked in Order of Percentage of Worker-Client Pairs Disagreeing on Item

| Issue | % Pairs disagreeing | % Workers | | % Clients | |
|---|---|---|---|---|---|
| | | Yes | No | Yes | No |
| 3B Guaranteed results* | 87 (13) | 23 (3) | 38 (5) | 46 (6) | 15 (2) |
| 9 Existence of hidden agenda | 73 (11) | 91 (10) | 9 (1) | 9 (1) | 91 (10) |
| 16 Expected duration of service† | 73 (11) | ... | ... | ... | ... |
| 4 Delineation of focus‡ | 67 (10) | ... | ... | ... | ... |
| 2 Delineation of focus | 60 (9) | 78 (7) | 22 (2) | 22 (2) | 78 (7) |
| 3 Delineation of focus | 53 (8) | 28 (3) | 63 (5) | 50 (4) | 38 (3) |
| 3D Delineation of focus | 53 (88) | 13 (1) | 38 (3) | 25 (2) | 25 (2) |
| 15 Who attends | 53 (8) | 100 (8) | 0 (0) | 0 (0) | 100 (3) |
| 1 Delineation of focus | 40 (6) | 17 (1) | 83 (5) | 50 (3) | 17 (1) |
| 11 Self-determination | 20 (33) | 0 (0) | 100 (3) | 100 (3) | 0 (0) |

NOTE: Five workers and five clients did not answer item 3B: one client did not answer item 3; four clients did not answer item 3D; two clients did not answer item 1. Figures in parentheses represent actual numbers.

*This item does not fit the agreement-disagreement formula, in that a "yes" response by either one or both role partners yielded no credit for the item.

†The "yes"-"no" formula is not applicable to this item. However, eleven clients (73%) answered that they expected to be receiving counseling for a *shorter* period of time than their paired caseworkers estimated.

‡Worker and client pairs did not agree on the present focus of the work they were doing together.

percent of our study sample was under the false impression that workers had the power and/or authority to guarantee improvement in the client's situation. These findings suggest that some workers and some clients tend to be overly optimistic about outcome or results and/or invest an excessive degree of omnipotence in the worker.

   2. *Existence of a hidden agenda.*—Do workers have certain ideas about the goals of treatment that they do not tell the client? Seventy-three percent (eleven pairs) of the sample pairs disagreed with their partners on this item. Ten workers in the sample indicated "yes," while their role partners answered "no." Thus in the ten worker-client pairs the clients were not aware of the existence of a hidden agenda and in fact indicated that they did not think workers had any goals other than those that had been made explicit. Such figures suggest the possibility that workers and clients may be working at cross purposes if workers have objectives in mind which they do not share and thus fail to enlist the client's commitment to a joint pursuit of these objectives.

*3. Estimation of length of service.* —When clients and workers were asked the question, "How long do you think ["you" or "the client"] will be coming to the agency?" 73 percent, or eleven worker-client pairs, answered differently. Eight clients indicated that they expected to be in treatment for a shorter period of time than their paired caseworkers indicated. Three mismatches in paired caseworker and client responses occurred in the other direction, with the caseworker expressing an expectation of a shorter involvement than the client. These findings indicate that in a majority of cases workers overestimate (or clients underestimate) the length of time clients expect to be receiving service. This raises important issues in terms of how workers reconcile this discrepancy. In discussing such findings with workers both at the VA clinic and at other mental health facilities in the New York area, I was struck by the extent to which workers insisted that the discrepancy was due to the fact that the clients had not yet been seduced into a longer form of treatment and that this goal would be accomplished as the treatment progressed. I suspect that this discrepancy in time perspective relates to the previously discussed issue of the hidden agenda, in that workers feel justified in keeping long-term treatment objectives to themselves if they are expecting the client to pursue a long-term, open-ended, and unfocused course of treatment.

*4. Delineating a problem focus of service.* —When workers and clients were asked to write what they believed to be the focus of the work with ("your caseworker"-"your client") at the present time (item 4), ten pairs (or 67 percent) of the study sample did not agree on the focus. Since credit was given for paired statements that were rough approximations of each other, this 67 percent represents a conservative estimate of the extent of lack of clarity and explicitness within pairs with respect to the focus of the work.

Moreover, when clients and workers were asked if the worker made a "conscious deliberate attempt to engage [the client] in a discussion of the focus of the work you are doing together," nine, or 60 percent, of the worker-client pairs disagreed. Seven workers answered affirmatively, but their role partners answered negatively, indicating that workers may overestimate the impact of their attempts to zero in on a problem area as an explicit focus of treatment. Worker-client mismatches on the items related to the deliberate engagement of the client in delineating a focus of service indicate that, when misperceptions exist within a pair, they exist in the direction of clients missing workers' attempts to focus. These findings strongly suggest that workers tend to be too subtle and possibly indirect in the aspect of contracting which includes the explicit definition of a focus.

5. *Who in the family is involved in counseling.* —When workers and clients were asked, "Are other family members besides ["you"-"the client"] expected to come to sessions?" eight worker-client pairs indicated a lack of agreement. In each pair a misperception occurred with the worker expecting other family members to attend counseling, while the client in the pair maintained that only he was expected to attend sessions. This suggests that clients may be reluctant to include other family members in their treatment, while workers are thinking of the "client" in a larger context than the identified patient alone. One wonders why clients are reluctant to include spouses, parents, and children and what part the setting plays in reinforcing their perception that they only are "the client." In view of the impact of family and ecological systems on development, this finding suggests the necessity of further exploration of the nature of clients' resistance.

6. *Self-determination.* —When workers and clients were asked whether the client has an *un*important role to play in determining the course of the service he is receiving, three worker-client pairs were mismatched. In each mismatched pair the worker, subscribing to the principle of self-determination, answered negatively, indicating that the client did indeed have an important role to play in his treatment; but the client in each pair answered affirmatively, indicating his belief that the course and evolution of his casework service was not under his influence. While this mismatch occurred in only three (or 20 percent) of the fifteen pairs, it is significant that some clients in this setting underestimate or devalue their right to influence the nature and course of the service they are receiving.

## Expectations of Client Role as a Dimension of Contracting

We now turn to the second dimension of contracting having to do with expectations of client role. Table 2 ranks the items in section II of the questionnaires in terms of disagreement within pairs. Questions, phrased from the client's point of view, which are potential areas of misperception between workers and clients are the following: Do you expect to relate important dreams to your worker? Do you expect to share your deepest thoughts with your caseworker? Do you expect to be embarrassed by things you tell the caseworker?

Table 2   Items from Section II of Questionnaires Ranked in
Order of Percentage of Worker-Client Pairs Disagreeing on Item

| Issue: Worker/client expectations of client | % Pairs disagreeing | % Workers | | % Clients | |
|---|---|---|---|---|---|
| | | Yes | No | Yes | No |
| 6 Relate Dreams | 67 (10) | 30 (3) | 70 (7) | 70 (7) | 30 (3) |
| 18 Do what worker tells him* | 67 (10) | 10 (1) | 90 (9) | 80 (8) | 10 (1) |
| 10 Depend on worker | 60 (9) | 22 (2) | 78 (7) | 78 (7) | 22 (2) |
| 27 Depend on worker* | 60 (9) | 11 (1) | 89 (8) | 89 (8) | 0 (0) |
| 36 Be embarrassed | 60 (9) | 100 (9) | 0 (0) | 0 (0) | 100 (9) |
| 31 Share deepest thoughts* | 53 (8) | 0 (0) | 100 (8) | 88 (7) | 0 (0) |
| 8 Be careful what he says* | 47 (7) | 57 (4) | 43 (3) | 43 (3) | 43 (3) |
| 17 Bring out reactions to caseworker | 47 (7) | 71 (5) | 29 (2) | 29 (2) | 71 (5) |
| 19 Hold back feelings | 47 (7) | 100 (7) | 0 (0) | 0 (0) | 100 (7) |
| 35 Tell other family members | 47 (7) | 100 (7) | 0 (0) | 0 (0) | 100 (7) |
| 29 Discuss experience with drugs | 47 (7) | 57 (4) | 43 (3) | 43 (3) | 57 (4) |
| 1 Experience intense feelings | 40 (6) | 17 (1) | 83 (5) | 83 (5) | 17 (1) |
| 12 Do most of talking | 40 (6) | 100 (6) | 0 (0) | 0 (0) | 100 (6) |
| 14 Tell caseworker when he disagrees | 40 (6) | 17 (1) | 83 (5) | 83 (5) | 17 (1) |
| 26 Prepare for session | 40 (6) | 33 (2) | 67 (4) | 67 (4) | 33 (2) |
| 30 Change* | 40 (6) | 50 (3) | 50 (3) | 33 (2) | 50 (3) |

*One client did not answer this item.

These three questions, which were highly vulnerable to mismatches between clients and workers, reflect the pervasive and fundamental gap between the workers' philosophical and theoretical allegience to psychoanalytic theory and the clients' pragmatism, consciously experienced "openness," and willingness to be cued by workers with respect to sharing dreams. Workers and clients attach different meanings to the notion of sharing one's "deepest thoughts," with workers assuming that this is a painful and laborsome process. Pursuing this argument, the worker's perspective, influenced by psychoanalytic theory and equations between deepest thoughts and unconscious ideation, clashes with that of the client, who consciously intends to cooperate fully in counseling by sharing all and does not understand or respect the existence of unconscious motivation. We might hypothesize that what happens under such circumstances is that workers do not sufficiently capitalize on what clients are ready to bring to and share in the session because of their prejudice in favor of underlying and more inaccessible thoughts and, moreover, that their interventions are geared to uncover rather than discover the richness of clients' conscious thoughts, ideas, conflicts, and concerns.

Other ambiguities, confusions, and misunderstandings of client role occur within pairs with respect to the activity or passivity of the client. Studying the large percentages of disagreement within pairs on items 18 (67 percent), 10 (60 percent), 27 (60 percent), and 12 (40 percent) reveals that, when there is a disagreement between workers and clients on the extent to which a client should depend on his worker for direction, it is usually the case that clients are expecting *more* direction than workers want to provide, and workers are expecting clients to take more initiative than clients are willing to assume. These issues remain unresolved for a majority of worker-client pairs after the third interview.

## Expectations of Worker Role as a Dimension of Contracting

With respect to the third dimension of contracting, we can ask what areas relating to worker role are characterized by a discrepancy between workers and clients (Table 3). In the high-ranking items, two themes emerge. The first is that clients expect workers to offer

Table 3  Items from Section III of Questionnaires Ranked in Order of Percentage of Worker-Client Pairs Disagreeing on Item

| Issue: Worker/client expectations of worker | % Pairs disagreeing | % Workers | | % Clients | |
|---|---|---|---|---|---|
| | | Yes | No | Yes | No |
| 18  Be a friend | 80 (12) | 25 (3) | 75 (9) | 75 (9) | 25 (3) |
| 21  Mostly listen* | 80 (12) | 50 (6) | 50 (6) | 50 (6) | 42 (5) |
| 7  Give rules to follow | 67 (10) | 30 (3) | 70 (7) | 70 (7) | 30 (3) |
| 36  Get another family member to clinic | 67 (10) | 90 (9) | 10 (1) | 10 (1) | 90 (9) |
| 23  Bring up service experience | 60 (9) | 44 (4) | 56 (5) | 56 (5) | 44 (4) |
| 30  Remind client of past mistakes | 60 (9) | 22 (2) | 77 (7) | 78 (7) | 22 (2) |
| 3  Cheer client up | 53 (8) | 38 (3) | 63 (5) | 63 (5) | 38 (3) |
| 6  Tell client what problem is | 53 (8) | 50 (4) | 50 (4) | 50 (4) | 50 (4) |
| 16  Get client's mind off his troubles | 53 (8) | 0 (0) | 100 (8) | 100 (8) | 0 (0) |
| 19  Provide solution | 53 (8) | 0 (0) | 100 (8) | 100 (8) | 0 (0) |
| 11  Interrupt client | 40 (6) | 33 (2) | 67 (4) | 67 (4) | 33 (2) |
| 15  Arrange specific services | 40 (6) | 83 (5) | 17 (1) | 17 (1) | 83 (5) |
| 28  Get angry | 40 (6) | 100 (6) | 0 (0) | 0 (0) | 100 (6) |
| 32  Provide information | 40 (6) | 100 (6) | 0 (0) | 0 (0) | 100 (6) |
| 34  Help client feel better | 40 (6) | 33 (2) | 67 (4) | 67 (4) | 33 (2) |

*One client did not answer this item.

friendship, concrete advice, and relief and to provide solutions, whereas workers do not plan to do so. On the other hand, potential areas of misunderstanding exist when clients expect workers to be more directive and the latter fail to demonstrate what is directive within the scope of their role such as arranging specific services; providing information about disability payments, loans, and insurance; and locating resources. These are noteworthy findings, since they point out that clients tend to wait for social work activity that will never be forthcoming and may eventually become frustrated and dissatisfied, while workers fail to communicate some aspects of their role which relate to their willingness to provide concrete services.

## Verbal Participation in Contracting

Audiotape recordings were made of the first three interviews after case assignment, in order to collect data on verbal participation in the contracting process. Content relating to verbal contracting activity of worker and client was analyzed and coded. The research design operationalized verbal participation of the client and worker by locating statements which fall into any of the following six categories of social worker's and/or client's attempts: to clarify expectations of agency, to clarify agency function, to explore and deal with any discrepancy between agency service and client's expectation, to clarify expectations of client role, to clarify social worker's role, and to deal with discrepancy in role expectations. The researcher listened to each of the forty-five-minute audiotapes (forty-five tapes) and counted the frequency of verbal contracting activity for worker and client in each pair. Total scores were available reflecting sums of verbal contracting activity for each worker and each client in each of the three interviews and cumulatively for the series of three interviews.

A two-way analysis of variance was performed, using the two groups (caseworkers and clients) and the three interviews as the two variables. The results indicate that the frequency of total worker participation in contracting is significantly different from the frequency of total client participation ($F$ [1/28] = 6.101, $P < .025$), a finding which is consistent with the hypothesis that workers carry major responsibility for contracting. Second, taking interviews as the variable, a statistically significant difference was found between the frequency of participation for the two groups over the three interviews, with caseworker activity distinguishably more frequent than client activity in each of the three interviews ($F$ [2/56] = 12.442, $P < .001$). Third, the interaction between groups and interviews did not indicate that caseworkers and clients move in different directions or at different rates, implying that, though clients make fewer comments in each of the three interviews with respect to contracting, they follow the rhythm and pacing of their workers and are thus responsive to workers' leads.

These findings suggest an apparent dominance of worker activity which may overshadow the determinant of client involvement and raise the issue of whether striving for more mutual interaction and feedback would be desirable for casework practice.

Furthermore, a definite pattern emerged, showing that the major proportion of contracting activity is done in the first interview. This finding raises important questions about the desirability of expanding and elaborating the contracting process as a sequence of interactions involving negotiation between worker-client pairs over time. The loosely defined "initial phase" of service during which contract negotiation should be established remains an ambiguous period in the literature. My data suggest that contracting may be short circuited and discontinuous if it remains a one-session endeavor. A systematic process-oriented approach would seem to be advantageous in maintaining a focused service.

## CONCLUSION

In spite of the limitations of this study, including sample size and restrictions of setting, I believe that the study provides concepts and findings applicable to the first phase of casework service. First, the concept of contract negotiation which has achieved widespread support from various theoretical models of social work practice has not been developed with any systematic rigor. Defining the contract is the first step in developing a consistent theoretical approach to planned interventions in the first phase of service. As implied by the study, the tasks of contract negotiation can be specified for workers and clients, since by definition contract negotiation exists as the mutual and active engagement of both role partners to reach agreement on what they will do together and how they will go about it.

Findings concerning contract status show a statistically significant correlation between agreement on worker role and other dimensions of the contract (client needs and client tasks), suggesting that an understanding of the worker's tasks is pivotal to successful contract negotiation. However, the translation of client needs into a problem focus and an understanding of client responsibilities (client role or tasks) were revealed in this study as underdeveloped aspects of contract negotiation which did not develop in relation to one another. The study thus raises an important issue concerning how contract negotiation could benefit from the interrelationship of client-identified needs and client tasks.

Though in this study worker and client consensus on expectations of each other was fairly high, disagreement, when it occurred, was generally in the direction of clients wanting to lean more on workers for concrete help and workers wanting clients to take more initiative and be more introspective.

Findings on verbal participation in contracting indicate that workers carry major responsibility for contracting, clients follow workers in the rhythm and pacing of contracting, and most contracting activity occurs in the first interview. They suggest that worker activity tends to overshadow client involvement in this area. Furthermore, the findings imply that contracting is not pursued as a continuous process and may be merely a one-session endeavor. An ongoing, process oriented approach would seem to offer more opportunity for maintaining a focused service.

Thus our data suggest that a greater degree of mutuality could be achieved by worker activity which shifted in the direction of pursuing the participation of the client in delineating focus and establishing the parameters of his involvement. This seems particularly true in light of contemporary social work practice, which targets a wider client population in prevention and consumer approaches.

## NOTES

The research in this article was supported by a grant from the Veterans Administration.

1.  Ann Shyne, "What Research Tells Us about Short-Term Cases in Family Agencies," *Social Casework* 38 (1957): 223–31.

2.  Frances B. Stark, "Barriers to Client-Worker Communication at Intake," *Social Casework* 40 (1959): 177–83.

3.  John E. Maver and Noel Timms, *The Client Speaks: Working Class Impressions of Casework* (New York: Atherton Press, 1970).

4.  William J. Reid and Ann W. Shyne, *Brief and Extended Casework* (New York: Columbia University Press, 1969).

5.  William J. Reid and Laura Epstein, *Task-oriented Casework* (New York: Columbia University Press, 1972).

6.  Edwin J. Thomas, "Behavioral Modification and Casework," in *Theories of Social Casework,* ed. Robert W. Roberts and Robert H. Nee (Chicago: University of Chicago Press, 1970).

7.  Carel B. Germain, "An Ecological Perspective on Casework Practice," *Social Casework* 54 (1973): 323–30.

8.  A discussion of dimensions of the contract can be found in Anthony Maluccio and Wilma D. Marlow. "The Case for the Contract," *Social Work* 19 (1974): 28–37.

9.  I am indebted to Dr. William Schwartz for his assistance in my gaining a conceptual grasp of relevant dimensions of the contract.

10. Adapted from Leonard Brown, "Social Workers' Verbal Aids and the Development of Mutual Expectations with Beginning Client Groups" (D.S.W. diss., Columbia University School of Social Work, 1970).

*Chapter 14*

# A STUDY OF PRACTICE SKILLS

## Lawrence Shulman

Efforts to investigate the effectiveness of social work practice and that of other helping professions have led more often than not to frustrating results. Fischer's controversial article on casework reviewed a number of studies of social work and found that in most instances, casework had not been proved effective.[1] Fischer pointed out that the treatment variable had been poorly defined in many of the studies. A review of the literature undertaken in connection with the study to be reported in this article supported Fischer's view. Definitions of treatment included workers' aspirations (to help clients function in a desirable way), type of service (marriage counseling), intensity of service (3.5 contacts per week), or provider of service (psychoanalyst, psychologist, or social worker).[2] The critical variable, often left unexplained, was the specific interaction between the client and the worker. The studies assumed implicitly that all trained workers dealt with clients in the same way.

Before the effectiveness of practice can be judged accurately, it is necessary to clearly define and measure the practice being evaluated. However, efforts to focus on the skills of social workers are not numerous in the literature, although there is some evidence that this line of inquiry might be productive.[3] For example, research in the field of psychotherapy has identified specific behaviors, such as empathy, relevant self-disclosure by the therapist, and facilitative confrontation, that appear to positively affect outcomes.[4]

This article reports the results of a four-year project that investigated the helping process and examined the relationship between the helping professional's behavior in an interview and the results of his or her efforts.[5] Varying elements in the helping process are introduced by the professional's function, by the purpose of the encounter, and by the specific service that the setting offers. However, this researcher believes a single underlying process operates in all helping relationships, and it is this process the study sought to examine.

The project was guided by a specific theoretical frame of reference—the mediating theory developed by Schwartz.[6] Although the study was not a test of this theory, its constructs helped shape the strategies used and determine which skills were examined. However, all the skills generated by this framework can fit comfortably within other theories of the helping process.

The model of the helping process used in this study is common to many approaches. Stated simply, the worker's behavior, in interaction with the client, contributes to the development of a working relationship, which is a precondition for effective helping. This model generates a number of important questions: Which of the worker's skills lead to a positive working relationship? Is the function of some skills primarily to build a relationship whereas other skills are helpful after relationships are developed, and still others serve both functions? Will some skills have a negative impact if used before a positive relationship is developed?

These questions, which explore the internal dynamics of the model of the helping process, were the focus of this study. Specifically, it examined the associations between the independent variable, specific skill of social workers, and the two dependent variables, the relationship between worker and client and the worker's helpfulness.

## Questionnaires

The first phase of the study was to develop instruments to measure the worker's practice behavior and effectiveness and to test the instruments for reliability and validity. The Social Worker Behavior Questionnaire was designed to obtain feedback from the client on the frequency with which the worker made use of 27 specific skills, which were chosen using the theoretical framework guiding

## Table 1  Social Worker Behavior Questionnaire

| Skill | Questionnaire item[a] |
|---|---|
| Clarifying purpose | In our first meeting, my worker explained the kinds of concerns we might be discussing. |
| Clarifying roles | My worker explained how we would work together, describing the kind of help a social worker could give. |
| Encouraging client feedback | During our first meeting, my worker asked me for my ideas on specific subjects we would discuss together. |
| Displaying worker's beliefs in the potential of the work | During our first meetings, my worker told me she really believed I could get help with my concerns from this agency. |
| Holding to focus | When we began to discuss a particular concern, the worker kept me on the topic. |
| Direct contact with other significant people | When I had trouble talking to someone, the worker would meet with them to make it easier for me to speak to them. |
| Viewing people involved in institutions, organizations, and other systems in new ways | The worker helped me to understand the behavior of other people in new ways. |
| Moving from the general to the specific | When I raised a general concern, the worker asked me for examples. |
| Connecting feelings to work | My worker helped me to see how my feelings affected the way I acted. |
| Reaching for between-session data | The worker began our visit by asking if anything had happened between visits that I wanted to talk about. |
| Pointing out the illusion of work | When the worker thought I was not working hard in our discussion, she let me know. |
| Reaching inside of silences | When I was unusually silent during our visits, the worker tried to find out why. |
| Supporting client in taboo areas | The worker helped me to talk about subjects that were not easy to talk about. |
| Sharing personal thoughts and feelings | The worker shared her personal thoughts and feelings, which helped me to get to know her better as a person. |
| Understanding client's feelings | When I told my worker how I felt, she understood. |
| Dealing with the theme of authority | When I was upset about something my worker did or said, she encouraged me to talk about it. |
| Checking for artificial consensus | When I agreed with an idea too quickly, the worker asked me if I really meant it. |

Table 1    (Continued)

| Skill | Questionnaire item[a] |
|-------|----------------------|
| Putting the client's feelings into words | The worker seemed to understand how I felt without my having to put it into words. |
| Partializing client's concerns | The worker helped me look at my concerns one at a time. |
| Supporting client's strengths | The worker believed I could handle the situations we discussed. |
| Identifying affective obstacles to work | The worker would point out when my feelings about something made it hard for me to talk during our visits. |
| Providing data | The worker shared her suggestions about the subjects we discussed for my consideration. |
| Displaying feelings openly | The worker let me know her feelings about the situations we discussed. |
| Pointing out endings early | Sometime before our last visit the worker explained that our visits would be ending soon. |
| Sharing ending feelings | The worker let me know how she felt about our finishing. |
| Asking for a review of learning | The worker asked me what I got out of our visits together. |
| Reaching for client's ending feelings | The worker asked how I felt about ending our visits. |

[a] The examples used in each version of the questionnaire have been omitted.

the study. These skills were translated into questionnaire items using terms that clients could understand. For example, the skill of "holding to focus" appeared on the questionnaire as follows: "When I began to discuss a particular concern (for example, my child's difficulty at school), my worker kept me on the topic." The client could chose one of the following responses: (1) often, (2) fairly often, (3) seldom, (4) never, (5) no answer. Since the study was set in two bilingual Canadian child welfare agencies, five versions of the form were developed in which the examples were varied to suit the potential respondents—natural parents, adolescents, unwed parents, adoptive parents, or foster parents—and the questionnaires were prepared in both French and English. Table 1 lists the skills and the corresponding questionnaire items.

A second instrument, the Service Satisfaction Questionnaire, was designed to obtain clients' perceptions of the content of the practice, the status of their relationship with the worker, and the worker's helpfulness. The key items on this questionnaire were:

1. How satisfied are you with the way you and your worker get along?
   A. Very satisfied
   B. Satisfied
   C. Not very satisfied
   D. Not satisfied at all
2. In general, how helpful has your worker been?
   A. Very helpful
   B. Helpful
   C. Not very helpful
   D. Not helpful

There were also five versions of this questionnaire in both French and English.

Obviously, it was important to the results of the study to assess the accuracy of the client's perceptions of workers' behavior. To determine the degree of error involved, a representative selection of 100 clients assigned to 10 workers were sent appropriate versions of the Social Worker Behavior Questionnaire. Of the 81 who responded, 50 were sent an identical questionnaire two weeks later, and 45 of these were returned. An average score on all items was computed for each client's questionnaire. The Pearson's correlation between the average scores on the two test was .75 ($SD$=0.29). When responses to individual items on the two tests were compared, 7 had correlations of less than .30, 9 correlations were between .30 and .50, and 13 were between .51 and .86. (Low correlations may have been degraded by the small variances for some items.)

In a second test, internal consistency was examined by dividing each respondent's returns into two roughly equivalent sets of questions (split-half method). An average score was computed for each half and a correlation computed, using the Spearman-Brown correction, between the two sets of scores obtained. The resulting correlation of .79 offered support for the questionnaire's internal consistency. Although some support for reliability was obtained, the instrument is still considered to be in an early stage of development.

Face validity of the forms was explored by conducting a series of interviews with respondents, workers, and supervisors to determine the clarity of the final version. In addition, two bilingual supervisors were asked to translate the French versions into English without having seen the English versions. The results supported the validity of the questionnaire.

Additional subdesigns explored criterion validity. In one, the 15 workers whose clients had given them the most positive average scores on the Social Worker Behavior Questionnaire and the 15 with the least positive scores were selected from the total of 118 workers. Workers with positive scores on this questionnaire also scored higher on relationships with clients ($F = 5.6$, $df = 29$, $p \leq .05$) and were seen by clients as more helpful ($F = 7.42$, $df = 29$, $p \leq .02$). In another procedure, three trained raters using an observation system developed for the project rated videotapes of 11 social workers during 120 hours of practice. The raters' analysis was compared with questionnaire returns from the videotaped clients. Although strong correlations were found, they were not high enough to be significant with the small sample of workers.

A third procedure to test validity involved comparing 20 workers' average scores on each skill with their own ratings of their skills. Workers were asked to rate themselves after data for the study had been collected but before they knew their own results. On the overall questionnaire, workers scored themselves the same as their clients' average rating or one category apart 81 percent of the time. However, this finding warrants a cautious interpretation since many items had a small range of variation in responses, which would contribute to agreement between workers and clients.

Similar procedures were used to test the five versions of the Service Satisfaction Questionnaire. In the analysis of test-retest returns with 27 respondents, the correlation was .68 between the two sets of returns on worker-client relationship and .56 on the worker's helpfulness. In a validity test of this questionnaire, 20 workers were asked to report on their perceptions of their work with specific clients. Their responses were then compared with the actual returns of these clients. On the two specific questions discussed in this article, the workers agreed with their clients or were one category apart on 95 percent of the responses for both items. Once again, low variations in responses limit the inferences possible from this finding.

## METHOD AND SAMPLE

This study was carried out in two child welfare agencies—the Children's Aid Society in Ottawa and the Children's Service Centre in Montreal. The total staff of 118 workers in both agencies was included in the study. The agencies' records were used to identify the caseloads for each worker. Each case concerning adolescents over fourteen years of age, natural parents, unwed mothers, adoptive parents, or foster parents was listed on a separate card. These cards were randomly sorted into two groups, each reflecting the overall characteristics of the worker's total caseload. One group received the Social Worker Behavior Questionnaire, and the other received the Service Satisfaction Questionnaire. The random division of the caseload insured that all respondents had an equal chance of receiving either questionnaire. This meant that the data on a worker's behaviors were provided by one half of his or her caseload and the data on the relationship and helpfulness variables by the other half. This procedure was followed to maintain independence between the two questionnaires so that the results of one questionnaire would not be influenced by the respondent's having completed the other.

Over 4,000 questionnaires were mailed to potential respondents, who received the version suited to their category and to their language. All cases were open at the time the mailing list was developed; however, a number of cases closed during the six-week period required to prepare the mailing. Respondents were assured of confidentiality, and a coding system was used so that names were not on the returns. A return rate of fifty-three percent provided over 2,000 responses. This was a surprisingly high rate since the mailing coincided with a postal strike and since a significant number of relatively inactive cases we were included in the original mailing. Respondents' comments on the questionnaire indicated that they were eager to provide feedback, and many felt the questionnaire was overdue.

Table 2 provides a description of the social workers in this study. The largest group of workers were female, English speaking, and working with families or children. Sixty-one percent of the workers had some form of social work training. Table 3 describes the sample of clients who responded to the questionnaire. Three categories, natural parents, foster parents, and adolescents, comprised 75 percent of the sample. The age breakdown indicates that 65 percent of the respondents were over 25, and 82 percent had had contacts with their worker for more than two months.

Table 2   Sample of Social Workers ($N = 118$)

| Variables | Number | Percentage |
|---|---|---|
| Sex | | |
| Male | 20 | 17 |
| Female | 98 | 83 |
| Language spoken | | |
| English | 105 | 89 |
| French | 13 | 11 |
| Agency department | | |
| Family services | 42 | 35 |
| Children's services | 52 | 45 |
| Unmarried mothers | 11 | 9 |
| Adoption | 13 | 11 |
| Social work education | | |
| Junior college | 14 | 12 |
| BSW | 18 | 15 |
| MSW | 40 | 34 |
| Other education | | |
| High school | 3 | 3 |
| BA | 19 | 16 |
| Other | 24 | 20 |
| Social service work experience | | |
| Low (up to 3 years) | 44 | 37 |
| Medium (3–9 years) | 48 | 41 |
| High (over 10 years) | 26 | 22 |

Cross-tabulation of the data using the chi-square test of significance was used to analyze the impact of the characteristics of the workers and clients on the outcome measures. Although the details cannot be reported in this brief article, some of the variables that did not appear to influence the results raise interesting questions for future study. For example, the professional training of the worker by itself did not significantly affect the worker's scores on skills, relationship with clients, or helpfulness. However, differences in the results were observed when training was considered in combination with other variables, such as work experience and participation in agency consultation groups led by the researcher.

A number of limitations in the study result from the basic design, each of which can be considered as a challenge to the validity of the results. First, since the focus of the study was the worker's behavior, other important variables in the helping process, including other of the worker's skills (such as assessment), size of caseload, client's motivation and opportunities, and the impact of agency or

Table 3   Sample of Respondents ($N$ = 1,784)

| Variables | Number | Percentage |
|---|---|---|
| *Category* | | |
| Natural parents | 417 | 23 |
| Foster parents | 596 | 33 |
| Adolescents (over 14) | 332 | 19 |
| Unmarried mothers | 133 | 8 |
| Adoptive parents | 304 | 17 |
| Missing data | 2 | 0 |
| *Education* | | |
| Grade 13 or less[a] | 1,250 | 70 |
| Some college | 179 | 10 |
| College graduate | 158 | 9 |
| Other | 95 | 5 |
| No data | 102 | 6 |
| *Age* | | |
| Below 14 | 70 | 4 |
| 15–25 | 471 | 27 |
| 26–35 | 505 | 28 |
| 36–45 | 345 | 19 |
| Over 46 | 328 | 18 |
| No data | 65 | 4 |
| *Duration of contact with worker* | | |
| 2 months or less | 226 | 13 |
| 3–11 months | 808 | 45 |
| 1–2 years | 362 | 20 |
| Over 2 years | 299 | 17 |
| No data | 89 | 5 |

[a] Grade 13 is the highest grade in high school in Ontario.

social policy, were not included. Future research should include these variables because of their interrelationship with the interactional skill of the social worker. Second, variables related to the setting have a serious impact on the worker, on the client, and on their interaction. Therefore, generalizations to settings other than child welfare agencies must await replications of the study.

A third limitation was the lack of random assignments of clients to workers. Whatever biases existed in assignment procedures would have been present in the sample. For example, the general absence of differences between professionally trained and untrained workers in the scores on social work skills may be the result of a biased assignment of more difficult cases to trained workers. These difficult cases might have rated the trained workers lower on their use of skills. Self-selection of respondents represents another threat to validity. Analysis of the returns also indicated a lower than expected response by clients who were contesting the agency's decisions. Such clients who were angry at the agency, might also have rated their workers as less helpful. Although many of them did respond, their limited numbers may have caused the sample to be more favorable to the social workers than might actually have been the case.

Finally, this is essentially a study of the respondents' perceptions. Although extensive work was undertaken to explore reliability and validity, the questionnaire is still being developed, and further study with more objective outcome data is needed. Efforts to pursue this line of inquiry in this study were hampered by the limitations of the agencies' record-keeping systems.

## CORRELATIONS

The central line of inquiry in this project was exploration of relationships of specific social work skills to the development of a working relationship with the client and to the worker's helpfulness. Variables for this analysis were computed from the raw data by averaging the scores for each skill and for relationship and helpfulness on all the returns for each worker. By using averages, the reliability of the scores was increased. An additional step to strengthen the reliability of the returns was to exclude from this analysis workers who had less than four returns on either questionnaire.[7] The final number of workers included in the analysis was eighty-eight, reflecting exclusion of workers with less than four returns and the automatic exclusion of workers when data was missing on variables (the normal option for the programs used). All reported findings were significant at the .05 level.

Table 4 lists the skills that had significant positive associations with either the relationship or the helpfulness variables. The skills are listed in the order of the strength of their association. It should be noted that correlations below .29 are too low to be regarded with confidence. In addition, the skills of partializing the client's concerns and dealing with the theme of authority had questionable individual reliability scores.

Sharing personal thoughts and feelings is the first skill on both lists, having the strongest association with both relationship and helpfulness. The similarity of the correlations between skills and

Table 4   Correlations of Worker's Skills with Relationship
and Helpfulness ($N$ = 88)[a]

| Relationship | | Helpfulness | |
|---|---|---|---|
| Item | r | Item | r |
| Sharing personal thoughts and feelings | .45 | Sharing personal thoughts and feelings | .47 |
| Understanding client's feelings | .41 | Understanding client's feelings | .46 |
| Clarifying roles | .34 | Supporting client in taboo areas | .33 |
| Displaying feelings openly | .33 | |  |
| Putting the client's feelings into words | .31 | Putting client's feelings into words | .32 |
| Providing data | .30 | Encouraging client feedback | .31 |
| Partializing client's concerns | .29 | Partializing client's concerns | .27 |
| Dealing with the theme of authority | .26 | Providing data | .25 |
| | | Clarifying roles | .23 |
| Supporting client in taboo areas | .24 | Reaching for between-session data | .21 |
| Reaching for between-session data | .23 | Displaying feelings openly | .21 |
| Encouraging client feedback | .20 | Dealing with the theme of authority | .18 |

[a] All correlations are significant, $p < .05$.

relationship to those between skills and helpfulness is not surprising, since relationship and helpfulness are associated with each other ($r$ = .76). It is quite possible that a specific skill correlates with helpfulness because of its association with relationship. Therefore, a partial correlation procedure was introduced to allow the researcher to make inferences about whether particular skills appeared to contribute to the relationship-building process, to the worker's helpfulness, or to both simultaneously.[8]

Table 5 illustrates the results of this further analysis for six skills selected for their theoretical importance and their illustration of the analysis. The first column provides the simple correlation of the skill with helpfulness as shown in Table 4. Partial correlation was used to recompute the correlation between the skills and helpfulness while removing the impact of the relationship variable. For example, the correlation between the skill of putting the client's feelings into words with helpfulness was $r$=.32. When controlled for relationship, this correlation almost disappeared. The change in correlation level may be considered to indicate that this skill actually contributes to relationship-building and not to helpfulness, since the association

Table 5   Partial Correlation of Skill with Helpfulness ($N = 88$)

| Skills | Correlation with helpfulness ($r$) | Correlation with helpfulness, relationship controlled ($r$) |
|---|---|---|
| Sharing personal thoughts and feelings | .47[a] | .24[a] |
| Understanding client's feelings | .46[a] | .32[a] |
| Putting client's feelings into words | .32[a] | .04 |
| Clarifying roles | .23[a] | .07 |
| Identifying affective obstacles to work | −.17 | −.24[a] |
| Supporting client in taboo areas | .33[a] | .17 |

[a] Significant, $p < .05$.

with helpfulness was lost when the impact of relationship was removed.

Such a finding suggests that relationship was an intervening variable between the skill and helpfulness. In cases such as this a second test was conducted to examine the association between the skill and the relationship variable while controlling for helpfulness. In all cases the correlation between skill and relationship was unchanged, suggesting that relationship was, in fact, an intervening variable.

Different interpretations of the function of a skill in the helping process can be made according to whether, when relationship is controlled, the correlation between the skill and helpfulness increases, decreases slightly, or even reverses from positive to negative. The following discussion of the results of this analysis for the six skills shown in Table 5 represents the researcher's logical inferences, but other inferences may be equally reasonable.

The skill of sharing personal thoughts and feelings appeared to add equally to building relationships and to helpfulness with clients. When a worker is open and personal with a client, this may break down some of the barriers preventing clients from being open about their own feelings. As the worker becomes more multidimensional, there is more "person" for the client to relate to. In addition, the thoughts and feelings of the worker may provide information that can be of use to the client, thus contributing to the helpfulness factor.

This finding supports the theory that only by developing skill at being personal in pursuit of a professional function can social workers be helpful. The model that social work borrowed from the medical profession, which stresses clinical detachment and objectivity, may have introduced an artificial dichotomy between being personal or being professional. One client illustrates this point in his comments on the questionnaire, stating: "I like Mrs. X. She isn't like a social worker, she's like a real person." Of course, the importance of sharing personal thoughts and feelings does not imply that workers should use sessions with clients to work out their own problems.

The skill of understanding clients' feelings also appeared to contribute to both the relationship and helpfulness factors; however, the emphasis was on helpfulness. The function of this skill may be to free the client to understand his or her own feelings. It also contributes to relationship-building, but less strongly than does sharing personal thoughts and feelings. When a worker can genuinely empathize with a client without judging him or her harshly, then the client is free to be honest, and the relationship is strengthened.

The data on the skill of putting clients' feelings into words suggests (although less convincingly than the results for other skills, because of the lower original correlation) that the essential contribution of this skill may be to relationship-building. This is interesting because one view of practice cautions against articulating the client's feelings too early in the relationship, for fear that a worker may overwhelm the client or create defensiveness. On this assumption, workers will sometimes hold back their affective hunches and fail to communicate their sense of the client's feelings. However, the findings indicate that this skill could be particularly important in the beginning stage of the helping process when clients are wary of revealing too much of themselves. This skill's special contribution to relationship-building may be in giving clients the message that the worker understands them. According to this interpretation, a worker might be better off to risk being slightly ahead of the client than being too far behind. This researcher suspects that clients' defensiveness is raised not by genuine empathy but rather by interpretations of behavior offered in the guise of empathic responses.

The figures in Table 5 indicate that the skill of clarifying roles is more closely associated with the relationship-building process than with helpfulness, although the low original correlation requires caution in interpretation. This finding is important theoretically, since some practice strategies suggest the need to build a relationship before direct discussions about purpose and role takes place. If this skill is central to relationship-buiding, however, it would confirm the notion that a real working relationship can develop only with clarity of role, which allows the development of a clear boundary within which the client can use the worker. Ambiguity about purpose and role can lead to heightened concerns and greater defensiveness on the part of the client. When this researcher has discussed the issue of clarifying roles in training workshops with social workers, he has found that workers' reluctance to be direct in the beginning phase of work is often related to their inability to describe their function without using jargon, to their difficulty in describing their agency's services, or to their embarrassment over direct discussion of the client's problems.

Another skill, identifying obstacles to work, originally showed a low negative correlation with helpfulness, which was amplified when the relationship variable was taken into account. Although caution is required in interpreting this finding, because workers and clients disagreed on the analysis of validity on the frequency of this skill's use, one interpretation is that the use of this skill is not helpful to the client. In fact, the negative effect of this skill on helpfulness may have been suppressed by otherwise positive relationships between workers and clients. This finding raises a major question about the subtleties involved in the process of pointing out obstacles and making demands on the client for work. Pointing out directly to clients that their feelings seem to block their ability to work may be experienced by the clients as a harsh criticism and thus serve to close them off.

A skill with a similar purpose, the more gentle skill of helping a client discuss taboo areas, appears to be more closely associated with helpfulness. Rather than having their failures pointed out to them, clients may need help in dealing with the problem. A number of findings in this study support the idea that some demands of work help clients to open up, and others may close them off. Further study is needed to clarify the distinction between these two types of demands.

## FUTURE RESEARCH

Future research into social work practice must include the study of skill as a central factor, since logically a professional's skill has a powerful impact on the outcome of his or her work. This study was on effort to deepen understanding of how that impact is made and to increase the ability to measure the social worker's skill. Additional research can explore this line of investigation in other social work settings and with other helping professions to identify both common and varying elements in the helping process. In developing a theoretical generalization, a number of replications of the results would strengthen support for the initial findings. Even relatively low correlations, for example, if repeated in diverse studies take on greater significance. The findings of this study should be viewed with its limitations in mind and should be seen as one step in an ongoing process.

With workers' skills operationalized and open to measurement, studies of social work effectiveness may yield different results. Rather than concluding that social work practice is ineffective, researchers may discover that positive findings have been obscured as the impact of skilled workers has been offset by those with less skill. In a follow-up study undertaken by this researcher, for example, initial analysis of some key outcome measures found no significant differences between the effectiveness of social workers with different patterns of service. When the analysis was repeated using the workers' scores on the social work skills as a control variable, significant differences emerged that would not have been uncovered if the workers' skills had been ignored.

The helping process being studied is a complex one, with each variable somewhat dependent on the effects of the others. The researcher cannot examine one level of analysis, such as the worker-client interaction, without viewing it within the context of a second level—the agency or institution—which, in turn, must be seen in the context of a third level of social policies and structures. As understanding of how each level works is developed and refined, computer models can be constructed to explore the interdependence between them. This would strengthen the work of the client, the social worker, the administrator, and the social policy analyst. The study of skill is an important key in the development of a science of helping that will free the individual artistry of each social worker to operate more effectively.

## NOTES AND REFERENCES

1.  Joel Fischer, "Is Casework Effective?" *Social Work,* 18 (January 1973), pp. 5–20.

2.  J. McVicker Hunt, Margaret Blenkner, and Leonard S. Kogan, *Testing Results in Social Casework: A Field Test of the Measurement Scale* (New York: Family

Service Association of America, 1950); Robert Ballard and Emily Mudd, "Some Theoretical and Practical Problems in Evaluating Effectiveness of Counseling," *Social Casework*, 38 (December 1957), pp. 533–538; Walter B. Miller, "The Impact of a Total Community Delinquency Control Project," *Social Problems*, 10 (Fall 1962), pp. 168–191; and Maude M. Craig and Phillip W. Furst, "What Happens after Treatment? A Study of Potentially Delinquent Boys," *Social Service Review*, 39 (June 1965), pp. 165–171.

3.  For examples of such studies, *see* Henry S. Maas, "Group Influences on Client-Worker Interaction, *Social Work*, 9 (April 1964), pp. 70–79; Florence Hollis, "Exploration in the Development of a Typology of Casework Treatment," *Social Casework*, 48 (June 1967), pp. 335–341; and William J. Reid and Anne W. Shyne, *Brief and Extended Casework* (New York: Columbia University Press, 1969).

4.  *See*, for example, B. G. Berenson and Robert R. Carkhuff, eds., *Sources of Gain in Counseling and Psychotherapy* (New York: Holt, Rinehart & Winston, 1967); Charles B. Truax, "Therapist Empathy, Warmth, and Genuineness, and Personality Change in Group Psychotherapy: A Comparison Between Interaction Unit Measures, Time Sample Measures, and Patient Perception Measures," *Journal of Clinical Psychology*, 22 (April 1966), pp. 225–229.

5.  For a full report of the study *see* Lawrence Shulman, *A Study of the Helping Process* (Vancouver, British Columbia, Canada: School of Social Work, University of British Columbia, 1977). The theoretical model, research design, and findings are also presented in a series of six videotape programs, *The Helping Process in Social Work: Theory, Practice and Research* (Montreal, Quebec, Canada: Instructional Communications Centre, McGill University, 1976).

6.  William Schwartz, "Social Group Work: An Interactionist Approach," *Encyclopedia of Social Work*, Vol. 2 (New York: National Association of Social Workers, 1971), pp. 1252–1263; and Schwartz, "The Social Worker in the Group," in *New Perspectives on Services to Groups: Theory, Organization, Practice* (New York: National Association of Social Workers, 1961), pp. 7–29. *See also* Lawrence Shulman, *Skills of Helping Individuals and Groups* (to be published by Peacock Press in 1979); Shulman. *A Casework of Social Work with Groups: The Mediating Model* (New York: Council on Social Work Education, 1968); and Shulman, "Social Work Skill: The Anatomy of a Helping Act," *Social Work Practice* (New York: Columbia University Press, 1969), pp. 29–48.

7.  Analyses were performed using the programs from Normal H. Nie et al., *SPSS: Statistical Package for the Social Sciences* (2d ed.; New York: McGraw-Hill Book Co., 1975).

8.  This approach used a strategy for third variable analysis suggested in Morris Rosenberg, *Logic of Survey Analysis* (New York: Basic Books, 1968).

Chapter 15

# DISCUSSION OF THE SELECTED STUDIES

## Donald D. Dobbin

We are now going to review the three papers reprinted in Part III, in particular with regard to the data-gathering techniques the researchers used.

### WODARSKI AND PEDI: ANTISOCIAL AND PROSOCIAL CHILDREN AT A COMMUNITY CENTER

Evaluating outcomes of youth services programs provided by such agencies as community centers and settlement houses has proved to be a very complex and methodologically demanding research undertaking. The authors' approach to evaluation in terms of changes in antisocial behavior demonstrates the skilled use of a number of data-gathering strategies and techniques.

The term *antisocial,* like *predelinquent, deviant,* and *asocial* is a relative phenomena difficult to operationalize. To measure antisocial behavior the researchers must first construct an index or set of criteria to differentiate it from other forms of behavior. This is done systematically by operationalizing the concept in terms of motor behavior, physical contacts, verbalizations, object interference, and distracting behaviors. Other forms of behavior are then operational-ized as prosocial or nonsocial.

A multimeasurement strategy is employed to assess impact of the intervention, the community center experience. Based on a checklist of antisocial behaviors, the researchers designed three data-gathering instruments, an observational scale, self-inventories to be completed by the child, and an inventory on the child's behavior to be completed by the group counselors. The observational scale was administered by trained nonparticipant observers. This unobtrusive approach to data gathering was designed to insure reliability. Ob-servers were systematically trained to carry out their assignments through the use of videotapes of children's behaviors and interob-server agreement on classifying behaviors was measured repeatedly.

The authors compare and contrast the outcomes as measured by the three different but related data-gathering approaches. In doing so they point up the limitations of such studies in relation to threats to the validity and reliability of study findings.

Data collection in the study is well focused to answer the re-searchers question but it also accomplishes their second objective, to assess the degree of consistency between the various self-rating scales and the independent behavioral observations of the nonparticipant observers.

## RHODES: CONTRACT NEGOTIATION IN THE INITIAL STAGE OF CASEWORK SERVICE

The research by Rhodes intended to ascertain to what extent contracting processes were implicit in practice and which dimensions of contract negotiation contributed to variation among paired case-workers and clients. Original data were called for. The appropriate sources were the contracting parties. Without formal written con-tracts to call upon, the author had to assume the existence of a verbal or implied contract.

Two data-gathering strategies are employed. One focuses on the basic dimensions of the contract, the problem to be worked on, the role to be played by the client, and the role to be played by the worker. The other addresses itself to a content analysis of audiotapes to identify and count the frequency with which specified elements of contracting appear in the treatment process.

In the first instance, the researcher develops two analogous questionnaires, one to be completed by the client and the other by the worker. To collect data on the three focal points of contracting selected for investigation, the questionnaires were constructed to draw data from the respondents on the problem focus, expectations of client role, and expectations of worker role.

The first section of the questionnaire addresses the level of agreement between client and worker on the work they are presently involved in. Rhodes provides examples of the ideas and concepts used to guide data collection: realistic focus, agreed-upon focus, expectations relating to attendance, duration of service, involvement of family members, and so on. These constitute the basis for sets of questions making up the first section of the questionnaire.

The same strategy is employed in designing section two of the questionnaire, client role, and section three, worker role. This research is among the first to investigate client/worker roles in contracting. Therefore, the researcher has to construct her own frame of reference and rationale for developing a series of individual questions with "yes" and "no" answers to draw data. She uses a wide range of client and worker behaviors in the interviewing situation, expectations that cover a range of theoretical preferences from psychosocial to the problem solving to the existential approaches, as well as idiosyncratic and stylistic differences among workers and cultural differences among clients.

Using these two questionnaires the development of contracts along the three dimensions under study is investigated. The determining factor is the extent of agreement between worker/client pairs on each of the three subscores that summed determine the overall status of the contract.

A second interest of the researcher was in specifying the nature and extent of verbal participation that characterize contract negotiation. This was accomplished through another data-gathering approach. The 45 interviews constituting the basis for the worker/client questionnaire were audiotaped.

A content analysis of the tapes was carried out by encoding participation of the client and the worker attempts at verbal contracting. Using a schedule of six categories of verbal attempts at contracting the researcher counted the frequency of contracting activity for worker and client in each pair. This independent objective content analysis of the audiotapes was free of the subjective perceptions of the client and worker. It served well the secondary objective of the research project by producing useful information on the structure and process of verbal contracting.

## SHULMAN: A STUDY OF PRACTICE SKILLS

Two emerging concerns of casework constitute the subject matter for the researchers' fields of investigation. Both areas, measuring outcomes or results of casework intervention and analyzing the relationship between the helping process and outcomes, are in their embryonic stage of development. This is what sets the conditions for the choice of strategies and techniques to be used in data gathering.

With mediating theory as his specific theoretical frame of reference, the researcher selected 27 individual practice skills identified in the helping process. This phase of data collection zeros in on a process independent of product: measurement of effectiveness. To analyze the use of these skills as perceived by client and worker, the researcher operationalizes each skill by translating it into a descriptive statement of practice behavior as it might be observed or felt by the client.

The data required were successfully collected from the clients and workers. But the individual measurements and scales embodied in the data set are in the vanguard of the sequence of research in this area. This is also the case in the second phase of the study. Therefore, the issues of validity and reliability of the instrumentation and data collection process are critical.

To assess the accuracy of the clients' perceptions of workers' behavior, the Social Worker Questionnaire is sent to a sample of clients. Respondents are retested two weeks later and through the use of appropriate statistical procedures measurements of the accuracy of clients' perceptions are determined. Internal consistency in the questionnaire, an aspect of reliability, was analyzed through use of the split-half method on the data items collected.

Face validity of the forms was explored through another exercise in data gathering. Interviews with respondents, workers, and supervisors were conducted to improve the clarity of the final form. They offered the additional advantage of allowing the researcher to probe beyond the structured questions and follow-up on leads and cues that might contribute to refining the instrument.

Independent observers, serving as raters were employed to encode worker practice skills as reflected on videotapes of actual interviews. Their ratings were then compared and contrasted with questionnaire returns.

Similar statistical procedures based on additional data sets collected by the researchers were used to address the issues of validity and reliability on the second phase of the study. Here the primary instrument used was the Service Satisfaction Questionnaire, a briefer, less complex form but too new to the field to stand on reputation.

The wide variety of data-gathering approaches employed in this study help to give credence to the findings and confidence to the validity and reliability of the scales and measurements on which they rest.

Data gathering is viewed as an important tool in research. The nature of the problem being studied and the research design selected have a direct bearing on the data sources to be tapped and the strategies to be employed in collecting data. The research reports reprinted in Part III provide examples of various types of data gathering as part of the research process. The real test of this aspect of research is how well the data collected served the goals of the project.

## ARTICLES REPRINTED

Rhodes, S. L. Contract negotiation in the initial stage of casework service. *Social Service Review,* 1977, *51*(1), 125–140.

Shulman, L. A study of practice skills. *Social Work,* 1978, *23*(4), 274–280.

Wodarski, J. S., & Pedi, S. J. Antisocial and prosocial children at a community center. *Social Work,* 1977, *22*(4), 290–296.

Part IV

# EVALUATIVE RESEARCH

*Chapter 16*

# THE EVALUATION OF HUMAN SERVICE PROGRAMS

## Henry Wechsler

Perhaps the most widely conducted type of research in the field of human services and social work is related to the evaluation of programs. Some confusion exists on the differences between evaluation and evaluative research. *Evaluation* is the general process of judging whether some activity is worthwhile. It is a general term, not related to the method employed to make such a judgment. *Evaluative research,* on the other hand, indicates specifically the use of the scientific method for the purpose of making an evaluation. Research skills are not required to make an evaluation, but they are necessary for the conduct of evaluative research.

Because of the dependence of human service programs on public funds, and the need for public accountability, most programs today include an evaluative component. While such evaluation is by necessity tied to action programs, evaluative research has the same basic scientific requirements as any other form of social research.

The one basic additional ingredient required for evaluative research is the specification of goals against which programs may be evaluated.

### DETERMINATION OF GOALS

Human service programs are established in order to meet certain goals. These goals vary in type and specificity. James (1962) and

221

Suchman (1967) have discussed various different types of goals that programs in the human service field may have. Evaluations of programs have been classified as dealing primarily with the following aspects of the programs: *effort, performance, impact, efficiency,* and the *process* involved.

Evaluations of effort pertain to the quantity of labor and resources invested in the program. This type of evaluation is the one that most commonly appears in the annual reports of voluntary service organizations. "We saw 10,487 clients; conducted 45,392 interviews; visited 6,584 families; and placed 18,515 children in foster homes . . . ," and so on. This kind of report indicates what was done, but not what these actions accomplished.

An evaluation of performance examines the accomplishments brought about by the efforts of the program. Such accomplishments are examined in terms of the special goals of the program. They may relate to the improvement of the mental or physical health of the client, a reduction in antisocial behavior, or restoration of a broken family. It is important to recognize and deal with the fact that such measures reflect more than the specific actions taken by an agent.

Evaluation of impact examines the adequacy of the performance. In this form of evaluation, the performance that is accomplished by the program must be viewed within the context of the total needs of the clients and the overall size of the problem being treated. Thus, a very time-consuming and expensive form of psychiatric treatment may be found to result in successful outcomes for only a very limited number of patients. The outcome in terms of performance would be rated as successful; but in terms of the overall problem—the large number of patients who need psychiatric care— the impact may be negligible.

An analysis of efficiency is being more widely introduced into today's evaluation of programs. This type of evaluation is most useful when different programs with similar goals are being compared. Funds are limited, and different programs are competing for support; hence, it must be determined which programs are being used in the best possible way. In this fashion, cost-benefit analysis has become part of evaluative research. Programs may be found to have successful outcomes and significant impacts, but their personnel and budgets may still be handled in inefficient ways. The question asked in efficiency evaluation is whether the output warrants the input.

A final aspect of evaluative research is an analysis of the process involved. On a simple level, this can be detailed examination of the intervention methods. In examining the process, evaluations can also move into an area that has been designated as systems analysis. This type of overall evaluation helps us to get away from simplistic, black-and-white notions of whether or not programs work; instead they describe the ways in which the programs do work. Thus, such evaluations examine the program components, the staff and the interrelationship of the staff conducting the program, the conditions that surround the administration of the program, the program recipients, and the effects of the program.

## DESIGN

Evaluative research is subject to the same limitations and problems in design and method as are other types of social research. Because it is a study of the effects of intervention, evaluative research requires a design that approaches the traditional experimental design. As mentioned earlier in this volume, this design includes a pretest of the experimental group, their exposure to the treatment, and a posttest. It should also include a control group, which receives the pretest and the posttest but not the treatment. The conditions required for experimental studies include the random assignment of persons to the control and experimental groups. This is seldom possible in research designed to evaluate human service programs. It is not feasible, and perhaps not ethical, to assign some people randomly to an active program and others to a nontreatment group. At times, the impossibility of such an experiment may hold back progress. This is particularly true when certain ineffective forms of treatment are thought in the light of "common sense" and tradition to be effective. Take, for instance, the case of extensive bedrest after certain illnesses and surgery. When surgeons became willing to experiment with shorter, limited bedrest, they found it to be more effective than extensive rest in speeding recovery. If they had not tried this method, they would never have known the result.

Regardless of the merits of the inquiry, however, random assignment to a nontreatment control group is often not feasible. Thus other strategies have to be used. These are described in detail by Campbell and Stanley (1963) and Cook and Campbell (1979) in their discussion of quasi-experimental studies. Researchers may, for example, use the waiting list as the control group, or they may use comparison rather than control groups from other equivalent populations. In longitudinal studies, the patient may be his own control when a treatment is alternately given and withdrawn for various periods. A variety of research designs, including time series designs originally employed in behavioral research, are being increasingly used to evaluate different modalities.

A second major problem that arises in evaluative research is the biased selection of subjects. In selecting patients for treatment programs, human services providers tend to favor those who will most benefit. And since patients must make an effort to seek treatment, they in a sense select themselves: motivated clients with better prognoses come for treatment, while passive clients with poorer prognoses stay at home. It is impossible to change the client composition, but an evaluation should examine the possibly limited, selective nature of the client population when considering whether the findings about the program can be generalized from this population to the broader population of persons afflicted with the same problem.

An item often neglected in evaluative research is a description of the program that is being evaluated in order to determine which of its facets are associated with its outcome. Programs are usually complex sets of actions, administered by a number of individuals. If a program is found to have a positive outcome, it would be important to know which of its aspects contributes to its success. This information would serve to make the program more efficient.

The three studies reprinted in this section are excellent examples of attempts to evaluate human service programs through the use of research methods. All three show some of the basic characteristics of evaluative research, including their approaches and the basic methodologic problems they encountered. Additional examples of evaluative research in human services can be found in Struening and Guttentag (1975); Schulberg, Sheldon, and Baker (1969); and Schulberg and Baker (1979). Other recommended readings on evaluative research include Rossi, Freeman, and Wright (1979) and Weiss (1979).

## REFERENCES

Campbell, D. T., & Stanley, J. C. *Experimental and quasi-experimental designs for research.* Chicago: Rand McNally, 1963.
Cook, T. D., & Campbell, D. T. *Quasi-experimentation: design and analysis issues for field settings.* Chicago: Rand McNally, 1979.

James, G. Evaluation in public health practice. *American Journal Public Health,* 1962, *52,* 1145–1154.

Rossi, P. H., Freeman, H. E., & Wright, S. R. *Evaluation: a systematic approach.* Beverly Hills: Sage Publications, 1979.

Schulberg, H. C., Sheldon, A., & Baker, F. *Program evaluation in the health fields.* New York: Behavioral Publications, 1969.

Schulberg, H. C., & Baker, F. *Program evaluation in the health fields, Vol. II.* New York: Human Sciences Press, 1979.

Struening, E. L., & Guttentag, M. *Handbook of evaluation research, Vols. 1 and 2.* Beverly Hills: Sage Publications, 1975.

Suchman, E. A. *Evaluative research.* New York: Russell Sage Foundation, 1967.

Weiss, C. H. *Evaluation research: methods of assessing program effectiveness.* Englewood Cliffs, N.J.: Prentice-Hall, 1972.

*Chapter 17*

# SHARED PERSPECTIVES
## A Community Counseling Center for Adolescents

## Helen Reinherz
## Marguerite Heywood
## Joy Camp

In the face of diminished public concern about the "drug crisis" combined with the increased demands for accountability from supporting sources, many community-based programs created at the height of the panic over adolescent drug use in suburban communities are fighting for survival. These agencies are particularly vulnerable because they constitute new care delivery systems which are not part of established social service networks. Incorporating a variety of treatment approaches and a combination of professional and paraprofessional staff, adolescent counseling centers try to meet needs of youth within their own communities. In addition, because these centers deal with a highly charged issue, adolescent drug abuse, community attitudes and demands have been both ambivalent and unrealistic.

In most instances community supporters regard drug abuse as the target problem for the agency, whereas staff see drug abuse as symptomatic of wider personal and societal problems, and the adolescent clients, themselves, often do not view drug use as problematic. Since the disparities between community views, agency

This two year study was sponsored by the Division of Drug Rehabilitation of the Massachusetts Department of Mental Health as one of four studies of prototypical agencies using a variety of treatment modalities.

views, and those of adolescent clients may complicate the issue of accountability, community-based agencies have difficulties in meeting community demands for precise and specific reports of successful outcome (17).

This paper describes one community-based agency, its goals, the expectations of its clients, and their progress one year after intake. Some hypothesis will be presented to account for positive impact attributed to the agency by its youthful clientele as well as specific attitudinal and behavioral changes noted in the adolescents.

The community in which the agency was located established the Counseling Center at the height of publicity surrounding the "drug crisis" in suburban America. In the late spring of 1970, in spite of active opposition, a coalition of teenagers, upset by the dramatic death by overdose of a classmate, and a group of influential townspeople investigating drug use among youth obtained a treatment facility for their town. Adolescents, acting in concert with town adults, chose the first staff members who included two social workers, a psychiatrist, and several paraprofessionals. The research to be reported here began in the winter of 1971, soon after the Center entered its permanent quarters so that throughout the study the Center was in the process of growth and evolution. The research staff followed the agency through program, "initiation," "contact," and "beginning implementation" (14).

Key elements of the system including the community, the staff, and the clientele were examined through a variety of research methodologies from winter 1971 to January 1973. The total population of clients who came to the agency during a six-month period from February 1971 to August 1971, 59 adolescents, were studied at intake and 48 (81%) were reinterviewed one year later. Young male and female trained interviewers saw each of the adolescents individually at both intake and follow-up. Data was collected on drug and alcohol use, school and work performance, family interaction, peer relationships, and constructive use of time. Attitudes toward many of these variables as well as treatment at the Center were also sought. In addition, at intake and at the year's follow-up, each subject completed a self administered Self-Concept Scale (4,5).

## The Clientele of the Consultation Center

The clientele of the agency included adolescents with criminal records and histories of long-standing antisocial activity, as well as others who represented models of conformity at home and school. The majority of youth using the Center, however, could be characterized as alienated teenagers on the fringe of their adolescent subculture who were having difficulty in coping with major developmental tasks. During the period of study a large majority (3/4) of new clients were 14–18. The mean age was 17 and the total age range was 14 to 23. The proportion of males and females coming to the agency in the months studied was almost equal with 31 males and 28 females. At intake most of the youths told interviewers that they spent much of their time in aimless or passive pursuits, using a variety of drugs including alcohol.

Although their drug behavior and other actions deviant from community norms might make them appear to belong to the counter-culture, many of the characteristics describing the adolescents and even their expressed attitudes and values reflected the middle class character of their town. Evidence indicated that, in spite of expressed alienation, they were still deeply rooted in their community. Most clients lived at home with both parents, and were high school students. Their orientation to middle-class values could be seen in the fact that although they actively disliked school, they had no plans for dropping out as they felt education was "necessary for getting ahead." They also anticipated working in the future and expressed positive attitudes toward the concept of working.

## STAFF TREATMENT GOALS

The research staff, aware of well-documented difficulties of obtaining formulated treatment goals by "one shot" direct questioning of agency personnel (7), examined the goals of the staff through semistructured interviews repeated at intervals throughout the study, supplemented by notes of staff meetings and marathons. Although most of the agency's community supporters saw the Center as the panacea which would eradicate the drug problem from the town, from the beginning, the staff interpreted their role more broadly, regarding themselves as mandated to serve any troubled adolescent. Despite the fact that 81% of the clients coming to the agency used some drugs, the staff never focused solely on durgs as the major issue.

Basically, the staff considered drug abuse to be symptomatic of wider problems. Staff goals emphasized total development, including achievement of independence, growth of a clearer sense of identity, and increased self-understanding. Criteria by which staff members evaluated clients' progress were rooted in behavior and development, such as ability to work, to cope with school, to handle family difficulties, and relate to peers. Successful outcome incorporated diminution of drug use, but staff placed highest priority on indications of maturational progress and change.

Thus, staff orientation reflected the views of Brotman, who emphasizes the importance of general rehabilitation of drug users with abstinence a subsidiary goal (1), rather than other writers who believe that treatment goals for adolescent drug users must focus directly on the drug use itself with abstinence a central aim (2).

## ADOLESCENTS' EXPECTATIONS OF TREATMENT

Client-expressed expectations were reflective of the staff viewpoint. Of those clients who could state what they "expected" at intake, the majority (30 out of 33) thought the most valuable outcome of coming to the Center would be "getting their heads together." Thus, over 50% of the teenagers coming to the Center had treatment expectations which made them good candidates for therapy designed to increase self-understanding and improve relationships. This figure is in contrast with Lubin's finding that less than 10% of the clients at an urban mental health agency had expectations of treatment appropriate for psychotherapy (8).

At the same time, on coming to the Center, 26 youths were vague in their expectations for treatment and could not define what they anticipated. However, the Center offered easily accessible entry to services so that troubled adolescents without clearly defined treatment goals could enter and participate in the system comfortably.

## THE TREATMENT PROCESS OF THE YOUTH CONSULTATION CENTER

Staff treatment repertoire encompassed a wide range of modalities, including traditional psychotherapy, group activities and therapeutic community techniques, thereby creating a highly flexible and varied treatment program. There was no waiting list for treatment.

For many teenagers who spent hours playing ping-pong, watching T.V., and "rapping," the Center with its casual ambiance became a second home.

The staff also accepted uncertain commitment to therapy and tolerated impulsive and erratic behavior. Most important, both professionals and paraprofessionals maintained the appearance of having a "friendly" non-clinical relationship with their clients. As Werkman has observed, contemporary adolescents "want to be seen as seekers and learners not as patients in need of treatment" (16).

Although 21 subjects had come from professional referrals (five by court commitment), the majority, 38, came at the suggestion of a friend or relative choosing the Center because "it was there" thus validating the rationale for a community based agency.

The flexible and informal nature of treatment at the Center was evidenced by the treatment status of clients at follow-up. Among those followed up, 26% had completed treatment in mutual agreement with their counselor, and 33% were still in treatment. Treatment length varied from several interviews to continuance at time of follow-up with an average (mean) of 9½ months of treatment. Of the 41% who had left the Center on their own, over one half of these continued informal contact with the Center staff, and over 90% of the "drop-outs" said they would return to the agency if they felt they needed further help.

## CHANGES IN YOUTH AT FOLLOW-UP

When seen a year after first coming to the Center, 59 adolescent clients in the study had undergone considerable attitudinal and behavioral change. Of particular importance were meaningful changes in major areas of functioning: drug use; motivations for drug use; constructive use of time; number of arrests; and self-concept, an area of particular relevance in a study of this age group.

Besides acting as one indicator of emotional health, the Fitts Self-Concept Scale may be used as a measure of change in therapy (4). It has been stated that self-concept shifts as a result of influential life experiences, including therapy, and in turn, such changes are reflected in behavior (13). According to a recent study, delinquents in an intensive rehabilitation program who showed the greatest rise in self-concept also maintained the most modification in social behavior upon leaving the institution (13). A strong relationship, then, appears to exist between improvement in self-concept and improved social functioning.

At intake, the Center's clients scored well below the norm in self-esteem as measured by the Fitts scale. Thomas has reported several studies that show adolescents normally test about 20 points lower than the national mean of 346.6 (13). However, the mean score of the Center sample was 286.6, almost two standard deviations from the norm and considerably below the mean of 336 scored by a comparison group of "non-client" community teenagers. The Center's adolescents also scored below a group of 54 teenage boys, the majority with a history of school failures, who achieved a mean of 326 (11).

The adolescents' initial low total self-esteem scores derived strongly from those subscores which indicated an extremely weak sense of identity, self-deprecatory feelings about behavior, and discomfort in roles as family members. These low scores were mirrored in the subjects' total functioning, with collaborative evidence from other sources of data including client self-reports, staff comments, and research staff observations.

As may be seen in Table 1, the increase in self-esteem among the 43 who completed the scale a year later was highly significant. Both the total scores and all its components showed statistically significant change in a positive direction. Moreover, these new self-

Table 1   Differences at Intake and Follow-up of Mean Scores
of Adolescents in Components of Self-Concept*

| Components of self-concept | $\bar{X}$ at intake | $\bar{X}$ at follow-up | $t^{**}$ | Level of significance |
|---|---|---|---|---|
| Total self-concept (Total P) | 287.6 | 317.1 | 4.24 | < .001 |
| Identity*** | 104.1 | 114.9 | 3.33 | .002 |
| Self-satisfaction | 91.8 | 102.4 | 2.81 | .008 |
| Behavior | 91.6 | 99.8 | 3.22 | .003 |
| Physical self | 59.9 | 64.2 | 2.23 | .031 |
| Moral-ethical self | 59.4 | 65.6 | 2.67 | .011 |
| Personal self | 54.6 | 61.5 | 3.41 | .002 |
| Family self | 51.9 | 59.3 | 5.04 | < .001 |
| Social self | 62.7 | 66.4 | 2.30 | .027 |

*N = 43
**Matched t tests were calculated for differences between Intake and Follow-Up scores.
***Each of the subscores has a different possible maximum score and cannot be compared.

images coincided with improvements in behavior and changes in attitudes—as reflected not only in interviews, but also by collaborative evidence from therapists and others in the clients' environment.

The adolescents' use of their spare time, when first seen, had indicated considerable alienation and boredom, as well as asocial and anti-social activity. A substantial minority, 25 (or 42%), had been arrested at least once, with eight having five or more arrests. At follow-up the sample had increased their constructive activities substantially. They participated in more sports, hobbies, outdoor activities and reading, and were involved in less "hanging around," "doing nothin'," and "doing dope." Related to this was the finding that there was a statistically significant reduction in the number of arrests.*

At the intake period 48 (81%) of the sample were using some form of drugs. Nearly all who used drugs smoked marijuana, while a sizable proportion, almost two thirds of the drug users, were using more dangerous drugs such as barbiturates, hallucinogens and amphetamines at least once a week or more often. At intake, 35 youths, 73% of those using drugs, reported they used drugs in order to escape difficult life situations with which they felt unable to cope.

By follow-up there was a statistically significant decrease in drug-taking, with ten youths ceasing drug use altogether.* A number of others switched from "hard" drugs to marijuana. The abuse of barbiturates, a frequently used drug at intake, diminished greatly. Those who continued to use drugs used them less frequently and for significantly different reasons, reflecting a decrease in need for blotting out difficult life situations or as many clients said they were no longer "using drugs as a cop-out."*

## CLIENTS' PERSPECTIVES ON TREATMENT AND CHANGE

Interest in the expressed opinions of consumers of help-services has been a growing theme of recent research (9, 12). Mayer and Rosenblatt point out the need to ". . . pay more attention to the opinions of patients. Whatever else can be said, the patient not the practitioners is experiencing the difficulty." (10). The research staff was interested in the adolescents' own perceptions of their treatment as well as that of their own progress as may be seen in Tables 2 and 3.

*<.05 (McNemar Test)

Table 2    Subjects' Self-Rating of Improvement

| Area of change | Better (%) | Same (%) | Worse (%) | N |
|---|---|---|---|---|
| Work | 67 | 33 | 0 | 36 |
| School | 57 | 43 | 0 | 35 |
| Friends | 67 | 24 | 9 | 45 |
| Parents | 64 | 32 | 4 | 44 |
| Drug use | 64 | 31 | 5 | 39 |
| Self-understanding | 89 | 11 | 0 | 45 |

Table 3    Subjects' Rating of Center's Effect

| Area of change | Helpful (%) | No effect (%) | Harmful (%) | N |
|---|---|---|---|---|
| Work | 49 | 51 | 0 | 37 |
| School | 46 | 54 | 0 | 39 |
| Friends | 60 | 40 | 0 | 43 |
| Parents | 68 | 30 | 2 | 44 |
| Drug use | 57 | 35 | 8 | 37 |
| Self-understanding | 89 | 9 | 2 | 44 |

The clients had listed "getting my head together" as a major treatment goal and expectation. Tables 2 and 3 indicate the clients' perceptions of areas of positive change in themselves and their assessment of the Center's role in these changes.

Specifically, Tables 2 and 3 reveal that in line with their initial expectations, clients rated "self understanding" both as most improved and as most influenced by their contact with the Center. By improved "self-understanding," the adolescents said in part that they had a better sense of who they were and were conscious of resulting positive changes in their self-esteem:

Coming here . . . made me become a person, and stand up for my own thing.
Basically the Center helped me know myself and come to reality with myself.

As may be seen, several other areas of change were also aknowledged, with the Center listed as most influential in helping create improved relationships with peers and parents.

It has been demonstrated that what happens in their peer group strongly influences adolescents' lives and drug behavior (2, 15). At follow-up, two-thirds of the clients felt that their relationships with friends had improved and nearly the same proportion felt that the improvement resulted from coming to the Center. They reported more self confidence in their own opinions, which enabled them to drop harmful friendships and to inititate new relationships. Some adolescents continued to experience interactional difficulties and acknowledged the need to work further in this area.

At intake, the youths frequently reported conflict with parents, and other data sources also revealed considerable dysfunction among the families of the sample. Approximately two thirds of the clients thought the Center had helped them improve rapport with their parents. As one adolescent said: "We communicate more. They no longer just listen; they listen and hear what I say and the same with me. As a result, we understand each other." Other youths with problematic family situations that were unchanged reported learning to develop more independence from their disorganized families.

Although at intake, the clients had not considered drugs as a problem, nearly two thirds felt that they had "improved" in their drug behavior (a figure slightly under 71% who had actually changed position in drug behavior from intake to follow-up). In addition, slightly more than one half the follow-up respondents said that their attitudes toward using drugs had become more negative as they found more positive alternatives. As one said, "Drugs just don't fit into my life anymore."

## PATTERN OF CHANGE—TWO EXAMPLES

Looking at individual change, the data revealed that the largest proportion, 26, of the 48 youths seen at follow-up had made positive changes in at least two of the major areas. At the same time, over one quarter of the adolescents, 14, seen at follow-up had made changes in three or more outcome variables particularly self-concept, drug use, and constructive use of time, and eight youths had made little or no change and did not show improvement in any of the major indices of the study.

The case histories of Mary whose life changed in a number of ways after contact with the Center, and Jim whose life seemed little altered after entry into the agency, are presented to illustrate two divergent outcomes.

Mary was an 18-year-old who had originally come to the Center because her father had thrown her out of the house. She was in a state of turmoil—drinking, using barbiturates, and experimenting with a number of other drugs. Mary needed immediate help with housing but also requested help with her emotional problems. A social worker found her a temporary place to stay, and Mary was assigned to group therapy where she found support from peers and counselor in her efforts toward achieving independence. As she began to experience some sense of her own identity and feel better about herself, her drinking and drug use stopped. Mary commented that her contact with the Center had given her a breathing space so "I could get myself together." She continued to show improvement and change in all aspects under study.

Sixteen-year-old Jim came to the Center for several months as a participant in a paid work program but had never regarded himself as needing help with his personal problems. A heavy drinker and user of hard drugs, he had been arrested a number of times for a variety of petty offenses. When he was seen at follow-up, basically little had changed in his life. Most importantly, he still had a very low self-concept score, reflecting his poor self-esteem. He continued to have brushes with the law and to drink heavily. Jim kept up a sporadic contact with one of the paraprofessionals "as a friend to talk to." However, although he had reduced his drug use somewhat, and was marginally involved in a sports activity sponsored by the Center, neither Jim nor the Center felt that he could be said to have changed in any real sense.

## DISCUSSION: SHARED PERSPECTIVES AND CHANGE

The writers are aware of the inability in a descriptive study to directly attribute change to treatment without a control group. However, the direction of change occurring in areas of greatest mutual focus of staff and clients plus the observations of clients provide fruitful issues for consideration and raise hypotheses for further testing. The treatment philosophy at the Center focused on the total growth of an individual including meaningful social activities, healthier relationships with family and peers and enhanced self understanding. The clients' own assessment of change and the changes found by other measures are strikingly reflective of the staff's objectives. Indeed, the greatest improvement in the adolescents occurred in self-concept, with subscores of identity, behavior and family relations showing highly significant change—all areas of major treatment focus at the Center. Moreover, self-understanding which is closely related to sense of identity and family relations, were also the areas the teenagers reported as having been changed most by their contact with the Center.

The literature points to several factors which might have contributed to the successful outcome for many clients seen at the Center. Recent studies have highlighted the necessity of congruence of goals and expectations between client and therapist (12). Increasingly, both research and experience point to evidence that the cultural and class differences between worker and client can lead to lack of meaningful communication, resulting in client dissatisfaction, and high drop-out rate in therapeutic encounters (9, 10). Our study indicated that clients and therapists at the Center shared generally mutual treatment expectations and cultural values. As indicated earlier, the majority of clients came to get what the Center could offer. Those who came wanting to "get their heads together" were thus ready to enter into relationships, seek self understanding, and, in general, to deal with the sort of issues involved in the psychotherapeutic process.

Even more fundamentally, clients and staff shared an orientation to community values. Although the youth might fail to conform to some of the standards of their middle class suburban community, they were essentially in tune with them and had no real emotional or intellectual commitment to counter-culture values. Staff attempts to help adolescents within the existing cultural framework were thus compatible with the clients' world view.

It is also hypothesized that the community base of the agency was another factor that contributed to the satisfaction expressed by most clients. The philosophy behind the community mental health movement has underlined the usefulness of treating people within their own environment, and using existing community resources to augment the treatment process (3). The Center gained added strength from the historical fact that its adolescent constituency played an essential role in its establishment. A further element equally salient was the flexibility of the Center's approach. The staff met the clients "where they were," did not impose rigid requirements, and offered a variety of services which clients could use according to their needs and at their own pace. The community base and the flexibility together allowed teenagers to find help within their own community without having to define themselves as in some way "deviant" (16).

And most crucial to the survival of the agency was the fact that the clients' most outstanding changes—in self-esteem and in self-understanding—occurred in conjunction with significant behavioral changes such as fewer arrests, more constructive use of time and less drug use. Thus, the Center, in spite of not focusing directly on the goal of changing drug behavior, did in fact appear to help reduce drug use among its clients, fulfilling its initial mandate from the supporting community as it continued to fulfill its mandate to its most significant constituency, its adolescent clientele.

## REFERENCES

1. Brotman, R. and Freedman, A. *Community Mental Health Approach to Drug Addiction,* Washington, D.C.: U.S. Government Printing Office, 1968.

2. Caroff, P., Lieberman, F. and Gottesfield, M. "The Drug Problem: Treating Pre-addictive Adolescents," *Social Casework,* 1970, 51, pp. 527–532.

3. Cochran, M. and Jones, W. "Mental Health and the Community," *Community Mental Health Journal,* 1971, 7, pp. 161–168.

4. Fitts, W. *Tennessee Self-Concept Scale,* Nashville, Tennessee: Counsellor Recordings and Tests, 1965.

5. Fitts, W. *The Self Concept and Delinquency* (Research Monograph I), Nashville, Tennessee: Nashville Mental Health Center, 1969.

6. Gordon S. "Are We Seeing the Right Patients?", *American Journal of Orthopsychiatry,* 1965, 35, pp. 131–137.

7. Klerman, L. "The Potential Contribution of Research Projects to Comprehensive Programs for Pregnant Adolescents," in *Illegitimacy: Changing Services for Changing Times,* New York: National Council on Illegitimacy, 1970.

8. Lubin, B. et al. "Correlates of Initial Treatment Assignment in Community Mental Health Center," *Archives of General Psychiatry,* 1973, 29, pp. 497–500.

9. Mayer, J. and Timms, N. "Clash in Perspective Between Worker and Client," *Social Casework,* 1969, 50, pp. 32–40.

10. Mayer, J. and Rosenblatt, A. "Clash in Perspective Between Mental Patient and Staff," *American Journal of Orthopsychiatry.* 1974, 44, pp. 432–441.

11. Reinherz, H. and Griffin, C. *The Treadmill of Failure: Community Mental Health Monograph,* Boston, Massachusetts: Massachusetts Department of Mental Health, 1971.

12. Silverman, P. "A Reexamination of the Intake Procedure," *Social Casework,* 1970, 51, pp. 625–634.

13. Thomas, W. *Correlates of Self Concept* (Research Monograph VI), Nashville, Tennessee: Dede Wallace Mental Health Center, 1972.

14. Tripodi, T., Fellin, P., and Epstein, I. *Social Program Evaluation,* Itasca, Illinois: Peacock Publishers, 1971.

15. Wechsler, H. and Thum, D. "Drug Use Among Teenagers: Patterns of Present and Anticipated Use," *The International Journal of Addictions,* 1974, 8, pp. 905–912.

16. Werkman, S. "Value Confrontations Between Psychotherapists and Adolescents," *American Journal of Orthopsychiatry,* 1974, 44, pp. 337–344.

17. Westhues, K. "The Drop-In Center: A Study in Conflicting Realities," *Social Casework,* 1972, 53, pp. 361–368.

*Chapter 18*

# TESTING A BEHAVIORAL APPROACH
# WITH GROUPS

## Harry Lawrence
## Claude L. Walter

An abundance of research evidence now exists to validate the effectiveness of behavior modification with individual treatment approaches.[1] Therapeutic work with groups, regardless of theoretical orientation, has not been as well researched. Nevertheless, clinical experience and studies in social psychology attest to various special advantages of groups. For example, social reinforcement from group members can facilitate individual improvement, learning about others' problems can illuminate one's own, and new behavior and ideas can be tried out within the supportive setting of the group.[2]

In recent years, Lawrence and Sundel have developed a model of group work that combines some of the benefits derived from both behavioral and group interaction principles.[3] Adult group members who have various personal difficulties meet for eight weekly sessions. They are taught how to frame questions and comments to each other appropriately, to specify their own problems in terms of observable behaviors, and to apply behavioral principles in assessing these problems and gathering data about them. The group then devises strategies for each member to overcome his or her difficulty, and the members often use behavioral rehearsal techniques to develop the skill needed to carry out such plans.

An exploratory study of this model was conducted with three groups in a family service agency.[4] Of the 17 group members who were seen six months after treatment had ended, 12 (70.6 percent) reported that their treatment goals had been fully achieved and sustained. Two members had obtained partial success, and two noted no improvement.

Based on these promising results, the authors decided to test this group approach using an experimental design. The proposed study had implications beyond the evaluation of the model, however, because it had some features that had been subjected to little prior research: it was a controlled-outcome study of group work; it involved real clients in an open agency setting; and the groups were composed of members having a diversity of problems.

Sound outcome studies of treatment groups have been conducted that support the effectiveness of behavioral approaches, but these have not addressed all of the above dimensions. For example, Paul and Shannon treated "nonclient" groups of recruited college students with the homogeneous problem of speech anxiety.[5] Rose's innovative work with assertiveness training groups included agency clients but was not a controlled study.[6] Recent controlled research by Hand, Lamontagne, and Marks involved groups of outpatients being treated for agoraphobia, but the clients' problem was homogeneous.[7]

The study to be reported here posed both evaluative and ethical difficulties. The kinds of problems that impel people to seek an agency's help are generally more severe than those found in self-improvement programs, and the obligation to provide service of an acceptable standard precludes the use of placebo groups and limits the use of waiting lists for control purposes. Further, the heterogeniety of types of problems makes comparisons difficult. For the practitioner, however, it may be worth foregoing the greater precision of a laboratory study to evaluate a program as it operates in an actual agency.

## METHOD

The study attempted to assess improvement in the following areas of the clients' functioning, which were the focus of the group treatment:

Group members would receive training in assessing and solving social problems. Could these members demonstrate their behavioral problem-solving ability following the group's termination?

Based on previous experience, it was anticipated that most clients' problems would involve some inadequacies in "social effectiveness," such as timidity in asking for a joint checking account with a spouse or attempting in vain to shame a child into doing his or her chores. Training in social effectiveness—involving the giving and receiving of approval, criticism, and requests—would be a part of the group program. Would members be able to demonstrate an improvement in their social skills following group treatment?

Each client joined a group to alleviate a specifically identified problem. Would group treatment significantly improve this focal problem? These questions are interrelated, and a positive finding on all of them would lead to the highest degree of confidence in the effectiveness of the behavioral group treatment method.

Participants in the study were obtained by staff referrals from a family service agency and a community mental health clinic. Clients qualified as subjects if they were *adults* who evidenced *persistent* interpersonal *problems* with family members, acquaintances, or work associates or had problems of personal discomfort or inadequacy.

The prospective subjects were interviewed by one of the members of the research staff. The interview was structured and included listing the subject's problems and selecting one to work on and then defining the problem behavior in observable terms. In addition, the interviewer and the subject implemented a one-week baseline plan to measure the frequency or duration of the problem behavior that was selected. This might include recording the number of marital arguments that occurred during the week or the length of time the subject talked in a social situation without stopping.

Two pretests were also administered. The first, the Rathus Assertiveness Schedule, is a self-rating test in which the individual scores the degree to which his or her behavior corresponds to descriptions of assertive or unassertive actions.[8] This measure was used because the researchers viewed assertiveness as being a partial indicator of social effectiveness.

The second test, the Behavioral Problem-Solving Test, was designed to evaluate the subject's proficiency in identifying information most relevant to the assessment of a problem in personal relationships. In addition it tested the subject's skill in providing sound behavioral explanations for the existence of a problem situation, when given appropriate data.

The behavioral assessment part of the test provided the subject with two vignettes, one concerning a child management problem and the other a marital problem. The information given in the vignettes was incomplete. The subject was to indicate what further information he or she would need to best assess the problem by rank-ordering seven questions according to their relative importance in obtaining the needed information. Three of the seven questions were of high behavioral relevance designed to obtain specific, observable information pertaining to the problem presented, such as "Where, when, and how often does the couple argue?" Four of the questions in each vignette were of low behavioral relevance, because of their vague, speculative, or tangential nature, for example, "Why haven't they had any children?" Subjects were scored according to how many questions of high relevance were ranked as their top three choices.

The problem management part of the Behavior Problem-Solving Test contained enough information to formulate hypotheses about what was maintaining the problem behaviors and what courses of action might be taken to remedy these conditions. The test presented six forced-choice questions about each vignette with four possible answers.

A second interview was scheduled a week later. The client's baseline data were reviewed with him or her, and a new baseline assignment was made if the information was incomplete. Two Social Effectiveness Tests were also administered at this time. These tests were in the form of scripted role-playing in which the client was placed in problem situations with an actress and responded to her standardized comments. The subject's performance was evaluated for "social effectiveness" in giving a positive evaluation or responding to a negative evaluation.

In the first of these tests, the Positive Evaluation Test, the subject was instructed to act the part of a personnel manager and the actress portrayed a worker who had eliminated many poor work habits and had made improvement on others. The subject was evaluated on the extent to which he or she complimented, acknowledged, or praised the worker's improvements. In the Negative Evaluation Test the subject portrayed an employee and was subjected to some vague arbitrary criticism by a "boss." The subject was evaluated on how skillful he or she was in obtaining clear specific information concerning the criticisms without resorting to aggressive or self-effacing behavior.

Following these pretests, the subjects were divided into experimental and control groups on a stratified random basis. That is, an attempt was made to balance the groups for types of problems. The categories that were used were marital problems, child management problems, problems with social relationships (for example, excessive talking leading to avoidance by others), and problems with self-control (such as destructive skin picking or avoidance of work). Subjects within a problem category were randomly assigned to either the experimental or control group.

The experimental group was divided into four groups of five to six members, and they started treatment. The subjects in the control group were placed on a "waiting list" until posttests were administered nine weeks later. During the time the experimental group was in treatment, the control subjects were not to receive treatment on the problems they had selected for group work. Logs prepared by the agency staff revealed that, in fact, contacts with control clients were confined to six brief telephone calls pertaining to matters only tangentially related to these problems.

Table 1 shows the distribution of clients in the experimental and control groups by age, sex, marital status, and education at the time of the pretest and posttest interviews. Table 2 presents the distribution of subjects in the two groups according to types of problems at the time posttests were administered.

The subjects making up the experimental and control groups were similar in terms of age range, sex, and educational background at the time of the posttest. The one area in which the groups differed was with regard to marital status, with more married members in the experimental groups and more divorced clients among the controls (See Table 1.). To find out whether marital status had an important effect on treatment outcome, posttreatment self-ratings of perceived improvement in the focal problem were compared for married and divorced subjects. Divorced subjects in both groups indicated greater improvement in their problems than did married subjects. The treatment effects would have been confounded if the better performing divorced clients had been overrepresented in the experimental groups. Actually, the reverse situation was true. It is therefore unlikely that marital status had a negative effect on the results.

Some small differences existed between the experimental and control groups regarding the distribution of types of problems. How-

Table 1    Distribution of Subjects in Experimental
and Control Groups

| Characteristics of subjects | Subjects completing pretests | | | Subjects completing both pretests and posttests | | |
|---|---|---|---|---|---|---|
| | Experimental group ($n = 24$) | Control group ($n = 24$) | Total ($n = 48$) | Experimental group ($n = 18$) | Control group ($n = 17$) | Total ($n = 35$) |
| Age | | | | | | |
| 20–29 | 5 | 11 | 16 | 3 | 5 | 8 |
| 30–39 | 12 | 9 | 21 | 10 | 8 | 18 |
| 40 and over | 7 | 4 | 11 | 5 | 4 | 9 |
| Sex | | | | | | |
| Male | 3 | 1 | 4 | 2 | 1 | 3 |
| Female | 21 | 23 | 44 | 16 | 16 | 32 |
| Marital Status | | | | | | |
| Single | 2 | 1 | 3 | 1 | 1 | 2 |
| Married | 18 | 13 | 31 | 14 | 8 | 22 |
| Divorsed | 4 | 10 | 14 | 3 | 8 | 11 |
| Education | | | | | | |
| 8–11 years | 3 | 2 | 5 | 3 | 0 | 3 |
| High School Graduate | 8 | 12 | 20 | 4 | 7 | 11 |
| Some College | 10 | 7 | 17 | 9 | 7 | 16 |
| College Graduate | 3 | 3 | 6 | 2 | 3 | 5 |

ever, no correlation was found between types of problems and success in treatment.

## TREATMENT METHODS

Each group, consisting of five to six members, was led by two group workers, a trained leader from the research staff and an "apprentice," who was a member of the agency's staff. These apprentice group leaders were experienced social workers, whose therapeutic orientations ranged from the eclectic to a preference for approaches other than behavior modification, but who volunteered because of their interest in developing behavioral skills. Periodic staff training sessions and weekly supervision were provided for them. Each group met for eight weekly sessions, each meeting lasting approximately 2½ hours.

Table 2   Categories of Problems in Experimental and
Control Groups at Time of Posttests

| Problem category | Experimental group | Control group | Total |
|---|---|---|---|
| Social Relationships | 4 | 4 | 8 |
| Marital | 5 | 3 | 8 |
| Child Management | 5 | 8 | 13 |
| Self-Control | 4 | 2 | 6 |
| Total | 18 | 17 | 35 |

The group was used as a means for achieving the individual treatment goals of each member. To further these objectives, the therapists influenced the activities and relationships of the group members to accomplish the following tasks:

The group accepted and helped to enforce treatment norms that had been established by the therapists. These rules required regularity of attendance, discouraged socializing among members outside the meetings, focused discussion of members' problems on contemporaneous events occurring outside the group sessions and on observable data, and required performance of assignments outside the group. (The purpose of discouraging socializing outside the meetings is to prevent alliances that might impair the functioning of the group. Such associations can be especially volatile when individuals with marital problems are included in the group. Given a different group composition or range of problems, fraternization may be unavoidable and even desirable).

Each group member made a final decision on problem priorities and further clarified his or her goals in treatment. Selecting a problem to work on and clarifying goals in the group involved more discussion with some members than with others because of either altered life circumstances or previous concealment of other major problems during the initial interviews.

Group members contributed to the assessment of each other's problems. Members were taught the following essential components of behavioral assessment: behavior specification, recording response frequencies, and delineation of controlling antecedents and consequences of the problem behavior. Lectures, demonstrations, and role-playing techniques were used in teaching members to apply these concepts.

Members offered appropriate prescriptions for solutions to each other's problems. After an individual's behavioral assessment was completed, the group helped him or her decide on appropriate methods of changing the problem behavior.

Members of the group participated in training procedures to acquire the skills necessary for successful performance of the prescribed behavior in the problem situation. The group ascertained whether each member could appropriately carry out the intervention he or she agreed to. When they observed difficulties, behavioral rehearsal procedures were instituted until adequate performance was demonstrated.

Group members provided social reinforcement for each other. The workers prompted the members to provide evaluative feedback and social approval for each member's treatment accomplishments outside the group as well as for demonstrating appropriate behavior within the meeting.

To achieve the above tasks, the workers prepared detailed plans before each meeting that specified the behaviors each group member was expected to perform during the meeting and the interventions that would be used to achieve these objectives. These meeting plans were sufficiently flexible for the therapist to respond appropriately to suggestions of the members and to unpredictable events.

The following is a representative account of one group's fifth meeting. Each member read data he or she had recorded as a "homework" assignment. This was followed by discussion. The workers presented a lecture and demonstration on how to respond to criticism in which role-playing was used to show how to turn vague criticisms into specific requests. The group then evaluated the results of each member's current interventions and devised new strategies. For example, by initiating pleasant conversations with his wife, Mr. R had greatly reduced the frequency of her verbal attacks. The group proposed ways to handle her critical comments when his preventive efforts failed. Following this, the members engaged in behavioral rehearsal of the new strategies they planned to initiate. For example, Mrs. A practiced how to guide a recalcitrant daughter through the performance of chores without responding to insults. After this the workers designed a recording plan with each member to obtain data on the actions to be initiated during the week.

## POSTTEST PROCEDURES

The interval between pretest and posttest interviews for both groups was nine to ten weeks. All subjects were asked to record data on the frequency or duration of the original problem behavior for the week preceding the posttest interview. During this interview, all participants were given the same battery of tests they had received for the pretest. In addition, they completed a Client's Problem-Rating Form indicating the degree of perceived change in identified problems since the pretest. The experimental subjects rated the problem they had worked on in the group, and control subjects rated the focal problem they had selected to work on in the pretest interview.

The control subjects were then organized into four groups and started treatment within two weeks of the posttest interview. Although this treatment was not part of the controlled experiment, the data gathered from it provided supplemental support for the experimental findings as well as additional clinical information. The conditions and the format of treatment were essentially the same as for the experimental groups. The senior therapist in each group was an agency staff member who had previously served as the apprentice therapist with one of the experimental groups. Each was assisted by a new apprentice co-worker from his or her own agency.

One week after the treatment of the control group ended, those group members returned for an interview and completed the Client's Problem-Rating Form. Three months after completion of treatment, experimental and control group subjects were mailed another rating form and asked to indicate the current status of their identified problems.

For those completing treatment in the experimental group, attendance averaged only 6.8 sessions per member, despite their verbal agreements to attend all eight sessions. The attendance rule was subsequently revised for the control groups to call for the automatic termination of group treatment if a member missed more than one meeting. Attendance among the control subjects then attained an average of 7.3 sessions per member, with no subject falling below the seven-session minimum. One subject withdrew from treatment.

Twenty-four subjects were originally assigned to both the experimental and control groups following pretesting. In the ensuing 9 to 10 weeks before posttesting, 6 experimental and 7 control subjects dropped out of the study. Telephone inquiries produced the following stated reasons for discontinuing treatment: the problem had sufficiently improved, family crises, schedule changes, moving, dissatisfaction with the group experience and preference for individual treatment. The distribution of reasons given for discontinuance were similar for both groups, except for the two experimental subjects who were dissatisfied with the group experience.

## RESULTS

Table 3 presents the results of the Behavioral Problem-Solving Test and shows the changes in the average scores for both groups from the pretest to the posttest. On the behavioral assessment part, the experimental group showed a significant improvement, whereas the control group scores remained unchanged. This suggests that the experimental groups did learn to consider behaviorally specific questions as more important in assessing problems than nonspecific questions.

Comparison between the groups of the number of right answers given on the problem management part again shows a significant difference in the experimental group's scores, whereas the control groups did not improve. Apparently, the experimental group's improvement was a consequence of group treatment.

Table 4 contains a comparison of responses on the tests that measured social effectiveness and assertiveness. On the Rathus Assertiveness Schedule the experimental group's scores did improve and changes in the control group were negligible. The experimental group's improvement is noteworthy, but did not meet the standard $p<.05$ level of significance.

All role-playing on the two Social Effectiveness Tests was transcribed and was independently coded from blind copies by two judges. The total index of coder reliability was .86 on the Positive Evaluation Test and .88 on the Negative Evaluation Test. The Positive Evaluation Test was scored by the proportion of positive responses to the opportunities for making positive responses in the

Table 3    Responses on Behavioral Problem-Solving Test

| Test | Number of subjects | Pretest mean score[a] | Posttest mean score | t-test | Level of significance |
|------|------|------|------|------|------|
| Behavioral Assessment | | | | | |
| Experimental Group | 18 | 3.33 | 5.27 | 6.01 | .001 |
| Control Group[b] | 19 | 4.15 | 4.15 | 0.00 | N.S. |
| Problem Management | | | | | |
| Experimental Group | 18 | 2.33 | 4.00 | 3.39 | .01 |
| Control Group[b] | 19 | 2.94 | 2.84 | 0.33 | N.S. |

N.S. = not significant.
[a] Mean figures are based on a scoring range of 0–6 correct answers per test.
[b] Includes two subjects who withdrew before completing the full battery of posttests.

Table 4    Responses on Measures of Social
Effectiveness and Assertiveness

| Test | Number of subjects | Pretest mean score | Posttest mean score | t-test | Level of significance |
|------|------|------|------|------|------|
| Rathus Assertiveness Schedule | | | | | |
| Experimental Group | 18 | 87.67 | 92.50 | 1.7358 | .10 |
| Control Group[a] | 19 | 79.89 | 80.89 | 0.3777 | N.S. |
| Positive Evaluation Test | | | | | |
| Experimental Group | 18 | .27 | .41 | 2.0709 | .055 |
| Control Group | 17 | .26 | .30 | 0.6247 | N.S. |
| Negative Evaluation Test | | | | | |
| Experimental Group | 18 | .57 | .58 | —[b] | N.S. |
| Control Group | 17 | .57 | .54 | —[b] | N.S. |

N.S. = not significant.
[a] Includes two subjects who withdrew before completing the full battery of posttests.
[b] t-test not conducted because scores obviously did not differ significantly.

role-playing situation. A comparison of the pretest and posttest scores for the experimental and control groups indicates that the level of significance for the experimental group comparison essentially reached criterion, whereas a significant difference was not attained for the control group. (See Table 4.) It therefore appears that clients who received group treatment learned how to give more positive evaluations of others in a role-playing situation.

Table 4 also presents the proportion of appropriate responses to total responses given in the Negative Evaluation Test. By inspection, the data show negligible changes in both the experimental and control groups. Group treatment therefore did not effect any changes in responding to the negative evaluations in this test.

To evaluate the data from the pretest and posttest behavioral recordings of each subject, two members of the research staff made independent judgment changes in each client's problem behavior. Four categories were used: "worse," "no change," "better," and "insufficient information." Independent ratings of the two judges were in agreement at a .8 level of reliability. When there was a disagreement in ratings, the judges discussed their differences until consensus was obtained. The judges assigned a case to the "insufficient information" category if there was doubt about the outcome. Eight of the 35 cases could not be evaluated because the available information was too limited. Eleven out of 15 (73 percent) of the experimental subjects were judged to have improved from the pretest to the posttest. In contrast, 11 out of 12 (91 percent) of the control cases for which sufficient data existed failed to make any gains.

## SELF-RATINGS

Ratings on the Client's Problem-Rating Form were made on a seven-point scale ranging from "very much worse" (1.0) to "very much better" (7.0). Table 5 provides a comparison of mean ratings on change in the client's focal problems according to these self-ratings at the posttest period. Experimental subjects reported a mean improvement of 5.94, which corresponds to a rating of "better." The controls, who had not received treatment at that time, indicated an improvement of 4.41, which is between "no change" and "slightly better."

The ratings were condensed into two categories for purposes of statistical analysis. One category, "little or no improvement" included ratings of "worse," "the same," and "slightly better." The other category, "substantial improvement," included ratings of "better" and "much better." A chi-square test indicated that the ratings of "substantial improvement" in the experimental group were significantly greater than in the control group ($\chi^2 = 12.60$, df $= 1$, $p < .001$). Therefore, according to self-ratings, group treatment resulted in substantial improvement in the focal problems.

Following their group treatment, members of the control group completed another rating form, noting the degree of change that had occurred in their problem between the beginning and conclusion of

Table 5   Posttest Comparisons of Change in Focal
Problem on Client's Problem Rating Form

| Rating | Experimental group | Control group |
|---|---|---|
| Much better (7.0) | 3 | 0 |
| Better (6.0) | 12 | 3 |
| Slightly better (5.0) | 2 | 5 |
| No change (4.0) | 1 | 7 |
| Worse (3.0–1.0) | 0 | 2 |
| Total | 18 | 17 |
| Mean Rating | 5.94 | 4.41 |

group treatment. Twelve subjects gave higher posttreatment than pretreatment ratings on their focal problem. One subject rated his problem the same, and one gave a lower rating. The mean score for the control group after treatment was 6.43, a rating falling between "better" and "much better." According to the Sign Test, improvement in the focal problems for control subjects was significant ($p$ <.003).

Three months after completion of treatment for each group, subjects in the experimental and control groups were mailed another self-rating form to rate the degree of change that had occurred in the focal problem and other identified problems since termination of their groups. Ratings were made on a seven-point scale ranging from "much worse" to "much more improved." The average rating for the experimental group was 5.7, between "slightly improved" and "moderately improved," indicating that these subjects continued to make improvements after treatment of their focal problem ended. The control group maintained their previous treatment gains. The mean for this group was 4.07, equal to "improvement maintained."

Combining the data for both groups, the three-month follow-up revealed that 15 (48 percent) of all the subjects made further improvement, 9 (26 percent) maintained prior gains, and 8 (26 percent) did not maintain treatment gains. In all, 74 percent of the subjects either made further improvement or maintained what they had previously achieved.

## DISCUSSION

The original proposition of the study was that behavioral group treatment would effect substantial improvements in the focal problems of the clients. This was substantiated by comparisons between treated and untreated groups of self-ratings of improvement in the problems and comparisons of evaluations of pretest baseline and posttest problem frequency data. It was further supported by before-and-after treatment differences in the control group's self-ratings of the status of their problems, combined after-treatment self-ratings of both groups on change in the focal problem, and combined three-month follow-up ratings on further improvement in the focal problem. The evidence would have been stronger if more quantitative baseline data had been gathered. Unfortunately, the researchers were not successful in obtaining the degree of accuracy in and compliance with the baseline assignments they desired.

Confidence in the findings would have been further strengthened if possible placebo effects had been controlled. However, the
provision of pseudotreatment would have been unethical, given the
severity of the problems being addressed. The clients had problems
of sufficient concern to impel them to seek the agency's help. The
findings that 74 percent of the clients sustained substantial improvement for three months following treatment exceeds what reasonably
could be attributed to placebo influences.

Comparisons of treated and untreated subjects on before-and-
after performance on the Behavioral Problem-Solving Test and the
Positive Evaluation part of the Social Effectiveness Test (with some
support from the Rathus Assertiveness Schedule) indicated that
treatment improved the clients' skills in engaging in behavioral problem-solving and had some influence on the clients' display of socially
effective behavior. No significant difference was found on the section
of the test concerning responding to a negative evaluation. This may
have resulted from the fact that the principles of handling criticisms
and demands were not as systematically covered in the experimental
groups as was the principles of positive reinforcement. (This was
subsequently corrected when treatment was given to the control
group.) The test may also have been culturally biased.

However, the reader should note that the results must be interpreted with caution. The Behavioral Problem-Solving and Social
Effectiveness Tests were specially designed for this research, because
no standardized instruments existed that could be used to evaluate
the variables of concern. These tests have not yet been verified for
reliability or validity. Therefore, at this point the reader must judge
the apparent validity of these instruments in evaluating the outcomes
of this study.[9]

## RECOMMENDATIONS

The "piggyback" method that was used to train group leaders
proved to be a highly effective way to introduce a new treatment
technology to an agency. This training approach was serendipitous,
arising from an impasse in meeting research schedules. It is sufficiently promising to be a subject for study in its own right.

In conducting further research on the effectiveness of this
model, several improvements should be made. Clients should be
better trained in accurate observation and recording of their baseline

behavior, and the monitoring of compliance in recording assignments should be improved. The development of standardized recording forms to cover the full range of anticipated problem behaviors would facilitate this process.

The Social Effectiveness Tests and the Behavioral Problem-Solving Test should be verified for validity and reliability. Systematic training in "social effectiveness" should be incorporated into the group treatment curriculum. Instruction in social effectiveness was not introduced regularly in this study until after the control groups began treatment, and it appeared to strongly influence desired behavior change.

Additional tests should be developed to better evaluate generalization of problem-solving since a possible advantage of this behavioral group approach is that clients learn how to apply the principles of behavior modification to problems other than the one worked on in the group. One way of studying this would be to examine changes in how members talk about problems over a series of meetings. Another approach would be to compare individual behavior therapy with group behavioral treatment. On balance, the findings from this study are sufficiently encouraging for the authors to recommend the clinical use of this group approach pending further evaluative research.

## NOTES AND REFERENCES

1.  *See,* for example, Eileen D. Gambrill, *Behavior Modification: Handbook of Assessment, Intervention, and Evaluation* (San Francisco: Jossey-Bass, 1977); David C. Rimm and John C. Masters, *Behavior Therapy: Techniques and Empirical Findings* (New York: Academic Press, 1974); and Cyril M. Franks and G. Terrance Wilson, eds., *Annal Review of Behavior Therapy,* Vol. 5 (New York: Brunner/Mazel, 1977).

2.  *See,* for example, Dorwin Cartwright and Alvin Zander, eds., *Group Dynamics: Research and Theory* (3d. ed.; New York: Harper & Row, 1968); Robert Liberman, "A Behavioral Approach to Group Dynamics," *Behavior Therapy,* 1 (May 1970), pp. 141–175; Albert Hastorf, "The Reinforcement of Individual Actions in a Group Situation." in Leonard Krasner and Leonard P. Ullman, eds., *Research in Behavior Modification* (New York: Holt, Rinehart & Winston, 1965), pp. 268–284; Bernice B. Lott and Albert V. Lott, "The Formation of Positive Attiudes toward Group Members," *Journal of Abnormal and Social Psychology,* 61 (September 1960), pp. 297–300; and Paul Glasser, Rosemary Sarri, and Robert Vinter, eds., *Individual Change through Small Groups* (New York: Free Press, 1974).

3. Harry Lawrence and Martin Sundel, "Behavior Modification in Adult Groups," *Social Work,* 17 (March 1972), pp. 34–43.

4. Martin Sundel and Harry Lawrence, "A Systematic Approach to Treatment Planning in Time-limited Behavioral Groups," *Journal of Behavior Therapy and Experimental Psychiatry,* in press.

5. Gordon L. Paul and Donald T. Shannon, "Treatment of Anxiety Through Systematic Desensitization in Therapy Groups," *Journal of Abnormal Psychology,* 71 (March 1966), pp. 124–135.

6. Sheldon D. Rose, "In Pursuit of Social Competence," *Social Work,* 20 (January 1975), pp. 33–39.

7. I. Hand, Y. Lamontagne, and I. M. Marks, "Group Exposure (Flooding) *In Vivo* for Agoraphobics," *British Journal of Psychiatry,* 124 (June 1974), pp. 588–602.

8. Spencer A. Rathus, "A Thirty-Item Schedule for Assessing Assertive Behavior," *Behavior Therapy,* 4 (May 1973), pp. 298–306.

9. Copies of the test instruments are available on request.

# Chapter 19

# DAY TREATMENT AND PSYCHOTROPIC DRUGS IN THE AFTERCARE OF SCHIZOPHRENIC PATIENTS

Margaret W. Linn, Eugene M. Caffey,
C. James Klett, Gerard E. Hogarty,
H. Richard Lamb

In 1978, the American Psychiatric Association and the President's Commission on Mental Health concluded that the needs of chronic mental patients suffering from severe, persistent, or recurrent mental illnesses should be our most urgent mental health concern.[1] Deinstitutionalization and the increase in high-risk populations that generate chronic patients were cited as creating problems in the care of these patients that now constituted a national crisis.

Patients have been discharged from mental hospitals in recent years by the tens of thousands. At the same time, readmission rates have steadily increased to about 40% within the first year of discharge.[2] The high rates of readmission suggest an inadequate network of aftercare services that might help to establish patients in the community. The power of psychotropic drugs in reducing psychiatric symptoms has been realized most dramatically in shorter hospital stays. There is also little doubt that these drugs have helped to keep patients, particularly schizophrenics, out of the hospital longer. In fact, several studies[3-5] point to the efficacy of drugs without finding any strong support for the effectiveness of sociotherapies and forestalling relapse. Leff and Wing[8] and Hogarty and associates[4] suggested that there might also be a small subgroup of patients who function better without drugs, even though these patients are difficult to identify at the present time. Furthermore, these studies emphasized that antipsychotic drugs may essentially be prophylactic in that they tend to prevent relapse in the first year after discharge.

The question of whether other types of treatment add to the use of drugs has been explored. May[9] recently reviewed studies of drugs used with other types of treatments in schizophrenia. He pointed out that "it is almost universally held that drugs, psychotherapy, and psychosocial methods should play supplemental rather than competing roles." He concluded, in regard to studies that combined drugs and aftercare services, that aftercare programs helped patients to remain in the community if these programs were focused on problem-solving, social adjustment, living arrangements, employment, and facilitating cooperation with maintenance drug therapy, but not when they were focused on intensive psychotherapy.

At this time, there are many chronic mental patients in the community. Drug therapy has been one of the most effective means of preventing relapse. The fact that patients need more than prophylactic therapy would seem a reasonable premise, but questions of a cost-benefit nature, as well as questions concerning the appropriateness of certain treatments for certain patients, need to be addressed. One alternative to inpatient treatment for many patients is partial hospitalization. Partial hospitalization for psychiatric patients was first used in Russia in the late 1930s. The movement soon extended to Canada and to England. Interestingly, each of the three countries developed along slightly different lines, with Russia emphasizing work, Canada stressing psychotherapeutic methods, and England organizing along the lines of social clubs. This diversity is reflected in programs in the United States. Some select more acute and some more chronic patients, and therefore, programs in the centers vary accordingly.

A number of studies have evaluated partial hospitalization as an alternative to inpatient care. For the most part, these controlled studies answered the question of whether some patients could be treated with less than full-time care. The alternative, however, is not always that of full-time hospitalization. Day care has also been used as a transitional program and as an alternative to other types of community care. All Community Mental Health Centers, now numbering over 500, have partial hospital programs. Therefore, the question of whether day treatment provides alternatives or additions to other types of community care, such as drug maintenance, is important.

A large number of day-hospital studies have been reported. Table 1 shows characteristics of several major studies of partial hospitalization. The majority studied day hospital as an alternative to inpatient care. Only two were controlled studies of day treatment and outpatient care. One of these[10] evaluated day treatment as compared with the "usual" outpatient mental health care and found day treatment more effective. This study, however, represented only one center and was done without control for antipsychotic drugs. The other study[11] compared day with inpatient and outpatient care. The investigators, however, were unable to randomly assign all patients meeting the study criteria, and these patients were studied as a separate group. This study was one of the few that controlled for drugs by at least having all patients receiving antipsychotic drugs.

The remaining studies randomly assigned patients to day or inpatient settings with a one- to two-year follow-up after discharge. As May et al[12] have pointed out, follow-up studies are limited in what they can assess compared with studies in which the aftercare itself was randomly assigned and studied under continued control. Most two-year follow-up studies showed that the major day hospital gains occurred at six and 12 months, and that by two years the differences between groups had largely disappeared.[13–15] There were, however, some limitations in these studies. One[13] could test only a third of their patients at two years. Another[14] did not randomly assign to day care, but assigned to regular hospitalization, brief hospital care with discharge, and brief hospital care with an option to go to day treatment after discharge (and only half of that group elected to do so). The other[15] instituted new outcome measures after the patients had been in the study for one year.

In terms of relapse data, Wilder et al[16] found 85% of the day hospital and 81% of the hospital group in the community two years from admission to either setting. About half of each group had relapsed at least once. Sappington, and Michaux[17] reported very low one-year relapse rates—15% for day treatment and 17% for hospital patients. Herz et al[11] found shorter stays during day treatment patients than for those assigned to inpatient care. Two years later, the day group had a lower readmission rate than the hospital-treated patients. Guy et al[11] reported no difference in relapse rates between day and outpatient treatment; however, during a two-year period, the total inpatient days were less for day than for the hospital-treated group. Ettlinger et al[18] retrospectively compared 30 patients discharged from hospital to day treatment with 30 matched patients

**Table 1 Major Comparative Studies of Partial Hospitalization***

| Investigator | Randomly assigned | Groups | | n | Sex | | Diagnoses | | Control drugs | Cost data | Follow-up, yr | | Day care† | | |
|---|---|---|---|---|---|---|---|---|---|---|---|---|---|---|---|
| | | Day | Hospital | Outpatient | | M | F | One | Mixed | | | 1 | 2 | Better | Same | Worse |
| Ettlinger et al[18] | ... | + | ... | + | 60 | + | + | ... | + | ... | ... | ... | + | ... | + | ... |
| Guy et al[11] | + | + | + | + | 92 | + | + | ... | + | + | ... | + | ... | + | ... | ... |
| Herz et al[14] | +‡ | + | + | ... | 175 | + | + | ... | + | ... | + | ... | + | + | ... | ... |
| Kris[15] | + | + | + | ... | 141 | + | + | ... | + | ... | + | + | ... | ... | + | ... |
| Meltzoff and Blumenthal[10] | + | + | ... | + | 80 | + | ... | ... | + | ... | ... | +§ | ... | + | ... | ... |
| Michaux et al[20] | ... | + | + | ... | 142 | + | + | ... | + | ... | ... | ... | + | ... | +‖ | ... |
| Washburn et al[13] | + | + | + | ... | 93 | + | + | ... | + | ... | + | ... | + | + | ... | ... |
| Wilder et al[16] | + | + | + | ... | 276 | + | + | ... | + | ... | ... | ... | + | ... | + | ... |

* Positive.
† Only a general estimate of overall results.
‡ Herz et al randomly assigned to brief hospitalization, brief hospitalization with a later option for day, and longer term inpatient care (no random assignment made to day hospital per se).
§ Meltzoff and Blumenthal observed patients for 18 months.
‖ Michaux et al reported slightly better results for schizophrenics in the hospital, but somewhat favorable results for all patients in the follow-up period after hospitalization.

discharged directly to the community. No difference in two-year readmission rates were found.

None of the studies reviewed controlled for diagnosis in sample selection. Zwerling and Wilder[19] were perhaps the only investigators who had a large enough sample to perform meaningful subgroup analyses. They reported no difference in two-year relapse rates for schizophrenic male patients ($N = 60$) treated in day hospitals and those treated in hospital settings. Since their schizophrenic male patients had the poorest outcomes of any day hospital patients, they concluded that day treatment was of doubtful value for male schizophrenics, particularly in the acute phase of their illness. Guy et al[11] concluded the opposite, in that drugs plus day care was more beneficial for schizophrenics (male and female), and that drug therapy alone was a more rapid and effective treatment for nonschizophrenics. Michaux et al[20] concluded from studying matched groups of day and hospital patients that inpatient care provided more symptomatic relief for schizophrenic patients than did day treatment.

Studies examining cost of day treatment have compared cost with hospital care or have added these costs to the follow-up phase. As might be predicted, all favored day care cost over inpatient cost.[13-15]

Day treatment has yielded differential results for specific diagnostic groups, particularly schizophrenic patients. No study controlled for diagnosis in sample selection, and only one controlled for antipsychotic drugs. Most studied partial hospitalization as an alternative to inpatient care rather than its value as an aftercare program. None were multicenter studies. Therefore, the present study was designed to compare day treatment plus drugs with drugs alone for chronic schizophrenic patients discharged from ten hospitals throughout the country. As such, it is an attempt to further answer a principal question in contemporary psychiatry—whether the social therapies add significantly to the use of antipsychotic drugs alone in the posthospital care of schizophrenic patients.

## METHOD

The term "partial hospitalization" is the common rubric that classifies all day programs. What may be called day care in one setting can be called day treatment or day hospital in another. In the Veterans Administration (VA), two terms—day hospital and day treatment are used. They refer to distinct programs with different goals. The 35 day-hospital programs treat acute patients who primarily need vocational training along with other types of treatment. The present study focused on the day treatment centers (DTC) rather than day hospitals. Some of the DTC programs have been established for more than 30 years. In 1976, an average of 2,000 patients were treated on any given day. Compared with the day hospital program, the DTC treats more chronic patients, often as an extension of hospital treatment. The DTC goals emphasize enhancement of social functioning. In fact, a survey of the 47 programs was conducted to determine goals and objectives. The DTC staff most frequently listed the following three goals: (1) to improve or maintain abilities to interact successfully with family and others; (2) to provide patients a place to socialize, engage in productive activities, and thereby increase their psychological and social well-being; and (3) to provide a sheltered environment that sustains patients sufficiently so that they can live outside an institutional setting (e.g., will not require rehospitalization).

One issue faced from the beginning was whether there was too much variation among the DTC programs to make a multicenter study feasible. However, the similarity of veterans, goals of the programs, and common standards of operation within the VA structure seemed to have contributed to a somewhat uniform approach. Even though it was recognized that centers would differ to some degree— just as hospitals do in multihospital studies—the statistical problem of variance did not appear insoluble. It also seemed that a multicenter study was needed for two reasons: (1) most studies had been of single centers and did not permit broader validation of results; (2) most studies had included male and female patients as well as patients with mixed diagnoses, so that sample size for any subgroup was usually too small to provide definitive answers.

## Criteria of Success

A hierarchy of outcomes related to goals of DTC was specified to determine overall effectiveness of treatments. A primary objective of psychiatric aftercare is to help patients stay in the community as long as possible. This does not mean that hospital readmission represents failure. The philosophy of a revolving hospital door is sound, if brief periods of hospital care result in fewer total inpatient days during a given period of time. Therefore, the primary criterion of success in this study was time in the community.

A secondary set of criteria described psychosocial variables such as resocialization, psychiatric maintenance, and attitudes. Within this set, more value was assigned to resocialization and psychiatric maintenance, since these are assessed by behaviors. However, attitudes, indicate only a predisposition toward action. It was assumed that achievement of these secondary criteria would produce more community tenure.

A third level of outcome was cost. Cost was to be used in conjunction with the other variables in determining successful outcome. If no significant differences were found on any criteria, cost would become the most important outcome. If all criteria favored one program, naturally that treatment would be deemed superior, regardless of cost. If criteria were split between the DTC and outpatient drug management (ODM) groups, success would be judged by the program that favored community tenure and at least one behavioral assessment, with cost being one consideration. If community tenure did not differ between groups, the group with better outcome on secondary criteria would be judged at least partially successful and cost would again be a consideration.

## RATING TIMES AND MEASUREMENTS

A prospective randomized design was chosen. Since several studies questioned the long-term effects of partial hospitalization, a more rigorous two-year study was selected to address this issue. Ratings on the criterion measures were taken prior to random assignment and at 6, 12, 18, and 24 months. In addition, whenever a patient was readmitted to the hospital, criterion ratings were taken at the time of readmission. Patients were not terminated from the study at the time of rehospitalization. Relapse was defined as readmission, confirmed by clinical ratings on psychopathologic study. Whenever readmitted patients were discharged, they were returned immediately to the condition to which they had been randomly assigned.

Data were collected from several dimensions. Sources were professional raters (not involved in the operation of the DTC or outpatient care), patient self-reports, reports from relatives, and data from medical records. The five areas of outcome were days in the community, social functioning, psychiatric symptoms, attitudes, and costs.

**Community tenure** was measured by the number of days the person spent in the community during the two years. This excluded days in the hospital or days in jail. Days of rehospitalization during each six-month period or during the two years were also assessed, and days until first relapse were calculated for each patient.

**Social functioning** was assessed with the 21-item Social Dysfunction Rating Scale[22] (SDRS) by a project social worker using a semistructured interview guide. The SDRS draws heavily on evaluation of the person's interaction with his personal and social environments. Both the rater's assessment and the person's satisfaction with adjustment are taken into account. The items are rated on six-point degree of severity scales, with a higher score indicating more dysfunction.

Since it was desirable to have someone in the community also assess the patient, the patient was asked to name a relative, or someone who knew him well, who would be willing to answer questions about his adjustment. The Personal Adjustment and Role Skills Scale[23] (PARS III) was mailed to this person one week after the patient left the hospital and at the other follow-up times. This version of the PARS contains 57 items rated on five-point scales and provides factor scores for interpersonal involvement, agitation-depression, confusion, anxiety, alcohol abuse, outside social activities, and employment.

**Symptoms,** or psychiatric maintenance in relationship to symptoms, were measured by the Brief Psychiatric Rating Scale[24] (BPRS). The 16 items were rated on six-point scales by a project psychologist or psychiatrist.

**Attitudes** were assessed by six semantic differentials[25] completed by the patient. Concepts were selected with regard to the kinds of attitudes that DTC tries to shape in positive ways. Attitudes toward hospital, family, work, people, me, and me-as-I-would-like-to-be were measured with ten bipolar adjectives chosen from the evaluative factor. The evaluative factor is purported to measure an attitude dimension. Item ratings on each concept were summed, with a higher score reflecting more negative attitudes for that particular concept.

**Cost** of the two treatments was determined as follows. Each hospital submitted its per diem cost for inpatient psychiatric care and its unit (daily) cost for DTC every six months. For the DTC group, the number of days the patient attended DTC was multiplied by the daily DTC cost for that period of time, and any days in the hospital were multiplied by the appropriate hospital cost at that time. In the ODM group, the cost reflected only the number of days the patient had been rehospitalized.

In addition to these outcomes, demographic and diagnostic variables were collected from the medical records. The DTC staff screened all patients concerning goals, estimates on length of treatment, rehabilitation potential, employability, and attitudes toward the program. For these patients assigned to DTC, they completed initial and follow-up reports on the activities prescribed, degree of participation, and assessment of improvement. The project social worker completed data on work status, income, living arrangements, and drug compliance at each follow-up. The project physician supplied data on drugs by kind, level, and duration as well as estimates of compliance and overall adjustment every six weeks.

Process and structural variables that described DTC were completed initially and every six months for the ten centers during the four years of study. These variables described the staffing hours, patterns, programs, resources, types of patients treated, size of the program, turnover rates, and treatment philosophy.

*Procedures*

Ten hospitals were selected, representing at the time one fourth of all the DTC programs in the VA. The ten were chosen because of geographic location, size, and years of operation (average, eight). Two hospitals were located in California and three in Texas. The others were in Illinois, Florida, Iowa, Minnesota, and Tennessee. Principal investigators were selected in each hospital to supervise the study according to a common research protocol. Hospitals were visited before the study to train the raters so that reliability of data would be increased. Principal investigators met together before the study and every six months thereafter. An operations committee, with two subject matter experts and a biostatistician, was appointed for the purpose of monitoring the progress of the study every six months, and were the only persons to see unblinded results of the study as it was ongoing. A human rights committee also reviewed the progress of the study from their perspective at yearly intervals.

The project proceeded as follows in each hospital. If a patient met the entrance criteria, he was referred to DTC so that DTC staff could determine whether they would take the patient if he were assigned there, and to a project psychiatrist who adjusted medication to a maintenance level prior to the patient's discharge from the hospital. The same physician followed both groups of patients every six weeks. Medication remained the same unless side effects were encountered. All changes were documented. When the patient had cleared DTC and medication criteria, he was given a study number and received all of his baseline ratings. The principal investigator then opened a sealed envelope corresponding to the patient's number, and assignment to a DTC or ODM group was determined. The patient was discharged and treatments were initiated immediately. Each DTC was free to prescribe any DTC program for patients assigned to them. They could also discharge the patient during the two years if they deemed this advisable. Considerable discussion had centered on whether to prescribe a standard regimen for DTC patients in terms of activities and length of treatment, as well as whether to prescribe one type and dose level of medication. Although this would have provided a more tightly controlled study, it would not have been representative of treatment for these chronic patients. Therefore, a more naturalistic approach was taken.

*Sample Characteristics*

The sample was limited to schizophrenic patients receiving maintenance levels of antipsychotic drugs, who were referred for DTC at hospital discharge. Patients who had previously been treated in DTC were excluded, since a pure test of DTC was desired. Other exclusions included female patients (since VA has so few) and patients with a diagnosis of organic brain disease. Diagnosis of schizophrenia in the patients' discharge summary was also confirmed by the project psychiatrist by specified criteria. One hundred sixty-two patients were studied. The follow-up rate for time in the community was 100%, since this could be assessed by VA records as well as by patient contact. Seven patients died and two were dropped from the study at their own request. Follow-up study for purposes of doing the psychosocial ratings was 95% at six months, 85% at one year, 85% at 18 months, and 85% at 24 months. The major reason for loss of data was the patient moving from the area. Those subjects unavailable for follow-up did not differ significantly from their parent group on any of their baseline scores.

Patients were all male, averaged 37 years of age, two thirds were unmarried, and 64% were white. Almost half lived with parent(s). Only a third were less than high school graduates. Consistent with the diagnosis of schizophrenia, baseline scores of the BPRS showed higher ratings on conceptual disorganization, emotional withdrawal, and blunted affect than on other symptoms. Chronicity was reflected by an average of 4.4 prior hospitalizations and 158 days in the hospital during the year preceding referral to DTC. There were no significant differences between the two treatment groups on any background variables or baseline psychosocial data at the time they entered the study. Neither were there any statistically significant interaction between the ten locations and the group assignments.

## Treatment Variables

The most frequently used medications were chlorpromazine hydrochloride, haloperidol, and thioridazine (Mellaril). About 10% of the group had some medication change, either to another drug or an increase in their assigned drug. There were no differences between DTC and ODM patients concerning the estimates of drug compliance. Project social workers and physicians estimated that about a fourth of the patients in each group were noncompliant. The reliability of the physicians' and social workers' independent ratings was between 0.68 and 0.70 at each of the follow-up times. As previously mentioned, both groups were seen by the same project psychiatrist every six weeks for medication follow-up. The medication interviews were brief, and no attempt was made to offer more than limited supportive contact, which was the same for both groups. The ODM group was not treated in any other aftercare programs and remained essentially a drug maintenance group.

The DTC staff interviewed patients prior to random assignment to determine appropriateness of the referral. Those patients judged to be inappropriate for DTC by the centers did not enter the study or the DTC for treatment. Only 8% of the patients were judged inappropriate for DTC, the primary reasons being transportation problems or lack of interest. The DTC staff estimated that about a fourth of the patients had poor or very poor rehabilitation potential. They saw no potential for future employment for 30% of the group. About one fourth were classified as having "considerable" motivation as opposed to none (15%) or limited motivation (60%). No differences were found between those patients subsequently assigned to the DTC and those assigned to ODM on any of these variables.

The DTC group attended the centers an average of 60 to 70 days during each six-month period. Attendance was in line with the 80 to 85 days every six months that had been estimated by DTC staff as being needed. For 88%, a full day, rather than half day, of attendance was prescribed for each visit. The most frequently prescribed treatment were social-recreational (71%), group therapy (64%), individual counseling (48%), occupational therapy (32%), and work counseling and training (20%). About 10% of the sample had low attendance rates of less than three days a month. Data were reanalyzed, dropping the low attenders in both groups, and as expected, differences between the DTC and ODM groups were more pronounced when only the successes (attenders) were included. However, findings were essentially the same with no new main effect differences identified between groups. The results presented herein include all subjects randomly assigned to either group.

## Data Analyses

Data were analyzed in two ways. One series of analyses examined changes over time between the DTC and ODM groups for each of the nine outcomes separately by curve-fitting with orthogonal polynomials.[26] The other series of analyses examined the eight psychosocial adjustment variables together in a multivariate analysis of covariance at 6, 12, 18, and 24 months. While the first series of analyses probably represent the best test for change related to any single variable over time between the groups, there are some limitations to doing only that type of analysis. First, only subjects who have all four sets of ratings (84%) will be included. In the second type of analyses, all patients who have data at any follow-up time can be analyzed. For example, 94% of the sample can be included at six months. Second, and more important, the first curve-fitting type of analysis can only test one variable at a time. If a pattern of differences occurred between the groups, such an analysis would not be able to detect this. A multivariate analysis, which examined all of the outcomes together, would be able to determine such a difference if it existed.

Some features were common to both types of analyses. Baseline scores were always entered as covariates to increase the precision of the analyses.[27] In addition, analyses were performed with and without paranoid diagnosis controlled, since some studies suggested that paranoid schizophrenics had a different outcome from other schizophrenic patients.[11,19] Except in a few analyses, which will be explained later, data were always analyzed in a 2 × 10 factorial design with DTC and ODM being one factor and the ten locations another.

In the first series of analyses, the first step fits curves to the original means obtained at 6, 12, 18, and 24 months by orthogonal polynomials that transform the original means into four new means for mean, linear, cubic, and quadratic testing. The analysis tests for both the curve and levels of two groups. A split plot design was used with time zero included. Therefore, covarying out the initial scores, the rate of improvement, and any differences between the groups, were measured by fitting orthogonal polynomials at the four time points.

Alternately, a multivariate analysis of covariance was done at each of the four follow-up times testing all of the psychosocial adjustment variables for both univariate and multivariate differences between groups. In these analyses, the sample size at each follow-up corresponded with the number of subjects who had ratings at that time. As indicated, these analyses were done to see if a pattern (multivariate) difference would be found since the curve-fitting analyses examined one variable at a time.

The largest sample available for any analysis was 162. The number of patients varied for each hospital, and the number of subjects in each cell of the design also varied. However, precision of an experiment is generally indicated by the number of degrees of freedom for the error term in analysis of variance. In turn, degrees of freedom depends on the total sample size available for each analysis (not the number in each cell).[28] In this study, the samples for analysis ranged from 136 to 162, which provided more than sufficient degrees of freedom. Second, it was possible to do exact tests of significance with varying number of subjects per cell of the design.[29] Therefore, in each analysis, an exact test of significance is reported.

In general, the following questions are addressed by the analyses: 1) did DTC subjects differ from ODM subjects over time or at any point in time on any of their outcomes or on all outcomes taken together? 2) Were there differences among the ten locations? 3) Were there interactions between treatment groups and locations on any of the dependent variables? If the answer to the final question was "yes," could these differences be explained by process and structural variables that described the DTC programs?

## RESULTS

### Changes During the Two Years of Follow-up

The first series of analyses examined change over time on most of the outcome measures individually by curvefitting of the slopes of the lines. For time in the community, paranoid diagnosis was held constant. On all of the scale data, the prescores and paranoid diagnosis were covaried. The ten hospitals were treated as a factor in a 2 × 10 design.

TIME IN THE COMMUNITY.   Table 2 shows the average number of days in the community for each group every six months. In terms of total days in the community, the DTC groups spent 89% of the two years in the community and the ODM group spent 85% of the two years out, there being a difference of only an average of 19 days. There were no main effect group or hospital differences, but a statistically significant interaction was found between hospital and group for days in the community at the 5% level. The results among centers did not consistently favor the DTC group. In some centers, DTC patients did significantly better than the ODM group, but in other centers they did not.

OTHER RELAPSE DATA.   There are several other ways of looking at the data related to time in the community. For the most part, the opposite of community tenure was rehospitalization. Three patients in the study spent some days in jail; however, the remaining days, not accounted for by time in the community, were hospital days. The DTC group spent an average of 77.9 days in the hospital and the ODM group 95.9, an average of 18 more days for the ODM group. Although again in the expected direction, the cumulative number of days was not statistically significant between the groups. By the end of two years, patients in each group averaged 1.2 readmissions, and the cumulative relapse rates showed that 58.4% of the DTC and 65.8% of the ODM group had relapsed at least once as evidenced by rehospitalization. Survivorship curves for the two groups are shown in Fig. 1. In Fig 1, relapse is expressed as an exponential

Table 2   Days in the Community by Six-Month Intervals

| Months | Days in community | |
|---|---|---|
| | DTC (N = 80) | ODM (N = 82) |
| 6 | 167 | 162 |
| 12 | 158 | 156 |
| 18 | 160 | 150 |
| 24 | 157 | 155 |
| Total | 642 | 623 |

*DTC, day treatment centers; ODM, outpatient drug management.

function. The Life Table Method not only provides a better estimate of ultimate relapse or survivorship than simple cumulative percentages, but accounts for the speed of relapse during a period of time as well.[30] Patients administratively terminated can be credited for months of exposure by this method. As seen, at one year, 60.4% of the experimental and 53.3% of the control patients were surviving in the community. At 24 months, 44.5% of the DTC group and 33.4% of the controls were surviving. The difference between survivors in the two groups was not statistically significant.

Ratings taken at the time of readmission showed no significant differences between DTC and ODM relapsers in terms of their social functioning, psychopathology, and attitudes. It had been anticipated that if DTC patients were found to have better outcomes, it might be the result of DTC helping patients to take their medication more faithfully, but there seemed to be no differential rates in the estimates of compliance between these groups. Furthermore since relapse ratings did not differ between the two groups, it was unlikely that the DTC staff noticed that patients were slipping and, therefore, sent them back earlier to the hospital, or that DTC staff tended to hold their patients longer until the patients were more disturbed in an effort to abort readmission.

Those who relapsed each six months were compared on baseline symptoms with those who did not in the DTC and ODM groups

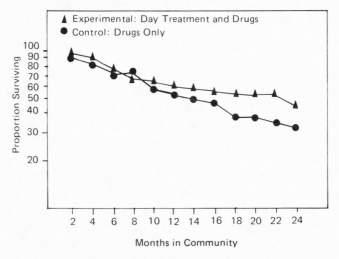

Figure 1   Survivorship Curves for Experimental
and Control Groups.

Table 3    Differential Predictors of Relapse From
Symptoms of DTC and ODM Groups*

| | DTC | | ODM | | |
|---|---|---|---|---|---|
| Symptoms (BPRS)[†] | Relapse | Non-relapse | Relapse | Non-relapse | Interaction F Ratio |
| Predicts relapse by 6 mo | | | | | |
| Emotional withdrawal | 3.18 | 2.48 | 2.63 | 3.02 | 5.10[†] |
| Motor retardation | 2.14 | 1.74 | 2.10 | 2.11 | 6.11[‡] |
| Predicts relapse by 12 mo | | | | | |
| Anxiety | 3.74 | 2.36 | 3.14 | 3.20 | 4.69[†] |

* DTC, day treatment centers; ODM, outpatient drug management. Higher scores are indicative of more symptoms. Interaction $F$ ratio refers to significant interaction between group assignment and relapse.
[†] $P < .05$.
[‡] $P < .01$.

(2 X 2 design) for analysis of variance. Table 3 shows that those who relapsed in the DTC group during the first six months scored higher on emotional withdrawal, whereas ODM relapsers scored lower ($P$ <.05). Second, at the .01 level, motor retardation was significantly associated with relapse in DTC subjects, but degree of motor retardation did not seem to influence relapse for patients receiving drugs alone. The DTC subjects who relapsed in the second six months had higher anxiety scores than DTC nonrelapsers ($P$<.05). No predictors were found for relapse in the second year.

SOCIAL FUNCTIONING.    Social functioning, measured by the project social worker with the SDRS, showed significant change in favor of the DTC patients. Figure 2 demonstrates the mean scores for the two groups during the two years of follow-up. At $P$<.02, with pretreatment scores covaried, the DTC produced significant improvement over ODM on social functioning. There were no interaction effects to suggest that these results were found in only some centers.

Patients had also been assessed by relatives in terms of adjustment as measured by the PARS III. Only 12% of the sample were unable or unwilling to identify a community contact; however, only 75% of those who had been identified returned usable data at the beginning of the study, and a decreasing number responded on each of the subsequent follow-up studies. Since the number of subjects who had all four of their follow-up ratings on the PARS was small (47%), the seven factor scores on the PARS were analyzed together at each of the follow-up times with all the available sample for any one time included. None of the seven factor scores differed significantly, at a multivariate level, between the DTC and ODM groups at any of the four times. In addition, there were no univariate differences on any factor except at 24 months, when the outside social factor favored the DTC group (*P*<.04). However, it should be noted that analyses on the PARS represented only a subset of the sample and that the PARS baseline ratings were not blind to treatment group, since patients had to be out of the hospital for at least one week before they could be assessed.

SYMPTOMS. The symptoms measured by the BPRS, like community tenure, showed that some centers were more effective than others in decreasing their patients' symptoms. There was a significant interaction at the .05 level between group and hospital when the BPRS was examined over time by the slopes of the lines.

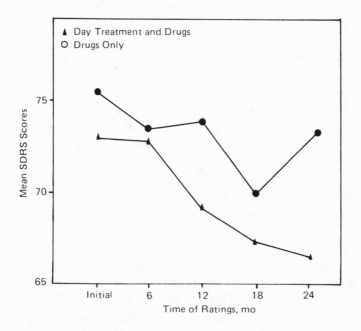

Figure 2   Changes Over Time on Social Dysfunction Rating Scale (SDRS). Higher Scores Mean More Dysfunctional.

ATTITUDES. Each of the six attitudes were compared individually between the two groups. Some attitudes were influenced by the DTC in a uniform way. Significantly more favorable trends were found for attitudes toward hospital ($P<.004$) and people ($P<.001$) for the DTC group. Some, but not all of the centers, also improved the patient's attitude toward work (interaction effect significant at $P <.04$). None of the centers significantly changed the attitudes that the patient had toward himself (me) or me-as-I-would-like-to-be or toward family and differently from that of the ODM group.

COST. There were no statistically significant differences between groups in terms of cost. It had been anticipated that cost for the DTC group would be more, even if the ODM group had more rehospitalization cost. Cost depended not only on each individual hospital's cost and DTC cost, but also on the DTC effectiveness in keeping patients in the community. The trend was toward higher cost for the DTC. The overall average cost for the two years for DTC patients was $5,895, which included an average DTC cost of $2,708 and a rehospitalization cost of $3,177. The readmission cost for the ODM patient averaged $4,437 for the two years.

## Multivariate Differences at Each Follow-up Time

For all the variables just described (except the PARS and Cost), differences between the groups had been tested individually for each outcome by curve-fitting of the lines. Another way of examining these data related to whether all of the variables together produced significant differences at any one point in time. Data were analyzed by multivariate analysis of covariance for all the psychosocial (scale) data together.

Table 4 shows means and significance levels for the four times of follow-up. The multivariate differences were $P<.12$ at six months, $P<.10$ at 12, $P<.08$ at 18, and $P<.004$ at 24 months in favor of the DTC group, using scores on SDRS, BPRS, and six semantic differentials. Although the differences are not statistically significant until 24 months, it would be added that they might be considered almost borderline statistically. At 24 months, the eight variables discriminated between DTC and ODM groups at $P<.004$ in favor of DTC. Covarying for paranoid diagnosis changed the significance levels more toward statistical significance at all points in time. For example, at 24 months, the significance level changed from $P<.02$ to $P$

## Table 4 Adjusted Means of Psychosocial Variables at Each Follow-up Time: Initial Scores and Paranoid Covaried for Main Effect of Groups in a 2 × 10 Analysis*

| Variables | 6 Months | | | 12 Months | | | 18 Months | | | 24 Months | | |
|---|---|---|---|---|---|---|---|---|---|---|---|---|
| | DTC | ODM | F | DTC | ODM | F | DTC | ODM | F | DTC | ODM | F |
| SDRS | 72.5 | 72.8 | 0.05 | 68.5 | 74.2 | 1.75 | 67.9 | 69.1 | 0.99 | 65.8 | 69.6 | 2.69 |
| BPRS | 37.4 | 38.1 | 0.11 | 36.0 | 36.6 | 2.37 | 35.4 | 36.3 | 0.17 | 31.3 | 38.4 | 8.08† |
| Semantic differentials | | | | | | | | | | | | |
| Hospital | 26.0 | 24.8 | 0.89 | 27.8 | 24.1 | 3.30 | 23.8 | 26.9 | 2.17 | 23.5 | 29.1 | 6.73† |
| People | 29.6 | 27.9 | 0.66 | 29.5 | 30.3 | 0.59 | 26.5 | 25.5 | 0.84 | 25.7 | 29.9 | 2.59 |
| Family | 23.1 | 27.0 | 3.00 | 26.1 | 26.4 | 0.08 | 22.1 | 21.9 | 0.20 | 24.3 | 26.2 | 0.77 |
| Work | 28.1 | 26.2 | 1.31 | 27.8 | 28.1 | 0.06 | 25.4 | 28.5 | 2.02 | 26.0 | 29.2 | 2.15 |
| Me | 27.5 | 30.8 | 2.52 | 28.1 | 29.4 | 0.01 | 29.7 | 29.2 | 0.16 | 28.3 | 28.2 | 0.01 |
| Me-as-I-would-like | 15.3 | 16.1 | 0.09 | 16.1 | 15.6 | 0.92 | 15.9 | 15.8 | 0.46 | 16.6 | 16.9 | 0.79 |
| Multivariate difference | $P < .12$ | | | $P < .10$ | | | $P < .08$ | | | $P < .004$ | | |

*DTC, day treatment center; ODM, outpatient drug management; SDRS, Social Dysfunction Rating Scale; BPRS, Brief Psychiatric Rating Scale. Higher scores represent more unfavorable ratings.
†$P < .01$ by univariate $F$ ratio.

273

<.004 when paranoid scores were held constant. At 24 months, there was no statistically significant hospital by group interaction ($P<.10$), although there was a .01 level of interaction for the BPRS score alone. Multivariate interaction effects for the multivariate tests were not significant at other points.

At 24 months, individual scores were usually in the expected direction, with the DTC group significantly different from the ODM group on BPRS ratings and attitudes toward hospital. The specific areas of significant improvement for DTC compared with ODM on the BPRS were conceptual disorganization, hostility, hallucinatory behavior, uncooperativeness, and unusual thought content. It is probable that the other six variables interacted with these two statistically significant ones in producing the multivariate difference. It should be emphasized that the variables analyzed together for the multivariate analysis of covariance represented only the psychosocial dimension and did not include time out of the hospital. It seemed more logical to examine days in the community separately, since the psychosocial variables probably influenced or overlapped with time out of the hospital.

## Identifying Centers with Good and Poor Results

Since the data on several of the variables analyzed over time indicated differential results related to the ten hospitals, graphs were plotted for each hospital separately, showing their mean ratings for DTC and ODM groups. The three major variables—community tenure, social functioning, and symptoms—were examined to find where outcomes on the three graphs had been in a less favorable direction for the DTC subjects or where it seemed that no differences occurred between DTC and ODM. Four centers were identified where at least two—and in one case all three—of the outcomes were either essentially the same between groups or less favorable for DTC patients. As indicated, the purpose in plotting results by hospital was to try to determine why significant interactions on some of the outcomes had occurred. It seemed to provide an opportunity to regroup the data by those hospitals where good outcomes had occurred for DTC and those where either there seemed to be no differences between their groups or where DTC subjects had actually done worse than ODM patients. It is recognized that such post hoc grouping has its limitations and that there is no ideal way to test statistically for differences; therefore, these data should be considered trends. In the data that follow, the six hospitals that seemed to have good results on the primary outcomes for DTC were grouped together, and those four where results did not seem to favor DTC were pooled. For the two variables in which interactions over time had been found (time in the community and BPRS), two graphs were done to show these variables by the hospitals with good and poor results. One thought, of course, was whether patients in these two groupings differed significantly on their baseline data and personal characteristics. No differences occurred when patients were analyzed in a 2 X 2 factorial design for analysis of variance (ODM and DTC being one factor and the good and poor result centers the others). Although not statistically significant, the hospitals with poor results tended to have control patients who were slightly worse at baseline. The fact that patients were similar in the good and poor result centers suggested that differences in outcomes between DTC and ODM groups in the two types of centers were not related to their having had different types of patients initially.

Figure 3 shows the relapse rates of patients in the six hospitals where results seemed superior and the relapse rates in the four hospitals where results were less favorable for DTC patients. As seen, the ODM groups have about the same relapse rates regardless of good or poor result hospitals.

However the DTC group, in the good result centers had about a 50% relapse rate by the end of two years and the poor result centers had about a 69% relapse rate.

The BPRS was another major variable that showed a significant hospital interaction effect by group. Figure 4 shows results on the BPRS plotted by the good and poor result centers. Inspection of the lines in Figure 4 shows that in good result centers, DTC patients improved by six months to about their optimal level. They show an increase in symptoms at about 18 months, but return to earlier levels by 24 months. In poor centers, they steadily decrease from what was a higher level of symptoms initially to about the same level as that of the good centers. The ODM patients in poor result groups change in about the same way during the first 18 months as their DTC groups, but at 24 months are more symptomatic. In good result groups, ODM patients increase in symptoms over time. This raises the question of whether it might be the ODM group that produced a significant interaction rather than the difference in DTC outcomes. In testing for baseline differences between good and poor result groups, it will be recalled that the BPRS was almost significantly

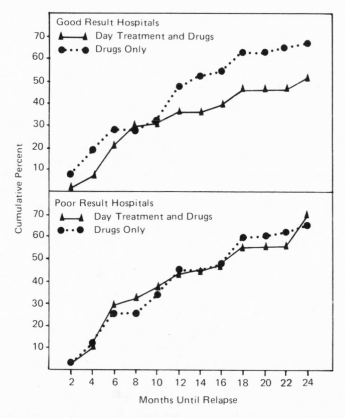

Figure 3   Cumulative Relapse Rates for Each Treatment Group.

different. In the analyses over time, the baseline differences were held constant. Thus, if initial means on the graphs were adjusted, the ODM groups would appear more similar. It is still possible, however, that it is the ODM groups that were really different in terms of symptoms. The thrust of the data for relapse rates, social dysfunction, and attitudes favors DTC. The outcome criteria related to the BPRS was maintenance of psychiatric condition, could DTC hold patients at their hospital discharge level? This seemed to be a relevant question for chronic schizophrenics. What we had anticipated was that DTC would help maintain patients and that ODM only groups would tend to become more symptomatic over time. The results suggest that this occurred, but more so in good result groups. Classification of types and amounts of drugs were similar for good and poor result groups. Compliance estimates did not differ significantly between the two. One explanation might be that good result DTC

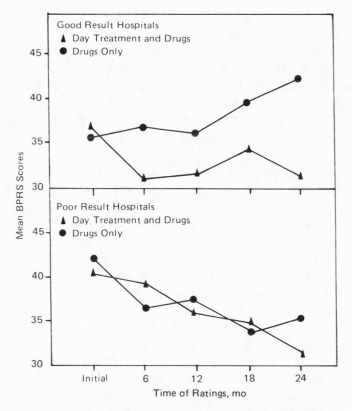

Figure 4   Changes Over Time on Brief Psychiatric Rating Scale
(BPRS). Higher Scores Mean More Symptoms.

centers also represented good result hospitals as well. They tended
to discharge their patients at better levels in terms of symptoms.
Their DTC programs were able to hold and even improve these levels
to a certain degree, but the lack of DTC for ODM patients resulted
in a trend toward more psychopathologic features for these patients.

## Identifying Center Variables Associated with Good Outcomes

Each DTC had nine separate ratings that described their
staffing, programs, and practices at six-month intervals. Staffing
hours were adjusted to a ratio depending on average daily attendance
in the DTC. In this way, variables that described the centers during
the four years could be compared between the six good result centers
and the four poor result centers. Certain variables were found to

differ significantly between the two groups of centers. Center variables are shown in Table 5.

The first four variables describe the flow of all patients in and out of centers. These numbers were adjusted to a ratio of the number of patients attending the center, so that higher numbers indicate more activity in terms of patient turnover. Poorer outcome centers had significantly more admissions, more discharges from their programs, more patients readmitted to the DTC, and more readmissions back to the hospital.

Staffing hours were also adjusted to the number of patients attending the centers, with higher numbers indicating more hours. Poor result centers had more psychologist hours and more social worker hours than good result centers. Good result centers had significantly more recreational therapy hours and more part-time staff hours. Total staffing hours and total number of staff per patient did not differ between the two types of centers.

In terms of patient mix, those centers who treated schizophrenics more often did better than those who did not. Poor result centers more often treated female patients (although the numbers are small in both groups) and patients who averaged about three years younger than the good result centers. Whether the centers treated alcoholics or patients with chronic brain disease did not matter in terms of their effectiveness with study patients.

Size of the center (either by patients on the rolls or average attendance), years of operation, and physical location in regard to the hospital, were not significantly different. Having private offices for staff did not differ, but more interviewing rooms were associated with poor result centers. Having a method to evaluate the patient's progress and assigning the patient to one person in the center for follow-up related significantly to the good result centers.

Poor result centers more often used group psychotherapy and more family counseling at a highly significant level statistically. Good result centers used more occupational therapy ($P<.05$). Other methods of treatment were similar.

Probably related to more professional hours, the poor result centers had significantly higher costs for the patients in the study than did the good result centers. This was found in spite of the fact that days of treatment in DTC did not differ between good and poor result centers. The average cost of care in the poor result centers was $7,170 per patient as compared with an average cost of $4,662 for the good result centers.

## Table 5 Characteristics of Good and Poor Outcome DTCs*

| | DTC | | |
| Variables | Good outcome | Poor outcome | F ratio |
|---|---|---|---|
| **Patient flow†** | | | |
| Admissions last 6 mo | 0.24 | 0.42 | 16.03‖ |
| Readmission last 6 mo | 0.15 | 0.29 | 9.01¶ |
| Discharge last 6 mo | 0.24 | 0.67 | 55.32‖ |
| Admitted hospital last 6 mo | 0.16 | 0.28 | 5.99# |
| **Staffing†** | | | |
| Psychiatrist hr/wk | 0.25 | 0.23 | 0.06 |
| Psychologist hr/wk | 0.19 | 0.71 | 42.08‖ |
| Social work hr/wk | 0.58 | 0.83 | 9.42¶ |
| RN hr/wk | 0.67 | 0.61 | 0.14 |
| Aide hr/wk | 0.59 | 1.01 | 2.52 |
| Recreational therapy hr/wk | 0.43 | 0.02 | 15.78‖ |
| Secretary hr/wk | 0.62 | 0.50 | 1.52 |
| Other volunteer/trainee hr/wk | 1.49 | 0.73 | 3.10 |
| Total hr/wk | 4.92 | 4.74 | 0.19 |
| No. of full-time staff | 0.10 | 0.10 | 0.02 |
| No. of part-time staff | 0.08 | 0.05 | 6.03# |
| No. of total staff | 0.18 | 0.15 | 3.26 |
| **Patient mix** | | | |
| Schizophrenic‡ | 0.85 | 0.69 | 5.42# |
| Alcoholics‡ | 0.05 | 0.07 | 1.94 |
| Chronic brain syndrome‡ | 0.08 | 0.06 | 0.48 |
| Average age treated | 46.67 | 43.15 | 17.07‖ |
| Female‡ | 0.02 | 0.06 | 13.80‖ |
| **The centers** | | | |
| Patients on rolls | 82.44 | 72.42 | 1.97 |
| Patients attending | 50.98 | 44.88 | 3.06 |
| Years of operation | 8.59 | 10.03 | 0.61 |
| Located within hospital‡ | 0.72 | 0.72 | 0.01 |
| Private offices for staff‡ | 0.64 | 0.72 | 0.57 |
| Interviewing rooms (mean) | 2.72 | 4.67 | 28.48‖ |
| Specific plan for evaluation‡ | 0.98 | 0.87 | 4.39# |
| One person assigned to patient‡ | 0.72 | 0.42 | 8.18¶ |
| **Programs used §** | | | |
| Individual psychotherapy | 1.56 | 1.55 | 0.01 |
| Group psychotherapy | 1.79 | 3.00 | 30.81‖ |
| Other type groups | 2.54 | 2.70 | 0.01 |
| Medication | 2.79 | 3.00 | 2.43 |
| Recreational therapy | 2.67 | 2.76 | 0.24 |
| Occupational therapy | 2.28 | 1.85 | 3.83# |
| Educational counseling | 1.88 | 1.85 | 0.03 |
| Special work training groups | 2.05 | 2.27 | 1.73 |
| Family counseling | 1.19 | 2.00 | 24.51‖ |

* DTC, day treatment center.
† Actual number divided by number of patients attending.
‡ Can be read as percent by disregarding decimal.
§ Degree to which programs were used, scaled 1 to 4, with 1, no patients, and 4 for most.
‖ $P < .001$.
¶ $P < .01$.
# $P < .05$.

An overview of the findings related to good and poor result centers suggests that high patient turnover and brief but more intensive treatment, particularly in terms of psychotherapeutic counseling by professionals, may lead to relapse for some schizophrenic patients.

## Treatments Received by Patients in the Study

In order to determine more accurately whether study patients had actually been treated similarly to other patients in the centers, patients in the study were compared between good and poor result centers in terms of their involvement in certain activities. Patients in the good result centers participated more in occupational therapy ($P<.05$). Patients in poor result centers participated significantly more in group psychotherapy ($P<.05$).

### COMMENT

The finding regarding the primary outcome variable of community tenure demonstrated that some centers were effective in forestalling relapse, while others were not. Furthermore, these same centers produced differential results in terms of symptom reduction. All centers were moderately effective in improving social function and attitudes about the hospital and people. Some centers improved attitudes toward work. None of the centers significantly changed attitudes toward me, me-as-I-would-like-to-be, or family any differently than did drugs. Reflecting on the hierarchy of variables set up for judging outcome, six of the centers could be considered successful in primary and secondary criteria as well as in cost. Four centers could be perceived as partially successful in that they influenced only levels of social functioning and some of the attitudes. If cost is also considered in these four centers, DTC costs were significantly more than costs for the ODM group.

It might be helpful to focus on the issue of effect size. The differences on social dysfunction were large enough to reflect clinical significance of change. Cost, however, might be a more dramatic effect. Extrapolating from our study of one fourth of the day treatment centers in the VA system, if all 40 operated as our "good" result centers, the cost for 2,000 patients (the average treated) per year would be about $4,662,000, as opposed to $7,170,000 if they were staffed as out "poor" result centers—a difference of two and one half million. Since six of ten centers studied were these lower cost centers, it might be assumed that the same proportion, 24 of the 40, also operated in this way. Therefore, if only the 16 other centers were reorganized, not only might outcomes for their schizophrenic patients be better but there would also be a saving of $1,846,000.

It must be stressed that classification of good and poor result centers was based on the center's success with our study patients. Poor result centers might be quite effective in working with neurotics, patients with affective disorders, or even with schizophrenics in the acute phase of their illness. The patients studied here were chronic schizophrenics, who may need a markedly different approach in treatment. We can only conclude that the DTC programs were not consistently effective in working with chronic schizophrenics.

In comparing results of our study with those of others, it must be re-emphasized that this was a study of alternative methods of aftercare and not a follow-up of patients assigned to day or inpatient settings. The study was carried out with strict control of day treatment plus drugs or drugs alone while the patients were living in the community. It is recognized, however, that patients from both groups were rehospitalized and that there were confounding effects of hospital stay, even though length of such rehospitalizations was brief. It should also be emphasized that ratings of adjustment and attitudes were essentially the same in terms of differences between the DTC and ODM groups when the relapsers from each group were removed and data reanalyzed.

The relapse rate of slightly more than 40% at 12 months in this study is in line with those of other studies for patients receiving neuroleptics.[6,30-34] Our relapse rate of nearly 70% for the drug-managed patients of 24 months begins to look more like those of placebo groups. However, it should be stressed that our sample included only male patients, who have notoriously higher relapse rates than female patients. Only about half of the chronic schizophrenics cared for in the good result centers relapsed by two years. This would indicate that day treatment, as practiced in these settings, could forestall relapse significantly for male chronic schizophrenics.

Our data also indicate that effects of day treatment are most pronounced at 24 months. This is contrary to the two-year follow-up data reported in other studies[14,15], however, it is often unclear in these studies whether follow-up began with discharge from day treatment or if it included at least some treatment days in the day center. If it was the former, it makes sense that long-term effects of hospital vs day treatment tend to wash out after two years. The initial results between drug and drug plus day treatment in this study were not as impressive at one year as they were at two. This delayed effect of DTC is similar to the delayed effect of major role therapy (MRT) with drugs seen in the two-year posthospital adjustment of schizophrenic patients reported by Hogarty et al.[7] Furthermore, relapse curves in our study also tend to approximate those described by Hogarty et al[7] in that a crossover of effects occurs at about six to eight months with DTC, and, in their findings, with MRT, relapse being somewhat higher initially. It might also be pointed out that both DTC and the drug only groups relapsed according to an exponential function. A similar observation has been made by Hogarty et al[7] and by Davis et al[35] who observed that both drug and placebo patients relapse according to an exponential function.

To simply conclude that some centers produced good results and others did not would leave many questions unanswered. Although not part of the original design, it seemed that characteristics of the good and poor result centers could be identified. Theoretically, in order to reach firm conclusions, patients would have to be randomly assigned to centers high or low on certain treatment characteristics or at least treatments randomly assigned within the centers. There are, however, some suggestions from these data that allow one to build a circumstantial case in explaining the findings.

Centers that were successful with chronic schizophrenics provided more occupational therapy, recreational activities, and in general treated their patients longer. Centers with poor results for chronic schizophrenics had more professional counseling staff and counseled more of their patients. They also had a higher patient turnover. Lamb[36] wrote regarding day treatment centers that:

> There is a tendency on the part of many mental health professionals to downgrade the importance of occupational and recreational therapies, and to see individual and group psychotherapy as the cornerstones of treatment. We feel that the activity program plays as important a role as any of the other treatment modalities, and in many ways sets the tone and establishes a therapeutic atmosphere in the day hospital.

Some of his other comments are pertinent concerning what might have happened in the poor result centers:

Another problem that frequently arises with individual therapy is the establishment of too close a relationship between the therapist and the patient which cannot be continued as an ongoing aftercare relationship.

For schizophrenic patients in particular, certain environments actually may be toxic. Our data showed that patients with symptoms of motor retardation, emotional withdrawal, and anxiety were a high-risk group for day treatment. These predictors of bad outcome in DTC—especially in the first six to 12 months—are in line with what Goldberg et al[37] have identified as critical residual symptoms. Goldberg et al[37] described predictors of poor outcome to MRT as: anxious intropunitiveness, motor retardation, anxious depression, disorganized hyperactivity (which include symptoms characteristic of withdrawal), and low insight. Findings from our own study tend to support differential effects of common environments on patients who differ in their vulnerability.

Ideally, one ought to be able to define characteristics of the psychological environment of the chronic schizophrenic that would protect against disorganization. One might begin with the work of such investigators as Shakow,[38] Silverman,[39] Mirsky and Kornetsky,[40] Venables and Wing,[11] and McGhie and Chapman.[12] From their work, an "interference" hypothesis has developed. It is suggested that process schizophrenics, who have nuclear, core, or poor premorbid histories, suffer from an inability to distinguish and filter out vast amounts of irrelevant stimuli. Too much stimulation results in a high level of arousal, which the patient attempts to reduce by restricting his cognitive field to a size that he can manage. Venables and Wing[11] found hyperarousal related to withdrawal in chronic schizophrenics. Brown et al[43] suggested that when the patient is unable to withdraw, latent thought disorders manifest themselves in delusions or odd behavior. They also cautioned that too enthusiastic attempts at reactivating long-term patients have been shown to lead to sudden relapse of symptoms.

Along these same lines, May et al[42] pointed out that milieu therapy can have toxic, antitherapeutic effects, particularly when techniques and methods developed for neurotics and character disorders are indiscriminately applied to psychotic patients. He wrote, "High stimulus input and role diffusion may be toxic for patients who have defects in perception, attention, and information processing or who are disorganized and hyperaroused." In his review and critique of studies that combined drugs and sociotherapies in aftercare, May et al[42] concluded that helping schizophrenics with limited social and vocational goals appeared to be of value. He found no support for combining drug therapy with insight and deeper psychological understanding. In terms of our findings, it is possible that the less intensively personal and more object focused activity of occupational therapy produced better outcomes than the intensive interpersonal stimulation often encountered in group therapy.

Further research needs to be directed at identifying characteristics of patients for whom either specific types of day treatment are toxic or for whom prolonged drug therapy is contraindicated. Results of this study suggest that certain types of day centers are effective for chronic schizophrenics and others are not. In regard to the large number of chronic schizophrenics discharged from mental hospitals, there is evidence that day treatment that is of a supportive and perhaps long-term nature can help to prevent relapse, enhance functioning, and decrease symptoms. Day centers need to be aware of the danger of high-turnover intensive treatment for some schizophrenics. Finding the environmental equilibrium between too much stimulation, which produces relapse, and too little stimulation, which fosters apathy, is a critical issue. What we are suggesting is a less costly method of care which, for once, is not synonymous with a lower quality of care. Day treatment in this context is seen as offering a sustained nonthreatening social support in the community care of chronic schizophrenia.

Participants in the Veterans Administration Cooperative Study included the following:

Study Chairpersons: Margaret W. Linn, PhD, Miami: and Eugene M. Caffey, MD, Washington, DC.

Veterans Administration Hospital Investigators: Haig Agigian, MSW, Palo Alto, Calif; Joan Carmichael, MSW, Miami; Ken Cox, PhD, Memphis; Musetta Gordon, PhD, Des Moines; George Faibish, PhD, Houston; A. J. Jernigan, PhD, Dallas; Robert Kooker, MD, Chicago; Frank Parodi; MD, Sepulveda, Calif; James Scarborough, MD, Waco, Tex; and Ron Williams, PhD, St Cloud, Minn.

Members of the Executive Committee: Eugene M. Caffey, MD, Washington, DC; Dean J. Clyde, PhD, Rockville, Md; Musetta Gordon, PhD, Des Moines; Gerard Hogarty, MSW, Pittsburgh; C. James Klett, PhD, Perry Point, Md; H. Richard Lamb, MD, Los Angeles; Margaret W. Linn, PhD, Miami; and James Scarborough, MD.

Members of the Operations Committee: Solomon Goldberg, PhD, Rockville, Md; Herzl Spiro, MD, Milwaukee; and Elliot Cramer, PhD, Chapel Hill, NC.

Members of the Human Use Committee: James A. Crothers, Rising

Sun, Md; Rev Maurice Moore, Aberdeen, Md; and William B. Calvert, Perryville, Md.
Statistical Analysis of the Data: Dean J. Clyde, PhD, Rockville, Md.
Veterans Administration Central Office: James A. Hagans, MD, PhD, Chief, Cooperative Studies Program.

## REFERENCES

1. *American Psychiatric Association Report and Recommendations to the President's Commissions on Mental Health.* Washington, DC, American Psychiatric Association, 1978.

2. Hogarty GE: Discrepancies in relapse rates among drug maintained schizophrenic outpatients: A methodological issue. Read before the Conference on the Role of Depot Neuroleptics in the Treatment of Schizophrenic Patients, Lucca, Italy, Oct 3, 1977.

3. May PRA: *Treatment of Schizophrenia: A Comparative Study of Five Treatment Methods.* New York, Science House, 1968.

4. Hogarty GE, Goldberg S, Schooler N: Drug and sociotherapy in the aftercare of schizophrenic patients: III. Adjustment of non-relapsed patients. *Arch Gen Psychiatry* 31:609–618, 1974.

5. Grinspoon L, Ewalt JR, Shader RI: *Schizophrenia, Pharmacotherapy and Psychotherapy.* Baltimore, William & Wilkins Co, 1972.

6. Hogarty, GE, Goldberg SC: Drug and sociotherapy in the aftercare of schizophrenic patients: One-year relapse rates. *Arch Gen Psychiatry* 28:54–64, 1973.

7. Hogarty GE, Goldberg SC, Schooler NR: Drug and sociotherapy in the aftercare of schizophrenic patients: II. Two-year relapse rates. *Arch Gen Psychiatry* 31:603–608, 1974.

8. Leff JP, Wing JK: Trial of maintenance therapy in schizophrenia. *Br Med J* 3:559–604, 1971.

9. May PRA: When, what, and why? Psychopharmacotherapy and other treatments in schizophrenia. *Compr Psychiatry* 17:683–693, 1976.

10. Meltzoff J, Blumenthal RL: *The Day Treatment Center: Principals, Application and Evaluation.* Springfield, Ill, Charles C Thomas Publisher, 1966.

11. Guy W, Gross M, Hogarty GE, et al: A controlled evaluation of day hospital effectiveness. *Arch Gen Psychiatry* 20:329–338, 1969.

12. May PRA, Tuma AH, Dixon WJ: Schizophrenia—a follow-up study of results of treatment: I. Design and other problems. *Arch Gen Psychiatry* 33:474–478, 1976.

13. Washburn S, Vannicelli M, Longabaugh R. et al: A controlled comparison of psychiatric day treatment and inpatient hospitalization. *J Consult Clin Psychol* 44:665–675, 1976.

14. Herz MI, Endicott J, Spitzer RL: Day vs inpatient hospitalization: A controlled study. *Am J Psychiatry* 127:1371–1381, 1971.

15. Kris E: Prevention of rehospitalization through relapse control in a day hospital, in Greenblatt M (ed): *Mental Patients in Transition*. Springfield, Ill, Charles C Thomas Publisher, 1961.

16. Wilder JF, Levin G. Zwerling I: A two-year follow-up evaluation of acute psychotic patients treated in a day hospital. *Am J Psychiatry* 122:1095–1101, 1966.

17. Sappington AA, Michaux MH: Prognostic patterns in self-report, relative report, and professional evaluation measures for hospitalized and day care patients. *J Consult Clin Psychol* 43:904–910, 1975.

18. Ettlinger RA, Beigl A, Feder SL: The partial hospital as a transition from inpatient treatment: A controlled follow-up study. *Mt. Sinai J Med NY* 39:251–257, 1972.

19. Zwerling I, Wilder JF: An evaluation of the applicability of the day hospital in treatment of acutely disturbed patients. *Isr Ann Psychiatry* 2:162–185, 1964.

20. Michaux MH, Chelst MR, Foster SA, et al: Postrelease adjustment of day and full-time psychiatric patients. *Arch Gen Psychiatry* 29:647–651, 1973.

21. Lorei T: *Definition of Day Treatment Center Goals by Staff Consensus: A First Step in Treatment Evaluation*. Department of Medicine and Surgery, Veterans Administration, Washington, DC, 1975.

22. Linn MW, Sculthorpe WB, Evje M, et al: A social dysfunction rating scale. *J Psychiatr Res* 6:299–306, 1969.

23. Ellsworth RB, Foster L, Childers B, et al: Hospital and community adjustment as perceived by psychiatric patients, their families, and staff. *J Consult Clin Psychol* (monograph) 32:5, 1968.

24. Overall, J, Gorham D: The brief psychiatric rating scale. *Psychol Rep 10:799–812, 1962.*

25. Osgood CE, Suci GJ, Tannenbaum PH: *The Measurement of Meaning*. Urbana, Ill, University of Illinois Press, 1957.

26. Morrison DF: *Multivariate Statistical Methods*, ed 2. New York, McGraw-Hill Book Co Inc, 1976, pp 216–222.

27. Bancroft TA: *Topics in Intermediate Statistical Methods*. Ames, Iowa, Iowa State University Press, 1968.

28. Cochran WG, Cox GM: *Experimental Designs*, ed 2. New York, John Wiley & Sons, 1957.

29. Clyde DJ: *Multivariate Analysis of Variance on Large Computers*. Miami, Clyde Computing Service, 1969.

30. Hogarty GE, Ulrich RF: Temporal effects of drug and placebo in delaying relapse in schizophrenic outpatients. *Arch Gen Psychiatry* 34:297–301, 1977.

31. Hirsch SR, Gaind R, Rohde PD, et al: Outpatient maintenance of chronic schizophrenic patients with long acting fluphenazine: Double-blind placebo trial. *Br Med J* 1:633–637, 1973.

32. Chien C: Drugs and rehabilitation in schizophrenia, in Greenblatt M (ed): *Drugs in Combination With Other Therapies.* New York, Grune & Stratton Inc, 1975.

33. Troshinsky CH, Aaronson HG, Stone RK: Maintenance phenothiazines in aftercare of schizophrenic patients. *Pa Psychiatr Q* 2:11–15, 1962.

34. Del Giudice J, Clark WG, Gocha EF: Prevention of recedivism of schizophrenics treated with fluphenazine enanthate. *Psychosomatics* 16:32–36, 1975.

35. Davis JM, Gosenfeld L, Tsai CC: Maintenance antipsychotic drugs do prevent relapses: A reply to Tobias and McDonald. *Psychol Bull* 83:431–447, 1976.

36. Lamb HR: Chronic psychiatric patients in the day hospital. *Arch Gen Psychiatry* 17:615–621, 1967.

37. Goldberg SC, Schooler NR, Hogarty GE, et al: Prediction of relapse in schizophrenic outpatients treated by drug and sociotherapy. *Arch Gen Psychiatry* 34:171–184, 1977.

38. Shakow D: Psychological deficit in schizophrenia. *Behav Sci* 8:275–305, 1963.

39. Silverman J: The problem of attention in research and theory in schizophrenia. *Psychol Rep* 71:352–379, 1964.

40. Mirsky AF, Kornetsky C: On the dissimilar effects of drugs on the digit symbol substitution and continuous performance tests. *Psychopharmacologia* 5:161–177, 1964.

41. Venables PH, Wing JF: Level of arousal and the subclassification of schizophrenia. *Arch Gen Psychiatry* 7:114–119, 1962.

42. McGhie A, Chapman J: Disorders of attention and perception in early schizophrenia. *Br J Med Psychol* 34:103–117, 1961.

43. Brown GW, Birley JLT, Wing JK: Influence of family life on the course of schizophrenic disorders: A replication. *Br J Psychiatry* 121:241–258, 1972.

*Chapter 20*

# DISCUSSION OF THE SELECTED STUDIES

# Henry Wechsler

Three studies have been included in this section to represent different types of evaluations of human service programs. These studies range in complexity from evaluations of programs without the use of control groups to evaluations that use random assignment of persons to control and experimental groups.

### REINHERZ, HEYWOOD, & CAMP: SHARED PERSPECTIVES—A COMMUNITY COUNSELING CENTER FOR ADOLESCENTS

Reinherz and her colleagues examine in detail the effect that participation in a community-based counseling center may have on "troubled" adolescents. An innovative aspect of their study was to evaluate the center on the basis of multiple goals. One major goal was set by supporters of the center: reduction of drug use. Center staff, on the other hand, envisaged a broader set of goals to help the troubled adolescent. The young people going through the program viewed it as "helping them to get their heads together." The program provided a variety of specific treatments, including traditional psychotherapy, group activities, and the establishment of a therapeutic community.

The study was descriptive in nature involving no control group against which the progress of adolescents going through the center could be compared. All adolescents entering the center program during a six-month period were asked to take part in the evaluation. Most of them (81%) could be followed up one year later. A wide variety of measures could be employed to study changes in the client population. Measures were made of drug use, constructive use of time, arrests, self-concept, and client's own evaluation of progress.

Although the findings indicated considerable improvement on the part of the teenagers, Reinherz, Heywood, and Camp were aware that their descriptive study could not directly attribute such improvement to the treatment at the counseling center because of the lack of a control group. It may be that such changes could be due to maturation—the teenager's "growing out" of the drug problem. The changes could also reflect the general waning of the social disrest in the community. Finally, it could be due to the attention the program paid to the teenagers. Without the use of a control group in the study, change that occurred could be attributed to any of these reasons, rather than to the intervention program of the center.

Because of the complex nature of the treatment program used at the center, even the use of an experimental design and control group would not permit attribution of change to any specific part of the program. Reinherz, Heywood, and Camp view this study as one that does not provide a final evaluation of this type of program, but rather as one which raises hypotheses for further testing.

### LAWRENCE AND WALTER: TESTING A BEHAVIORAL APPROACH WITH GROUPS

Lawrence and Walter utilize an experimental design to evaluate a group program of behavior modification that includes training in social effectiveness and in dealing with social problems. Lawrence and Walter devised this study following an earlier descriptive study in which the majority of group members reported improvement in social effectiveness. Unlike the earlier study, however, this evaluation used random assignment of persons to control and experimental groups. Since persons included in this study were agency clients who reported persistent interpersonal problems or feelings of personal discomfort or social inadequacy, a control group was justified only by placing persons on a waiting list and providing them with the group program after the experimental group had completed the eight-week program. This method is often the one that can be ethically employed in ongoing agencies. Under it, no one is denied a treatment program.

Lawrence and Walter utilized detailed pretest measures that included the clients' selection of a goal of the behavior change program, measures of the problem, scales of self-assertiveness and behavioral problem solving, and tests of social effectiveness. Although clients were assigned randomly to experimental and control groups, the two groups were stratified in order to provide an approximately equal distribution of the different types of problems in the two groups. Members of the experimental group received training in assessing and solving social problems and in social effectiveness as well as general group help and support.

The experimental group showed more improvement on a variety of measures than the control group. The use of the experimental design permitted this study to attribute changes to the active intervention. However, the need to treat the control group as a waiting list group provides a problem in the interpretation of the results. One group received special attention while the other was not seen. Is it the program or the attention to which change may be attributed? This potential complication has been called the "Hawthorne effect," named after a study conducted by Roethlisberger and Dickson in which any changes in the workers' environment, whether these included shortening or lengthening hours of work, resulted in increased productivity.

While relatively simpler treatment studies, such as those evaluating drugs, may use "double blind designs" in which neither the patient nor the researcher knows who is receiving the active drug and who is receiving the placebo, it is impossible to do this in the case of programs that use social or behavioral interventions. Thus, for example, the patient knows whether or not he is receiving an active, promising new form of intervention or whether he is simply on a waiting list or in a standard treatment program. This undoubtedly may influence responses to the rating scales.

Both these problems of interpretation are characteristic of evaluations of human service programs even when the studies are as well controlled as that of Lawrence and Walter.

## Linn, Caffey, Klett, Hogarty, and Lamb: Day Treatment and Psychotropic Drugs in the Aftercare of Schizophrenic Patients

Linn and her colleagues conducted a comprehensive evaluation of the day treatment program at ten Veterans Administration centers throughout the country. This study is an example of a full-scale, multiple goal, multi-institutional evaluation of a national program. The question studied was "whether the social therapies add significantly to the use of antipsychotic drugs alone in the posthospital care of schizophrenic patients." Patients discharged from Veterans Administration hospitals on maintenance levels of antipsychotic drugs were randomly assigned to a drug alone control group or to the day treatment plus drugs intervention group.

Because the aim was to evaluate the day treatment programs at Veterans Administration centers, ten programs varying in geographic location, size, and years of operation were selected in order to be representative of such programs in the Veterans Administration system. The day treatment programs in existence at these centers were not modified to make them uniform in order to evaluate the programs as they were currently operating.

The criteria for successful treatment involved: time spent in the community, level of social functioning, symptoms, attitudes, and the cost of the programs. Measures were developed to examine each of these variables. Approximately 80 patients in the drug maintenance and day treatment groups were followed for 24 months at 6-month intervals. Analyses were done for each separate variable as well as for multivariate differences. Linn et al. not only compared the day treatment group with the drug alone group, but also compared good outcome and poor outcome centers for the day treatment group in order to determine whether there were particular characteristics of centers associated with successful day treatment outcome.

One of the major advantages of this study was the analysis of program costs. It is today not sufficient to find that a particular social intervention program is more effective than either no intervention or an old form of intervention. If the program is successful, its cost must be compared with the cost of old procedures in order to decide whether the allocation of resources to that program on a full-scale basis will be feasible. The analysis of Linn and her co-workers found that the day treatment program is no more expensive than the cost of treating patients on drug maintenance alone when the readmission costs of the latter group is included.

## ARTICLES REPRINTED

Lawrence, H., & Walter, C. L. Testing a behavioral approach with groups. *Social Work,* 1978, *23*(2), 127–133.

Linn, M. W., Caffey, E. M., Klett, C. J., Hogarty, G. E., & Lamb, R. Day treatment and psychotropic drugs in the aftercare of schizophrenic patients. *Arch. Gen. Psychiatry,* 1979, *36*(10), 1055–1066.

Reinherz, H., Heywood, M., & Camp, J. Shared perspectives—a community counseling center for adolescents. *Adolescence,* 1976, *11*(42), 168–179.

Part V

# ANALYSIS AND INTERPRETATION

*Chapter 21*

# THE FINAL STEPS IN THE RESEARCH PROCESS
## Analysis and Interpretation

## Joseph M. Regan
## Helen Z. Reinherz

The researcher sits contemplating a mountainous stack of recorded interviews or sheet after sheet of computer print-outs. After hours and days of planning, replanning, and finally collecting the data, the process of summarizing and understanding the fruits of research efforts is finally at hand. Depending on temperament, the researcher may be beset with the fear that "nothing of significance will be found" or that "the data will be so rich, so full of interesting findings, that it will be impossible to fully explore and interpret it." Typically, the truth lies somewhere in-between.

Much of the groundwork has been set for the analytic process, but there may be some room for creative shifts and serendipitous discoveries in exploratory studies. The design (as indicated) must grow organically from the formulation of the problems. The process of data collection must also bear a direct relationship to the problem and the design. Of necessity, the requirements of analysis should have been considered through the earlier steps (particularly that of data collection), so that vital information could be gathered as the study proceeded. Although analysis in research includes the process of summarizing and making communicable the volume of material collected to answer the research questions posed at the beginning of the study, it also encompasses the search for meaning within the context of the study, and for linking findings with previous research. The period at the end of the study (as well as the beginning of the study) provides the researcher with an opportunity to enrich a single study by citing the work of other research investigators and to assess how the study's findings fit with the findings of others. Experience and knowledge of the subject area are crucial elements in the final stages of a study. If studies are based on a theoretical framework (and most good studies are), the researchers are in a good position to relate their findings to theory, as well as to comparable empirical studies (see chapters by Fraiberg and Plionis in Part I).

Some of the texts mentioned earlier have excellent chapters on analysis (Kerlinger, 1973; Polansky, 1975, chaps. 3, 9; Selltiz, Wrightsman, & Cook, 1976; chap. 14). At least one of them should be read in conjunction with this chapter. Additionally, many of the most frequently used statistical techniques reported in the social work research literature may be found in the statistical texts listed in the references at the end of the chapter. Blalock (1972) and Hays (1973) represent detailed texts designed specifically for the needs of social research students. Siegel (1956) has written a classic work with specific content in statistics appropriate for much of the data typically found in research in the social work field. The recently published text of Weinberg and Goldberg (1979) covers in a simple intuitive manner many of the current statistical techniques in the field of social research. Additional texts are listed to allow for a broader selection.

By using this research book and appropriate texts in social research and statistics the reader should gain an understanding of the analytic process. None of the usual texts or reports, however, convey both the challenge and often laborious work that are characteristics of this phase of the research process. If well done, this aspect of research makes all the prior work worthwhile.

## THE PROCESS OF ANALYSIS

Throughout this volume the selected articles contain a variety of approaches to the requirements of the analytic process adapted to the problem formulations and designs selected by the authors. An exploratory design, as exemplified by the Hanks and Rosenbaum study reprinted in Part II, may require the initial step of classifying the characteristics of a sample, in this instance battered women and qualities of their marriages. At times, the classification requirement in an exploratory study may constitute a major research goal leading to identification of significant variables for further study as in the first part (A) of the Fraiberg study reprinted in Part I. The Fraiberg study (Part B) reprinted in this section illustrates the change of approach from the initial exploratory phase to an elaborate analytic procedure developed in the subsequent descriptive phase of the study for coding the behavior of the infants.

In a number of studies on a descriptive or experimental level, interviewing tools may consist of precoded (preclassified) scales, when salient variables have been already identified and standardized instruments to measure them are available. For such instruments only a check or circle need be applied to record a response. The use of the Srole "Anomie" scale by Wolock and Horowitz and the Beck "Hopelessness" scale in the Mercer and Kane study (both in Part II) illustrate the use of preclassified measures.

For studies in which no precategorization or preclassification has been made, the first step of analysis always is to develop categories that are "exhaustive" (include all responses), "mutually exclusive" (allow only one possible category for each response), and are relevant to the purpose of the study as well as the respondents' frame of reference (Lazerfeld, Barton, & Katz, 1955; Selltiz et al., 1976).

## DESCRIPTION OF FINDINGS

A major initial goal of the analytic process is the presentation of the findings in a compact, understandable, and communicable format. A careful classification of qualitative and quantitative data must be presented to the reader. Many simple tables are merely presentations in summary form of facts about the group being studied; for example, Plionis presents the characteristics of a sample of children prone to repetitive accidents in a simple table of frequency counts (see Table 1). Table 1 of the chapter by Wechsler, Gottlieb, and Demone displays the social and economic characteristics of the study group by percentages. Additional tables in this study describe life-style and health habits, as well as personal problems of respondents. The tables also divide the population by place of residence (from core city to outer suburbs) allowing cross-classification or comparisons by place of residence along with the other characteristics listed in each table. It is essential that each reader of a research study spend time examining tables presented in reports to make independent judgments of content and meaning.

Other means of summarizing a large array of material include measures of central tendency, "average" or "typical" responses, or qualities (Polansky, 1975, Chap. 9; Selltiz et al., 1976, Chap. 14; Weinberg & Goldberg, 1979, Chaps. 3 and 4). As an example, in their study of adolescents Reinherz, Heywood and Camp (Part IV) compare the mean ($\overline{X}$) self-concept scores of the adolescents treated in the counseling center with scores of adults. They also compare treated adolescents with several other adolescent populations including a group of adolescents not treated by the center but from the same town. Such comparisons enable the authors to assess the self-concept levels of the adolescents studied relative to groups tested with the same scale.

Measures of variability or the dispersion of the characteristics studied are also necessary for a full understanding of a group's characteristics. The standard deviation and the range are often used in describing the characteristics of a sample or study population (Polansky, 1975, Chap. 9; Selltiz et al., 1976, Chap. 14; Weinberg & Goldberg, 1979, Chaps. 3, 4). Rhodes (Part III) presented the range of actual scores among the worker-client pairs studied for contract status. Thus, presentation of a measure of dispersion along with a measure of central tendency allows for a more complete description of a phenomenon. After all, the swimmer wants to know the depth of a pond from shallow edge to center (the variability) as well as the average depth before diving in!

## The Search for Relationships

In addition to a summary of central tendency and dispersion, the analysis may also include correlations and other measures of association between variables. Many of the articles reprinted in other sections of this book provide examples of correlational analyses. Correlations are useful not only in showing the presence of a relationship by the strength of the relationship. The Shulman chapter (Part III) explored the correlations between workers' skills and clients' estimates of workers' helpfulness and their relationship to the worker. In this part, the chapter by Rubin examines relationships between practitioner attitudes toward after care and characteristics of their experiences.

Contingency tables are often used as a method of looking at the relationship between two variables. Wechsler et al. reprinted in this section uses this approach. Additional examples of contingency tables are found in Wolock and Horowitz's study of child abuse and neglect (Part II). Both Wechsler et al. and Wolock and Horowitz used the chi square ($X^2$) statistic, an inferential statistic, to assess the "significance" of relationship between status on one variable with status on another. Such inferential statistics, based on probability theory, aid the researcher in decision making; they also allow the researcher to generalize from a sample (usually a relatively small group of individuals) to a population as a whole. The important differentiation between descriptive and inferential statistics is outlined in the next section. Selltiz et al. (1976), Kerlinger (1973), and some of the statistical texts listed at the end of the chapter present detailed discussions of the concepts and specific measures.

## STATISTICAL INFERENCE

Descriptive statistics are essential in reporting the actual magnitude of the quantities of any study's relevant variables, but they do not provide information on how seriously these quantities are to be taken. In other words, how meaningful are the reported results? Can they be attributed to chance or random variation or should they be accepted as indicating real differences? Inferential statistics are employed to answer these questions. If the differences are too large to be accounted for by chance, they are termed *statistically significant.* However, whether the results are significant or not is not determined in "yes" or "no" terms, but in the degree of their probability of arising from chance factors alone. Most investigators in the social science field treat findings as significant if their probability level is 0.05 or below, that is, if there are only five chances in 100 of their occurring by chance alone.

Among the most common statistical tests of inference utilized in the social work research literature are the $\chi^2$ (Chi square) and the $t$-test. The first is seen so frequently because it can be applied to all levels of measurement, while the latter has more stringent requirements (Polansky, 1978, Chap. 3; Weinberg & Goldberg, 1978). For example, Wolock and Horowitz (Part II) in the study of child maltreatment use the $\chi^2$ to compare the differences in the maltreating and comparison groups on the dimensions of parents' early childhood experience, current living conditions in the home, and the possession of major consumer items. The same study employs the $t$-test to compare the groups on the average (mean) number of children and the average age difference between children in the family. Wechsler, Gottlieb, and Demone use the $\chi^2$ to compare the differences in certain sociodemographic characteristics, major health habits, and various situational problems encountered in urban and suburban areas. There are a number of other tests of inference, including the Mann-Whitney U test used in the Plionis study (Part I) but basically these tests make the same determinations as the $\chi^2$ and the $t$-test. Choice of which test is the most appropriate depends on the nature of the sampling plan, the number of groups, and the level of measurement.

## Advances in Statistical Analysis Through Use of Computers

The development of predesigned computer programs, such as the Statistical Package for the Social Sciences (SPSS), has facilitated the ability of social work research to employ an array of complex techniques for statistical analysis. Indeed, as illustrated by some of the chapters in this book, one hallmark of the social work literature in the last ten years has been the gradual but emerging application of these techniques. Robertson (Part I) uses analysis of variance to examine differences in the elderly's activity preferences according to sex and marital and employment status. Wechsler et al. also apply analysis of variance in their discussion of difference levels of concern about specific neighborhood problems found in persons living in the inner city and the suburbs. Mercer and Kane (Part II) employ analysis of covariance to determine if a significant reduction occurs in hopelessness and a significant increase in activity level as the result of an experimental program for elderly in nursing homes. Wolock and Horowitz (Part II) use discriminant function analysis to determine which variables distinguish abusive parents from others. These tests and other statistical techniques, such as regression and factor analysis, appear more frequently in recent years than in the past in all social research reports including those in the social work literature.

These recent developments in the area of data analysis have far reaching implications for social work research. Increased access to computers will mean that large research data sets of substantial complexity can be processed more efficiently and managed more effectively. Packaged computer programs extend the use of sophisticated statistical techniques to research professionals who can learn their basic assumptions and proper use without having to be familiar with their complicated mathematical derivations. These techniques hold great promise for the social work research field. They are more powerful than the simpler techniques in the sense that more of the original information is included in the analysis. They also can make finer discriminations between the complex interdependency of variables so common in the issues that social work research addresses.

Although these analytic techniques can be very useful it is important to be aware of their limitations. No analytic technique, no matter how powerful, will compensate for a poorly formulated problem or deficiencies in research design. Also they may not be always necessary or indicated for the research problem addressed, and their use should not be equated with how "scientific" a particular research endeavor is. Fraiberg (Part B) considers their use and rejects them as inappropriate for the type of analysis her study required. Finally, these techniques are only part of the process of analysis. Nothing is more disheartening than to read a study that makes use of sophisticated statistical analyses but whose conclusions are quite limited in substance and meaning. Complex methods of statistical analysis operate best in conjunction with good theoretical formulations. Kaplan (1964) showed that they are tools for thought to which we turn because we need them not because they are there.

## PROTECTION AGAINST BIAS: ISSUES OF RELIABILITY AND VALIDITY

The research worker must guard against bias with as much tenacity as the disciplined professional guards against countertransference in the therapeutic encounter. Spurious findings can be avoided by earlier care in design, sampling, and data collection (discussed in detail in Part III in data gathering).

To ensure adequate reliability and validity of the analysis procedures, the researcher checks all aspects of the analysis from coding (classifying and/or quantifying) the data to handling the computations for reliability and accuracy. Vigilance is a small price to pay for accurate information!

Most important to the enhancement of the validity (i.e., meaning) of a particular study is concern with issues of both internal and external validity (Campbell & Stanley, 1963). Internal validity relates to uncontrolled aspects affecting results such as maturation or attrition of subjects. These factors can affect conclusions to be drawn from the data. External validity refers to the generalizability of results to other situations and samples. These issues should have been considered throughout the study. Because most studies have limitations in one or more areas, it is essential that the researcher clearly spell out some of the limitations for the reader.

## THE FURTHER TASKS OF INTERPRETATION AND UTILIZATION OF RESEARCH

Beyond the careful presentation of findings, the researcher has the final task in all studies, whether the health status and policy (Wechsler et al.), evaluation of therapy (Lawrence & Walter), or clinical theory (Fraiberg), to move beyond the data to the broader world of other studies and practice.

Fraiberg's "Muse in the Kitchen" (Part B) reprinted in this section illustrates how the creative imagination of the clinician-researcher infuses meaning into seemingly senseless responses of blind children. The analytic procedure represented by the inferences that are brought to bear on the carefully observed developmental processes of the babies in the study represents the culmination of years of theory developed by the psychoanalysts, Piaget, and other reseachers. Yet the study and its analysis would have been meaningless if the individual clinicians involved had not had the experience of intensive work with many kinds of children.

Additionally, Fraiberg (Part B) presents clear implications for action using the findings of the study. Along with the research, direct treatment had been given to the children and their parents to facilitate the optimal development of the blind children in the study. Thus, the results had been applied simultaneously with the ongoing research. Finally, plans were initiated for continued studies aimed at long-term results providing a model for longitudinal applied research.

In the study of the community counseling center for adolescents by Reinherz et al. in Part III the specific changes noted by staff and clients in the adolescents are compatible with the centers' goals. The authors link these findings to previous research findings on the relationship between congruent goals and expectations of therapists and patients and positive treatment outcome. The use of research literature to aid in the understanding of findings provides a means of linking the results of one piece of research with another providing external validation.

In interpreting their findings, Wechsler et al. present clear implications for the need for different health strategies for different population groups. They also indicate urgency in giving first consideration to improving social and environmental conditions that affect rather than simply spending more funds for medical care, an important consideration for social policy.

Rubin's study reported in this section examines the staffing needs of community based programs designed to provide after-care for deinstitutionalized patients who are often ill-equipped to exist without the supports after-care furnishes. His findings suggest patterns of staffing that may have benefits in lowering costs and enhancing all-important staff commitment to service.

The reader is advised to carefully assess the "discussion of results" and "interpretation of findings" sections of research articles. Important questions must be kept in mind. Do the implications arise directly from the findings? Even if the findings form the basis for the discussion, is the author stretching his material too finely and emerging with interpretations and, more important, recommendations that cannot be fully documented by the study's findings? In social work research, a field relating closely to practice, the informed reader must be aware of both the limitations and usefulness of findings. Through informed understanding the practitioner can select those findings and studies that will shape and enhance practice.

## REFERENCES

Blalock, H. *Social statistics,* 2nd ed. New York: McGraw-Hill Book Company, 1972.

Campbell, D., & Stanley, J. *Experimental and quasi-experimental designs for research.* Chicago: Rand-McNally, 1963.

Hays, W. L. *Statistics for the social sciences,* 2nd ed. New York: Holt, Rinehart and Winston, 1973.

Kaplan, A. *The conduct of inquiry.* Scranton, Pa: Chandler, 1964.

Kerlinger, F. N. *Foundations of behavioral research,* 2nd ed. New York: Holt, Rinehart and Winston, 1973.

Lazersfeld, P. F., Barton, A. H., & Katz, E. Some general principles of questionaire classification. In P. f., Lazerfeld, P. E. et al. (Eds.) *The language of social research.* Glencoe, Ill: The Free Press, 1955.

Polansky, N. A. (Ed.). *Social work research.* Chicago: University of Chicago Press, 1975.

Selltiz, C., Wrightsman, L. S., & Cook, S. W. *Research methods in social relations,* 3rd ed. New York: Holt, Rinehart, and Winston, 1976.

Siegel, S. *Non-parametric statistics: For the behavioral sciences.* New York: McGraw-Hill, 1956.

Weinberg, S., & Goldberg, K. *Basic statistics for education and the behavioral sciences.* Boston: Houghton-Mifflin, 1979.

## ADDITIONAL TEXTS AND REFERENCES

Campbell, D. T. Reforms as experiments. *American Psychologist,* 1969, *24*(4), 409–429.

Colton, T. *Statistics.* Boston Little, Brown, 1974.

Walizer, M. H., & Wienir, P. L. *Research methods and analysis: Searching for relationships.* New York: Harper and Row, 1978.

*Chapter 22*

# THE MUSE IN THE KITCHEN (Part B)

## Selma Fraiberg

A case history of the development of a research plan begins with the questions and proceeds logically to the methods and procedures which must be employed to obtain answers to these questions. I will try in the next few pages to give a sketch of our problems and the methods we employed. Then, in the last section some sample problems encountered in this research are analyzed in terms of the questions, the methods, and the results.

We can already see that the problems we have isolated for study have reciprocal and interlocking relationships throughout the course of development. Human object relations, the differentiation of a self and an outerworld, prehension, gross motor development, and language cannot be isolated as separate studies unless we first know the relationships which exist among these developmental schemas. In the case of the sighted baby we know a fair amount, which means that if we isolate areas for study we are working within a known framework. But if we are beginning the investigation of a previously uncharted territory, such as the psychological development of a blind infant, we cannot assume from the start that the relationships which exist among these sectors of development will be the same if vision is not available to the developing child. This means that we are practically obliged to conduct a systematic study of every sector of development in the blind infant in order to find the relationships which exist among them.

The methods and procedures for study which we worked out were the best methods, for us. They gave us, finally, the answers we were seeking. This means that they were valid methods for this study. But in this research as in any others, there is no such thing as "the correct" methodology. A quantitative study based upon a sample of 100 blind infants is not "better than" or "more scientific" than a qualitative study of 10 blind infants. Controlled experimentation is not "more scientific" than a naturalistic study. All of these are scientific approaches to problems. The best scientific method is the one that produces the answers to the questions. If we want to know how the developmental capacities of totally blind babies compare to those of sighted babies we must examine a large sample of this population and employ statistical measures for working out comparative norms. But if we want to know how totally blind babies make their human attachments, differentiate a self and an object world, learn to speak, learn to use their hands as fine perceptual organs, learn to locomote, one blind baby can inform us considerably and ten blind babies with a range of environments and a range of assumed differences in endowment can help us identify the variables at work.

Since many of the problems we were studying had never been systematically examined before, we had to begin data collection within the large complex of behaviors that constitute infant development. Since there were no instruments standardized for our population (totally blind from birth) and the existing instruments for blind children with all degrees of visual loss are not reliable in themselves, we had to work out a system of observation in which the observer's selection and recording of data could produce a body of information that would permit comparisons within the group of blind babies and between the group of blind babies and sighted babies.

At this point I will try to give you a brief summary of the research design.

## SUMMARY OF METHODS AND PROCEDURES

### The Sample

For our sample we chose babies who were totally blind from birth or who had light perception only; babies who had no other sensory or motor defects and no signs of central nervous system damage. Only by employing these restrictive criteria could we be sure that we were studying the visual deficit and its effects upon development. The total number of babies reported here is ten.

Blind babies who satisfied these criteria are rare even in a geographic range of 100 miles. In order to make home visits for observation we would need to travel in a radius of about 100 miles.

## Areas of Study

On the the basis of our pilot studies we selected these areas of infant development for study: human object relations; behavior toward inanimate objects, toys; feeding; sleep; affectivity; language; gross motor development; prehension; self-stimulating behaviors; object concept.

## Observational Procedures

Each baby was assigned to a team of two observers. The primary responsibility for observation was placed in a senior professional staff member who was present at each visit. Our senior professional staff was composed of psychoanalysts and clinical psychologists. By placing the primary responsibility for observation in trained clinicians we insured as far as possible a high degree of sensitivity and clinical judgment in the work of data collection.

Why clinicians? Because, I feel, the clinical eye is trained to examine fine details and to regard every detail in the pattern as significant. The clinical worker, if he is well trained, has learned to regard himself as an instrument for observation and to protect his observations from prejudice. The clinician is also a pathologist, which means that a deviation in behavior from the expected and the typical will be recognized and invite inquiry. Above all, if he is a well-trained and well-seasoned clinician, he will allow the data to tell their own story; he will not impose a design upon the patterns observed. He will be open to the novel and the unexpected and he will welcome surprise.

The most serious drawback to using beginners or trainees in psychological investigation is one that I can remember with pain but with charity in myself. When I was a young worker I could only see what I was trained to see. When something emerged in my work that did not fit the pattern, my tendency was to screen it out, or to try to make it fit. In my research plan I knew that this must not happen. There was danger enough for all of us in drawing inferences from behavior of children whose perceptual field was radically different from our own. If we added to this the danger of "making things fit," our investigation would be doomed from the start.

## Methods

The babies were visited in their homes at twice-monthly intervals. We chose a period in the baby's day, when he was normally awake and alert, when we might observe a feeding, a bath, a playtime with mother, a diapering or clothes change, and a period of self-occupation with or without toys.

One or the other of the observers recorded a descriptive narrative during the one-and-a-half hour observation period. In order to insure coverage of all items which must be gathered for comparative developmental study, the observers memorized our code schedule which included over 400 categories and subcategories of behavior. This was not as difficult as it sounds. During any one observational session, the number of items relevant for a particular baby's developmental level might range from 50 to 100. An experienced observer could cover all of these items in the normal course of the session without disturbing the baby's routine or imposing a pattern upon the session. We never brought a schedule to an observational session. We did not need or want a checklist. What we wanted was descriptive detail.

At monthly or twice monthly intervals (depending on the age of the child) we recorded film samples of behavior in the areas of mother-child interaction in feeding or play, prehension, gross motor development, self-occupation. Because the photographing did impose a degree of artificiality on the observational session, we tried to keep this within the minimum required for useful documentation and study (approximately 450 feet of film per month).*

## Evaluation of Data

All of the data recorded in the descripitive narratives can be treated in two ways. They can be tabulated in short-hand form using

*For a more detailed description of the procedures for data collection, see Fraiberg, 1968.

the code schedule. This gives us a quick summary of the achievements of any baby at any age which can then be compared with the developmental characteristics of all other babies in our sample. At the same time every item tabulated has a reference by page and line to the original protocol, so that the descriptive and qualitative aspects of the behavior entered can be given separate treatment.

## The Educational Program

It is important to mention that for all babies in our study we have provided concurrent educational and guidance services to families. We know that the early development of blind babies is perilous. As our own research progressed we obtained important insights into the developmental problems of blind infants and we were able to translate this knowledge into highly effective prophylactic and remedial measures. In providing an educational service for our babies we have certainly altered our field in this investigation. But I am sure this audience will agree that no benefits to the research could justify withholding this knowledge from our families. It is only necessary that those who use our findings add to their information regarding our sample that these babies were probably advantaged by our educational intervention. It is necessary, too, that our records show explicitly how and when we intervened so that these parameters can be read into the assessment.

It is worth mentioning that even when our guidance work demonstrably affected the development of certain blind babies, it never obscured the study of the deficit and its effects upon development. In each case the visual deficit created a temporary roadblock in development which we were powerless to remove; in each case we saw the baby and his mother struggle to find the adaptive solution; in each case we gave assistance when necessary to find the adaptive routes. But what we needed to know we learned fully even though we influenced the outcome.

On the side of assets to the research I should mention two very important benefits brought to us through our educational work. First, the caseworker's guidance records gave us the kind of intimate knowledge of our babies and their families which we could never have obtained through the observational sessions alone. Second, our interventions at many critical points became a form of hypothesis testing, truly an experimental procedure.

## SAMPLE PROBLEMS IN METHODOLOGY

From the brief summary I have given you in the preceding section you can follow the general lines of our study. Since this is a case history of the development of a research program I think it would be very proper for my colleagues to ask the questions: Why these methods and not others? This is surely the clumsiest, most unwieldy system for data collection ever invented. Had you thought of less complex procedures? Or did you consider taking only one of these developmental areas and submitting it to exhaustive inquiry?

These are fair questions and very interesting ones. In this section, then, I propose to take some sample problems, discuss alternative methods, present arguments for the methods chosen and see how the methods were linked to the result.

### Sample Problem 1: What is the Role of the Mother in Facilitating Successful Adapation in the Blind Infant?

If a blind child achieves a good level of adaptive functioning we will probably say that the mother of this child has done a very good job, and in colloquial terms speak of her as a "good" mother. If a blind child fails to make the grade we are inclined to regard his mother as a failure and to speak of her as a "poor" mother. If we want to elevate these notions to the status of science we could actually prove this. We could, for example, rate all our mothers on the Zweibach Maternal Warmth Scale, which I have just this moment invented, and rate all of our children on the basis of their developmental achievements. We would then find, predictably, that maternal warmth is highly correlated with the developmental achievements of blind children, in which case we would have spent a whopping chunk of taxpayers' money to deliver another cliché.

Now, of course, a provident nature has insured that almost any baby who is born with intact equipment will learn to walk and to talk, even if he has had the misfortune to get a mother who ranks low on the Zweibach Scale. This is just about what Hartmann means when he speaks of "the autonomous functions of the ego" and the guarantees for adaptiveness in "an average expectable environment" (Hartmann, 1958). But if a baby is born with a deficit in his equipment the "average expectable environment" has some built-in hazards. The minus on the side of "state of adaptiveness" will require pluses on the side of a mother who will have to substitute for the deficit and take over the role of facilitating adaptation where the intact equipment would have virtually guaranteed it. This requires a mother with a high degree of adaptive capacity herself, and while mother love is certainly a great facilitator in responding to an infant's needs, the birth of a defective child can test love cruelly. Often if love passes the test, there is no guarantee that love alone will open up all the pathways of development that are imperiled by the defect. Toni's mother would be rated as "superior" on anyone's scale, "a very good mother," we would say. When Toni reached nine months and lay for long periods on the floor nuzzling a rug, or when she was condemned for months to the futile navigation of a circle, did the "good mother" become a "poor mother" because her baby's defective equipment led her to an impasse? No, clearly the problem is more complex. We will not learn about the role of the mother in facilitating a blind baby's adaptation if we use the Zweibach Scale or any other measure available to us. Since no one had studied the complexities of a mother's relationship to her blind infant, we needed to begin at the beginning.

## Method

We would need to observe and record in a detailed narrative everything that could be observed in the nonverbal communications between a mother and her blind infant, to learn how the baby's signals were read by the mother, how the baby learned to discriminate his mother from others, how the love bonds between mother and blind baby were forged, how the mother provided experiences for the baby that substituted for visual experience, how the mother helped her baby find the adaptive solutions when blindness created roadblocks in development.

We also want to know the differences and similarities between the progressive course of human attachments in a blind infant and the sighted infant. For the sighted baby we have criteria, indicators of the sequential development of human attachments. We arranged these criteria from several sources on a scale, relying heavily on the work of Therese Gouin-Decarie (1965) in testing a population of ninety children in Montreal. Since many of these criteria are also standard items on infant developmental tests we were able to obtain age norms for sighted children for certain key indicators. We avoided, very carefully, any temptation to substitute nonvisual items for visual items in our own schedule and organized our data collection very simply on the basis of differential responses to mother, father, familiar figures, and strangers.

All of our data in this category (and in every other category) were recorded, you remember, in narrative form. Clumsy, but essential for this investigation. Only by following a narrative form could we give value to the behavior reported in context and in temporal sequence. If we only cut across our data for significant events we might falsify these data. For example, if an eight-month-old baby howls as soon as a stranger picks him up, one might score this as "stranger anxiety." But suppose we read the protocol and find in the preceding paragraph that the baby had been playing a lap game with his mother and the stranger inadvertently interrupted the game. We cannot score this as "stranger anxiety."

The data from every protocol are sorted and indexed by student assistants who are rigorously trained in our coding procedures. If an item is scored "stranger anxiety" it must be unequivocal. When the same item is tabulated as I-8b in the code book there is also a page and line reference which will lead us back to the descriptive material in the text, so that the qualitative aspects of the behavior can be examined.

## Findings

The detailed descriptive recording in the area of human object relationships provided data for two different problems. Abstracted from the recording was: (a) a qualitative analysis of mother-infant communication (the "dialogue" in Spitz's terms); and (b) a sequence of differential responses to mother and other human objects which permitted comparisons with sighted baby achievements in any given quarter of the first eighteen months.

MOTHER-INFANT COMMUNICATION. In the absence of that large repertoire of signals and signs which are normally provided by vision, nearly all of our parents experienced the feeling of being initially cut off from their blind babies. Since no educational help had been given any of our families before the time of referral to us, we can assume that the picture of mother-child interaction presented at the point of intake represented the mother's own unaided efforts to respond to her blind baby's needs and find her way into her blind baby's experience. In the sample that I am reporting, seven of ten babies were referred to us between the ages of three days and six months of life, and three babies were referred to us between six and nine months. (Ideally we would have wanted all babies referred to us as soon after birth as possible, but delays in diagnosis or referral gave us this distribution.) I cannot do more than summarize our findings in this rich and extraordinarily complex area. The following comments reflect the complexity of the problem.

"How will he know me?" was one of the first questions that these young mothers asked when they were still under the impact of the diagnosis of blindness. If the baby came to us as a newborn, we helped the mother to find a tactile-auditory language for communicating with her baby. When the baby came to us at four months or later, we were able to see at the point of referral how the mother found her way, or did not find her way, into her blind baby's experience.

Two of the older babies referred at eight months and nine months respectively, were well on their way to autism at the time we first met them. Jackie and Karen showed no differential responses to the mother or any human objects, were grossly retarded in all sectors of development, withdrew from stimuli and slept the better part of the twenty-four hour day. What kind of mothers were these? These were mothers who did not enjoy physical closeness with their babies. We saw this in their handling of their sighted children. Also they did not speak to their children except to make requests or give commands; having conversations with babies or young children was not their style. Were they "poor" mothers? That depends. Their sighted children were adequate, slow in speech development as you might expect with sighted children who are not encouraged to speak, and not inclined toward physical closeness, which you would expect, too. But the development of these sighted children was not imperiled by a mother who had a limited repertoire in the language of touch and speech. There was no danger of autism for these sighted siblings. Vision became a guarantor of development for these sighted children with a less than adequate mother; in the absence of vision, the blind baby with the same mother was cut off from all experience of knowing the mother. I should tell you that both of these blind babies were brought to normal functioning within a period of a few months through our education and guidance of the mother.

Now let's look at another baby, first seen by us at the age of four-and-a-half months. Robbie, at the time of our first observations, was an extraordinary blind baby. He smiled in response to voices, he cooed and gurgled in response and for self-entertainment, and he was beginning to sit independently for a few seconds; his adaptive hand behavior would place him in the very superior range for blind infants. His mother had had no help in rearing her blind baby before the time we first met her.

Was this mother a very intuitive mother? A very superior mother? Robbie's mother would be rated by us as one of the least empathic mothers in our group and one who presented the most severe pathological signs. She was dull and extremely obese. She showed clinical signs of a severe depression which she warded off through eating and excessive talking. What made her an adequate mother for a blind baby during the first five months of life? She enjoyed physical contact with her baby. "I can't leave him alone!" she would say. We reflected to ourselves that she would probably have worn out a sighted baby through the amount of gross tactile stimulation she gave the blind baby and her garrulousness, which we knew to be a defense against depression, made her known to her blind baby when she was not in physical contact with him! As long as she maintained her defense against depression, she could meet her blind baby's needs. During one brief period at the end of the first year, when the depression broke through, she removed herself from physical contact with Robbie, and for that period he regressed alarmingly. We helped Robbie's mother to reestablish her defenses and Robbie once again moved back to the level of good functioning.

This is not to say that a mother's pathology will not have effects upon a baby's development. When Robbie ran into trouble with his mother in the second year, it was through conflict over feeding, which we can understand from the role of food in the mother's pathology. But Robbie never became an autistic child and Robbie's ego organization was not imperiled as long as the mother's pathology did not isolate her from her baby. All things considered, an intact ego and a feeding disturbance are to be preferred to autism.

From these brief case examples with their contrasts of babies and mothers we can see how unprofitable it would be to rate our mothers on a scale of arbitrary values. If we multiply these examples many times we can begin to get the picture of extraordinary complexity that emerged from our qualitative analysis of data in human object relationships.

Even the most intuitive parents of our group encountered impasses and crises in their rearing of the blind baby that were unparalleled in the experience of good parents with normal sighted babies. The blind baby was helpless before the most ordinary dangers of infancy. Brief separations were experienced as traumas, occasioning in four babies severe regressions that required our assistance. Each step in the achievement of locomotion, which normal babies pass through on a developmental express train, was encountered by the blind baby as another roadblock, another detour, and always another move outwards into the terrifying void. And since the baby never did things the way other babies do, every roadblock created fresh alarms in the parents, and periods during which a mother and her baby were demonstrably out of rapport.

In our educational work we became the interpreters to the parents of the blind baby's experience, helped the parents establish a dialogue in non-visual terms.

COMPARISONS WITH SIGHTED INFANTS. Finally, how did our babies compare with sighted babies in the development of human object relations? Without any arbitrary substitution of nonvisual items for visual items on a sighted-child scale, all but one of our babies showed increasingly selective and well-differentiated responses to his mother and other important persons and to strangers, leading to what we speak of in psychoanalysis as libidinal object constancy. I can summarize with a few key indicators: the smiling response, differential vocalization, stranger reactions, separation anxiety, display of affection, and response to requests and prohibitions all appeared among our blind babies within the age range for sighted infants.

We must not generalize these findings to the blind infant population. Again we need to remember the selective criteria employed in choosing our sample and that the mothers of these babies received all the help we could give them in promoting the love bonds between the baby and themselves. But with all these cautions in interpreting our findings the result is a very significant one. This means, of course, that under the most favorable circumstances a blind baby need not be impeded in forming the vital human attachments. This probably means, too, that what we see in the sighted child as a sequence of differential responses expressed in visual terms must include every step of the way a large amount of non-visual experience, especially tactile and auditory experience, which is progressively organized under vision.

Having human object relations as a cornerstone in our investigation now permits us to draw inferences from our other data with a larger margin of safety. If, for example, the majority of our blind infants demonstrate adequacy in the area of human object relationships (even if we ourselves have influenced this) then any significant group deviation in other sectors of development can be treated more confidently as a possible effect of the visual deficit, or the restrictive experience of the blind infant, with relative independence of the variables in mothering.

*Sample Problem 2: How does the Blind Baby Coordinate Sound and Grasping in the Direct Reach on Sound Cue?*

We already know that Toni did not demonstrate directional reach for an object on sound cue until ten months of age. We cannot generalize this finding from one case of the blind infant population, but one case can tell us that the substitution of sound for vision is not guaranteed in the same way that vision guarantees that the thing "out there" can be attained through reaching and grasping at five months.

If we are only interested in the study of prehension in the blind child there are a number of valid approaches to the problem. We can, for example, conduct a testing program for all blind infants in the state of Michigan, at quarterly intervals in the first year. We would then obtain statistical information on the characteristics of prehension in blind infants in each quarter of the first year and the age range for all blind infants in the attainment of an object on sound cue. This would be a very interesting and useful study in itself. But it would not give us the answers to our questions.

In our psychoanalytic study of ego formation in the blind infant, we want to know how the hand serves ego development. If there is an extraordinary problem in the adaptive substitution of sound for vision, this will have effects not only in the development of prehension, but in contiguous and/or reciprocal lines of development. For all babies, the hand becomes one of the executive organs of the emerging ego, the bridge between the body self and the external world. In the case of the blind baby, the hand must serve all these functions and must also serve as a primary perceptual organ. We need to know the adaptive process as well as the adaptive solution.

In designing this aspect of the research I was helped by a clinical hunch. The hunch was derived from observations of Peter, my nine-year-old autistic boy in New Orleans.

When I first knew Peter I was struck by the fact that when he dropped an object from his hands or lost an object, he did not search for it. He did not even make a gesture of reach. From these and hundreds of other observations it was very clear that when he lost contact with an object, it ceased to exist. We are reminded now that the sighted baby under eight months of age will not search for an object that has been hidden before his eyes. As Piaget (1954) has demonstrated, the belief that an object exists independent of perception is obtained around the middle of the second year and only gradually during the first eighteen months does the baby begin to take into account invisible objects and deduce their movements in space.

Watching Peter, I was struck by the fact that this must be an extraordinary problem for the blind infant. In the absence of vision, the baby must learn to track objects on sound alone. How does the blind baby learn that when he does not hear a person or hear a sound object, it still exists? How does he build a world of permanent objects? And if he fails in this learning, if he cannot acquire the concept of objects which exist independent of himself and his perception, there will be no differentiation between self and object world; he will be, clinically speaking, autistic, meaning that all experience and all phenomena are experienced as part of the body self.

My hunch was that Toni's inability to reach for and attain an object on sound cue until ten months of age might be related to a conceptual problem for a blind infant. In the absence of vision it was possible, I reasoned, that the sound of an object would not connote substantiality or "graspability." The ten-month achievement in an otherwise healthy and bright blind baby might be the clue. At eight months the sighted baby on the Piaget object concept scale begins to search for an object under a screen, meaning that he is just beginning to get the notion that the object can exist independent of his perception. It was possible, I reasoned, that the blind baby must reach this level of conceptual development before sound connotes graspability, that is, that an object exists independent of his manual tactile experience of it and manifests itself through a sound "out there." If this is a conceptual problem for a blind baby, it is very likely that no blind baby could achieve the concept before a sighted baby, which would place reach on sound cue in the last third of the first year.

*Methods*

Our study of prehension, then, would include the testing of this hypothesis, but where nothing is known through direct observation of blind babies we must protect our investigation through designing experimental procedures that tested alternatives and variables without building in expectations. Also, since the factors we were seeking in this study were so complex and numerous, we needed to reduce the problems to manageable size.

There was a good solution, for which we are indebted to Piaget. Piaget's object concept scale, standardized in 1963 by Decarie (Gouin-Decarie, 1965) on a population of ninety children, deals with the same complexities for the sighted child that we were examining in the blind child. In every step of the development of the object concept, the test involves problems in prehension, coordination of sensory-motor schemas, behavior toward inanimate objects, recognition and mental representation, the differentiation of a self and an outer world, in a progressive sequence. This becomes a highly economical test for our purposes.

How can we use this scale? Clearly it would be hazardous for us to take Piaget's scale and make arbitrary substitutions of sound items for visual items when we do not know how sound can substitute for vision and when, in fact, the adaptive substitution is just what we are looking for. But if we followed Piaget's principles we would ask the blind baby to teach *us* how he learned to coordinate sound with directional reach and grasping.

This is what we did:

At twice monthly intervals we presented problems of search to our blind babies. The procedures were very simple. In the first year, for example, we presented sound toys and soundless toys, the child's own toys and interesting toys of our own. We allowed the child to hold them and play with them, and gently removed them from his grasp and placed them within easy reach. We worked out procedures that would tell us clearly how the baby reacted when the toy was experimentally silenced or moved from one place to another, what sensory information he used to discriminate objects and identify them. We also followed the evolution of grasping, mutual fingering, transfer, the coordinate use of hands, unilateral reaching and thumb-finger opposition. We provided only enough structure in the testing to assure us that we could study the variables at work.

We recorded all of the testing on 16-mm film. We then studied the film on a variable speed projector at approximately one-third speed or sometimes frame-by-frame. While viewing the film at one-third speed with the entire senior staff present, one of the investigators dictated a narrative record covering every gesture, every motion, in fine detail. If there was any disagreement on what was seen, we played the sequence over again until we had reached consensus. If there was no consensus, it was recorded as such. We then had a film record and a corresponding written document. The film protocol could now be used flexibly for coding and for sorting patterns.

This, too, is probably one of the clumsiest procedures ever invented. Yet it gave us all the answers we were looking for. I still do not know whether there were any short-cuts that we could have taken. Since nothing was known about adaptive hand behavior in blind infants we could not know what to look for. The situation is analogous to that of an archeological study of a site that is identified as potentially rich but has never been dug. Every fragment must be carefully examined, catalogued, and stored until the pieces can be arranged to tell a story.

## Findings

When we sorted our data on each child, this is what we saw:

(1) The biogenetic patterns of prehension appeared in the grasping mode in a clear evolution throughout the first ten months. The hand unfolds, and at ten months the index finger explores and thumb-finger opposition appears, which corresponds to the norms of sighted children.

(2) Adaptive hand behavior, the route to acoustically directed reach and attainment, followed a very different course from that of the sighted child. The coordination of hearing and grasping appeared in our blind babies in the last quarter of the first year. *The modal age for ten babies in our sample was ten months!*

These data tell us that there is no adaptive substitution of sound for sight at five months. The blind baby must find the adaptive solution via another route. How does the blind baby find the adaptive route? To answer this question we analyzed literally hundreds of miles of film and classified the data in stages. I will not attempt to give the details in this short report. But this is an interesting story and I can give you a summary by choosing one baby as a model.

At five months Robbie enjoys holding a bell in his hands and ringing it. If we withdraw the bell from his hands and ring it within easy reach of his hands there is no gesture of reach, the hands remain motionless.

At eight months of age we bring Robbie's oldest and most treasured musical toy within easy reach of his hands. It is playing its familiar music. Robbie looks alert, attentive, shows recognition on his face. He makes no gesture of reach. We finally give him his musical dog and he hugs it and mouths it. After awhile we withdraw the dog from his hands. He is angry at the loss. He can still hear the music. It is within easy reach. He does not make even a gesture toward the toy. In hundreds of experiments during this period we can demonstrate that whether we use a familiar sound toy or an unfamilar toy, whether mother presents the toy or the examiner presents the toy, whether sound is continuous or sound is discontinuous, there is no attempt to recover the toy.

At ten months of age if we sound the bell which Robbie is very fond of, there is still no gesture of reach. But now we see an interesting behavior of the hands. At the sound of the bell Robbie's hands go through the motion of grasping and ungrasping and once we see the hands executing the motion of ringing the bell. Still no reach, but now for the first time we can read the message in the hands that the sound of the bell connotes graspability and evokes a memory of bell ringing.

At eleven months and three days of age, Robbie hears the bell and for the first time makes a direct reach for the bell and attains it.

And now, from this model, we can reconstruct the problem for a blind baby. Sound alone does not connote substantiality for Robbie until eleven months. Until then the toy dog playing Brahm's Lullaby "out there" is not the same as the toy dog playing Brahm's Lullaby when held in the baby's hand. As a matter of fact, even the sighted baby at eight months will not search for a favorite squeaky toy if we cover it with a screen and cause it to squeak. But vision will unite the schemas of sound and touch so that the sighted child will soon take the sound to connote the object seen and grasped. The blind child has to make an inference that the familiar sound "out there" connotes the substantial object that he had held in his hands a few minutes ago. When, at ten months, Robbie's hands go through the motions of grasping and ungrasping and bell ringing we can see that he is getting the idea, and in a very short time we see him coordinate the schemas of prehension and sound in direct reach.

This means, of course, that the blind child has to reach a certain level of conceptual development before he can reach for and attain a sound object. The sighted child can achieve this on a much earlier level of conceptual development because vision will insure that the thing seen can be grasped at five months of age. This is not an advanced conceptual problem for the sighted baby; it is not even much of a memory problem. But for the blind baby, memory and an emerging concept of the qualities of things, independent of the self, are required for the solution of the problem.

We can now understand why many blind babies never find the adaptive solution and remain frozen on the level of body centeredness.

But now I should tell you, too, how the prehension study provided the vital clue to the problem of delayed locomotion in blind infants. Have you already guessed?

All of the babies in our sample were markedly delayed by sighted child norms in achieving locomotion through creeping, walking with support, and independent walking. As a group their achievements were very good for blind children; on a blind child scale their locomotor achievements would place them in the upper half of the blind infant population. This may reflect our educational interventions. But the developmental impasse which we observed in Toni appeared in each of our blind babies in the last quarter of the first year. There was maturational readiness for creeping which we can demonstrate through documentary films, showing a baby supporting himself ably on hands and knees, or pulling himself to a stand. These abilities testify for neuromuscular adequacy and "readiness" for locomotion. At ten months we see Robbie on film, supporting himself on hands and knees, acrobatically lifting one leg off the floor, maintaining beautiful balance. He has been "ready to creep" by all standards since nine months. For three months he maintains his posture, rocking back and forth on hands and knees. He is unable to propel himself forward. We had already guessed part of the story through observations of Toni. There was no external stimulus for reaching which would initiate the creeping pattern. But in those days we could not understand why a sound stimulus could not substitute for a visual stimulus. Now we knew.

Robbie demonstrated his first reach on sound cue at eleven months of age. Three days later while supporting himself on hands and knees he reached for an out-of-range sound object and began to creep.

This pattern or variations of it appeared in every child in our series. No baby learned to creep until he had first given us a demonstration of "reach on sound cue."

## COULD WE HAVE USED SOME SHORTCUTS?

The methods I have described in these sample problems brought us the answers we were seeking. If you now add to these two areas of study the ten other major categories of this investigation, you can see that the work of data collection and analysis has been very demanding. Could we have simplified our procedures? Could we have found shortcuts? I still don't know whether there were other methods that might have produced the same answers.

All of our data are coded and sorted manually. Two years ago as I saw the mountain of data grow, I considered the possibility of working out a system for computer sorting and retrieval of items in their descriptive categories. I sketched the problem and the plan, and our data processing people thought it was workable. We never used it.

As we moved into the evaluation phase of our work each of us had the most compelling need to see the story unfold before his own eyes. Our descriptive data in certain categories are transcribed on large cards, one item per card, of course, and we will have to spend hundreds of hours, all of us, playing solitaire with thousands of cards. So far not one of us has complained about the work. I think I know why.

By the time I have read and sorted a thousand cards in Section I, and re-read them and re-sorted them for the study of twenty-five subcategories, every card has been read hundreds of times. A large number of them have been practically memorized. Now, my mental storage and retrieval system is not nearly as efficient as the computer's system, but I have a useable past which the computer does not have. When the computer registers information on card 456, it will know immediately that card 456 belongs to the same group as card 243. This is very clever of the computer, but it only knows it because I told it so. Now when I look at card 456 I also will know that it belongs in the same category as card 243, which does not yet give me much of an edge on the computer. But perhaps the fourth time I look at card 456, something leaps out of the printed text, and I say, "That odd behavior in Sally! That ear pulling! Where did I see that before? Oh, yes. Artie at eight months. Where is Artie's eight-month file?" I reach in and pluck a card. I re-read it. It's the same manifestation. Now we have two examples of a piece of incomprehensible behavior. My mind wanders for a moment. The picture of a twelve-year-old boy, a patient long ago, comes into my mind. How did Ozzie get into the picture? I wait a moment. The patient in my memory picture is agitatedly plucking at his clothing. It's that frightful hour eight years ago when I was afraid he was heading for the hospital. He is clutching his own skin through cloth, in panic, as he describes dissolution of self-feeling. Ah, that's the connection. Affirmation of self-feelings through repetitive touching of the body. Is that what the two babies are telling us? I will wait now for more evidence.

This kind of sorting in human intelligence takes place on a preconscious level. The computer has no history, no record of experience that can do this work. Even if we improve the model, the computer will never learn to do this. It is not just the lack of clinical experience that limits the computer. A system of mechanical retrieval can never make such associative leaps. The associative paths that can lead you and me from two babies to a twelve-year-old boy are not part of a logical system. There were probably affective pathways in my own mental processes that led me from the picture of two babies, pulling at their ear lobes, to a memory of a boy plucking at his clothes. In layman's language we might say the process began by "feeling" a similarity, even when I could not yet know what the connections were.

All this belongs to what we call "clinical imagination," which is simply another form of the scientific imagination. The insights of a physicist or a mathematician or a poet emerge in much the same way, through a collaborative process in which a preconscious ferment of ideas produces a hunch, or a connection, which is then examined and tested objectively by the instruments of logical intelligence. It is this imagination that is nurtured and developed in everyday clinical work. When we move from clinical practice to clinical research, this imagination becomes our most valuable instrument for the study of human problems.

The research which I have described today is the work of clinicians. If good and useful things have come out of this investigation, it is because of the extraordinary advantages that came to us through our clinical experience and training. Even our prehension study, which brought all of us into an area far removed from our clinical experience, became the unexpected beneficiary of this clinical experience. What we brought from the clinic were eyes trained for subtleties in movement patterns; we watch hands, body postures, faces with the same kind of attention that we use in listening. Since the blind baby's hands were going to tell us a story, we developed hand watching as a specialty in the research, where it was only a kind of subspecialty in our usual clinical work. Then, in the way in which one thing leads to another in clinical research, the same clinical attention which was focused on hands was brought to bear upon other forms of motility, the trunk and head, for example. When we had analyzed these movement patterns in a group of normal blind infants, we found a scattered number of motility patterns that we will never see in normal sighted babies. Then we had the key to the so-called blindisms. We now know how they emerge, how they become stereotyped and how to undo them in the early years. But this story must wait for another time.

In the end, this study by clinicians of the development of blind infants gave us the answers to the questions that were raised at the beginning of the study, eight years ago in New Orleans. Since these were clinical problems we can test the validity of these findings in the clinic. If we have correctly identified the unique adaptive problems for the blind infant we should be able to translate our findings into methods of facilitating adaptive solutions for blind infants and young children.

The final stage of this research is application; which brings us back full circle. The clinical researcher is back in the kitchen—although, in a certain sense, he never left the kitchen. The research I have described is a kind of kitchen research, close to the source of supply, inventing with the materials on hand. It is plain in its design and functional. But then, science is not the practice of sacred arts. If we love science we can love it for its commonness, its everyday presence in the form of observing, questioning, examining—its everyday practice in our clinical work.

It was my husband who gave me the last line of this essay and the title. He paraphrased a line from Whitman. "Where is the muse? The muse is in the kitchen. . . ."

### REFERENCES

Fraiberg, S. Parallel and divergent patterns in blind and sighted infants. *Psychoanalytic study of the child.* (Vol. XXIII.) New York: International Universities Press, 1968.

Gouin-Decarie, T. *Intelligence and affectivity in early childhood.* New York: International Universities Press, 1965.

Hartmann. H. *Ego psychology and the problem of adaptation.* New York: International Universities Press, 1958.

Piaget, J. *The construction of reality in the child.* New York: Basic Books, Inc., 1954.

*Chapter 23*

# LIFESTYLE, CONDITIONS OF LIFE, AND HEALTH CARE IN URBAN AND SUBURBAN AREAS

**Henry Wechsler
Nell H. Gottlieb
Harold W. Demone, Jr.**

Proposals to reduce morbidity and mortality have been traditionally directed at the health care delivery system. Such approaches as restructuring the system, improving access to it, and increasing the supply, quality, and distribution of manpower have been suggested.[1] Government health policies reflecting these approaches have included the development of financing mechanisms (Medicaid and Medicare), neighborhood health centers, health maintenance organizations, area health education centers, and the National Health Service Corps.

Evidence regarding use of ambulatory health care services indicates that access is becoming more equitable. In contrast to the early 1930s when low-income people were seeing a physician half as often as high-income people, in 1976 people of low income were seeing physicians slightly more often than those of high income.[2]

More recently, attention has been directed to nonhealth service determinants of health status.[1,3,4] Health workers have begun to focus on individual behavior patterns, or "life-style," as major determinants of health status.[4-6] Exercise, diet and nutrition, smoking, use of alcohol and drugs, and stress are key components of this lifestyle approach.

Others have pointed out the importance to health of social, environmental, and economic factors.[7-10] The long-observed inverse relationship between morbidity and mortality and social class still remains, but it may be weakening with increased access to services and higher living standards.[7,11,12]

The determination of the relative contribution of these factors —access to care, preventive health behaviors, as well as socioeconomic and environmental differences—to health status has profound implications for decisions concerning health policy.

We examined the preceding variables from data collected in a survey of social needs of persons residing in different areas of Greater Boston. In Boston, as in other communities, geography is generally related to socioeconomic status, the latter rising progressively from the core city to the outer suburbs.[13] In addition, in a previous study higher mortality rates were seen for two mental health catchment areas in the core city of Boston.[14] We expected residents of the areas from Boston's core city to its outer suburbs to differ in reported health status, and we wished to compare the use of health services, lifestyle health habits, and everyday problems and concerns.

## METHODS

Data had been obtained through a comprehensive household survey in the Boston standard metropolitan statistical area (SMSA) conducted in late 1975 by the United Community Planning Corporation and the Combined Jewish Philanthropies. The survey employed an area probability sample designed to reflect the current population characteristics, attitudes, and needs of the Greater Boston community. The final sample included 1,043 randomly selected respondents (age 18 years or older) in 52 cities and towns.

We classified respondents according to their residence in one of four areas: (1) the core city, comprised of two mental health catchment areas that had been noted previously to have higher mortality rates than the rest of the city,[14] (2) the remainder of the city, (3) suburbs within the city's circumferential highway, and (4) suburbs outside this belt highway. For convenience, these areas are designated as the core city, other Boston, the inner suburbs, and the outer suburbs. We examined total population differences among the four groups, which were similar in age and sex composition.

## FINDINGS

SOCIAL AND ECONOMIC CHARACTERISTICS. For all social and economic variables examined, there were statistically significant differences ($P < .001$) among the four groups of respondents. As shown in Table 1, the core city and outer suburban respondents—almost without exception—were at opposite extremes on each indicator studied, and the proportions of respondents in each category decreased monotonically with increasing distance from the core city. The core city had the highest proportions of persons who did not complete high school; who were in semiskilled, service, and unskilled occupations; whose family incomes were less than $5,000; who were renters rather than home owners; and who were members of minority groups. These findings met our expectations that the geographic differences studied reflected major differences in socioeconomic conditions.

Table 1    Social and Economic Characteristics, by Place of Residence (Percentage of Respondents)[1]

| Characteristic | Core city | Other Boston | Inner suburbs | Outer suburbs |
|---|---|---|---|---|
| Education: less than high school graduate | 48.7 | 28.2 | 24.2 | 14.1 |
| Occupation: semiskilled, service, and unskilled | 52.6 | 35.6 | 27.5 | 22.7 |
| Occupation: neither respondent nor spouse of respondent is working[2] | 51.7 | 36.4 | 25.7 | 19.6 |
| Income: less than $5,000 | 47.6 | 27.8 | 14.6 | 11.5 |
| Low social class[3] | 51.4 | 33.0 | 26.9 | 19.9 |
| Rent home | 85.3 | 71.7 | 46.5 | 19.3 |
| Living in two-spouse household | 28.4 | 44.8 | 58.6 | 68.5 |
| Marital status: not married | 68.7 | 55.4 | 41.7 | 32.0 |
| Minority population | 58.6 | 24.1 | 3.1 | 4.2 |

[1] This table represents answers to 8 questions. With the exception of income, the numbers of respondents on which the percentages are based range from 111 to 116 in the core city, 200 to 214 in other Boston, 461 to 478 in the inner suburbs, and 226 to 235 in the outer suburbs. For income, the numbers of respondents were 103, 180, 411, and 208, respectively. Chi-square analyses revealed statistically significant differences ($P < .001$) for all variables.

[2] Includes unemployed, laid off, retired, students, keeping house, and those who have never worked.

[3] Hollingshead Social Class V (21).

HEALTH STATUS.   Among the four groups, perceptions of their health status—excellent, very good, good, or fair or poor—differed significantly ($P < .01$). Respondents from the core city were most likely to view their health as fair or poor (23 percent versus 17 percent in both the other Boston and inner suburbs groups and 8 percent of those in the outer suburbs).

USE OF HEALTH SERVICES.   The respondents were asked if a physician had been seen, if standard tests had been administered, and where medical care was obtained for themselves and their children. No statistically significant differences were seen among the groups on any of these measures of use of health services. In fact, although the differences were minimal, the core city residents were more likely—within the past year—to have had a consultation with a physician about their health (83 percent), a physical examination (66 percent), a blood pressure measurement (81 percent), a blood sample taken (71 percent), and a urine test (71 percent). Of the core city women, 83 percent had had a Pap test at least once, 67 percent within the past year.

Although use of health care services was basically the same, the four groups differed with regard to location of these services. Statistically significant differences beyond the .001 level were found among the groups concerning where they obtained medical care for themselves and for their children. Of the core city respondents, 45 percent went to a hospital clinic or emergency room, 18 percent used a neighborhood health center, and 26 percent used a physician's office. In contrast, half the other Boston respondents, 75 percent of those from the inner suburbs, and 82 percent from the outer suburbs used a physician's office. The same pattern of location of medical care was seen for the children of respondents, except for those in the core city who depended more on neighborhood health centers.

LIFESTYLE HEALTH HABITS.   Data were available on the four groups for each of four major areas of health habits—exercise, diet, smoking, and alcohol and drug use (Table 2).

For exercise, the difference in the proportion of respondents who reported participating in any physical activity was significant among all groups ($P < .05$), with the highest proportion in the outer suburbs group (69 percent). However, no differences were found among the groups on "very active during the day."

Table 2   Lifestyle Health Habits, by Place of Residence
(Percentage of Respondents)[1]

| Health habit | Core city | Other Boston | Inner suburbs | Outer suburbs | $x^2$ difference |
|---|---|---|---|---|---|
| Exercise: | | | | | |
| Very active during day | 43.9 | 43.6 | 43.8 | 50.2 | NS |
| Participates in physical activity(ies) | 59.6 | 57.3 | 58.5 | 69.3 | $P < .05$ |
| Weight: | | | | | |
| Weight is about right | 37.4 | 51.2 | 41.8 | 46.8 | NS |
| Would like to lose more than 15 pounds | 26.7 | 11.7 | 19.2 | 13.2 | $P < .001$ |
| Smokes cigarettes | 47.8 | 46.5 | 40.7 | 32.3 | $P < .01$ |
| Drinking behavior: | | | | | |
| Abstainer or infrequent drinker | 49.5 | 37.1 | 31.1 | 24.6 | $P < .001$ |
| Light or moderate | 25.2 | 38.1 | 47.8 | 50.7 | |
| Heavy | 25.2 | 24.8 | 21.1 | 24.7 | |
| Prescription drugs: | | | | | |
| Takes to relax | 15.7 | 14.6 | 16.2 | 11.2 | NS |
| Takes to sleep | 7.0 | 4.7 | 4.0 | 4.7 | NS |
| Takes amphetamines | 7.8 | 3.3 | 2.5 | 1.7 | $P < .02$ |

[1] This table represents answers to 10 questions. The numbers of respondents on which the percentages are based range from 107 to 116 in the core city, 202 to 213 in other Boston, 456 to 478 in the inner suburbs, and 219 to 235 in the outer suburbs.
NOTE:  NS indicates not significant.

We did not have specific weight and height information. However, we were able to ascertain whether respondents thought their weight was about right and, if not, the amount of weight they would like to lose. Although there was no statistically significant difference among the groups of respondents who reported their weight was about right, there was a significant difference ($P < .001$) in their desire to lose more than 15 pounds; 27 percent of the core city respondents expressed this desire compared with 13 percent of those in the outer suburbs.

The difference in cigarette smoking was significant among the groups ($P < .01$). The proportion of respondents who reported that they were cigarette smokers was highest within the city (close to half of both core city and other Boston respondents) and lowest in the outer suburbs group (less than one-third).

Based on responses to two general questions concerning alcohol use, respondents were classified by drinking behavior.[15] This classification resulted in a significant difference $(P < .001)$ among the groups. Although the proportions classified as heavy drinkers were basically similar for the four groups, core city respondents had the highest proportion of abstainers and infrequent drinkers (50 percent); the proportion decreased with increasing distance from the core city. The four areas showed the opposite trend for the proportion of light and moderate drinkers.

Three questions in the survey concerned the use of prescription drugs. Only for amphetamines was there a significant difference among the four groups $(P < .02)$; the core city respondents were most likely to report the use of this substance and the outer suburbs group the least.

LIFE PROBLEMS AND CONCERNS.   Although we could not measure stress directly in this study, we could measure one aspect of stress that might differ among residents of different geographic and social areas —that which is associated with social and neighborhood problems.

Compared with other respondents, a higher proportion of those

Table 3   Problems Encountered In the Past Year, by
Place of Residence (Percentage of Respondents)[1]

| Problem | Core city | Other Boston | Inner suburbs | Outer suburbs | $\chi^2$ difference |
|---|---|---|---|---|---|
| Within household: | | | | | |
| Money | 32.8 | 19.4 | 11.6 | 7.7 | $P < .001$ |
| Need for home nurse | 10.4 | 3.3 | 4.0 | 3.0 | $P < .01$ |
| Job | 30.2 | 24.5 | 19.1 | 18.7 | $P < .05$ |
| Personal, family, or marriage | 26.5 | 21.1 | 15.4 | 14.9 | $P < .02$ |
| Home uncared for during illness | 12.1 | 7.1 | 6.1 | 3.4 | $P < .02$ |
| Child | 27.7 | 16.3 | 20.3 | 25.8 | NS |
| Other: | | | | | |
| Drinking by close relative or friend | 19.3 | 13.7 | 12.5 | 10.6 | NS |
| Elderly relative living independently | 14.7 | 13.1 | 10.3 | 14.5 | NS |

[1] This table represents answers to 8 questions. With the exception of child problems, the numbers of respondents on which the percentages are based range from 113 to 116 in the core city, 211 to 214 in other Boston, 473 to 477 in the inner suburbs, and 234 to 235 in the outer suburbs. For problems with children, the numbers of respondents were 47, 49, 143, and 89, respectively.
NOTE: NS indicates not significant.

in the core city reported problems in each of eight problem areas examined (Table 3), and significant differences were found among the groups for five of these areas. Other analyses indicated that 69 percent of core city respondents reported problems in at least one area, whereas slightly more than half of all other respondent groups reported none; this difference was significant ($P < .001$). Among the core city respondents who reported at least one problem, the majority (60 percent) reported more than one.

Respondents' concerns about selected neighborhood conditions are summarized in Table 4. Significant differences ($P < .01$) among all groups were found for eight concerns and for a composite index of community satisfaction. In almost all instances, the respondents in the core city showed the greatest number of concerns; as distance from the inner city increased, the number decreased.

When asked to rate their overall satisfaction with their neighborhood as very, fairly, or not very satisfied, core city residents were less satisfied than other groups: 28 percent were not very satisfied compared with 18 percent of other Boston, 7 percent of the inner suburbs, and 3 percent of outer suburbs respondents. Conversely, the proportion who were very satisfied ranged from 71 percent of outer

Table 4   Mean Level of Concern[1]
About Neighborhood Conditions[2]

| Condition | Total sample | Core city | Other Boston | Inner suburbs | Outer suburbs | Analysis of variance: all groups |
|---|---|---|---|---|---|---|
| Crime rate | 5.09 | 2.86 | 4.30 | 5.69 | 5.76 | $P < .01$ |
| Cost of housing | 5.32 | 5.22 | 5.20 | 5.40 | 5.30 | NS |
| Air cleanliness | 5.72 | 3.96 | 4.08 | 6.00 | 7.47 | $P < .01$ |
| Street cleanliness | 6.01 | 3.54 | 4.53 | 6.52 | 7.53 | $P < .01$ |
| Public schools | 6.19 | 4.15 | 3.75 | 6.96 | 7.23 | $P < .01$ |
| Proximity of playgrounds and parks | 6.29 | 5.35 | 5.02 | 6.84 | 6.72 | $P < .01$ |
| How neighbors keep property | 7.09 | 5.01 | 6.45 | 7.36 | 8.14 | $P < .01$ |
| Convenience to work | 7.53 | 7.43 | 7.04 | 7.74 | 7.56 | NS |
| Convenience to shopping | 7.64 | 6.39 | 7.35 | 8.14 | 7.50 | $P < .01$ |
| Size of home | 7.70 | 6.89 | 7.34 | 7.91 | 8.00 | $P < .01$ |
| Composite community satisfaction | N.A. | 5.03 | 5.64 | 6.88 | 7.20 | $P < .01$ |

[1] The scale ranged from 1 ("don't like it at all") to 10 ("exactly as I like it").
[2] This table represents answers to 10 questions. The numbers of respondents range from 72 to 115 in the core city, 102 to 212 in other Boston, 303 to 474 in the inner suburbs, and 160 to 233 in the outer suburbs. Low numbers are for questions that exclude cohorts from responding (for example, public schools and convenience to work).
NOTE: N.A. indicates not applicable; NS indicates not significant.

suburbs respondents to 56 percent of inner suburbs, 41 percent of other Boston, and 26 percent of the respondents in the core city. This difference was significant ($P < .001$).

## DISCUSSION

This study provided an opportunity to examine the association of use of the health care system, lifestyle health behaviors, and socioeconomic factors with health status reported by residents of the Greater Boston SMSA.

Use of health services was similar among respondents from each of the four areas in the Greater Boston SMSA. Although not significantly different, respondents from the core city were the most likely to have used these services within the past year; yet, they were significantly more likely to report fair or poor health.

While patterns of use did not differ, sites of care did. The dependence of the inner-city population upon hospitals and health centers (which are available only in the city) for their care, as documented in this study, must be an important consideration in the formulation of health policy. This dependence requires health planners and administrators to examine how best to guarantee the continuation of these institutions or to provide acceptable substitutes.

In terms of the health habits that we examined, the findings suggest that respondents from the outer suburbs in certain respects have adopted healthier lifestyles than the respondents from the other areas. For example, of the four groups of respondents, outer suburbs residents were the least likely to report that they smoked cigarettes, the most likely to report participation in physical activity, and the least likely to take prescription drugs to relax or to take amphetamines. They were also not likely to wish to lose more than 15 pounds.

Although the lifestyle findings are presented by place of residence, they should also be viewed within the context of the social and economic differences among the groups of respondents. Our study replicated previous studies relating drinking behavior to social class,[16] smoking to education and social class,[17] and obesity to social class.[18] The difference noted with respect to exercise may reflect a greater opportunity and more facilities for exercise in the outer suburbs.

Overall, however, the differences among the groups in lifestyle health habits were not dramatic. Nonetheless, the potential for health improvement across all groups through healthful lifestyles should not be overlooked, since it is possible that health interventions might be better directed at behavioral factors than at health care. Further research in this area is needed.

The most notable differences among the core city, the rest of Boston, and the suburban areas were in the respondents' social and economic characteristics, problems, and concerns about one's neighborhood. These differences no doubt represent a realistic assessment by respondents of their situations. However, this study did not establish a causal line between these characteristics and the excess mortality for the inner city reported in another study[14]: it leaves unresolved the choice between the two alternative epidemiologic explanations of the findings—"drift" versus "social causation." Do people live in the core city because they have social problems and illness, or do they have these problems as a result of living there? However, whether or not the social problems cause stress, they are characteristic of populations residing in the core city.

One should note that our findings with regard to place of residence assume a constant age and sex differential across the responses to each question. Although our data did not show age and sex differences across the four geographic areas, such differences may exist with respect to specific questions.

It is clear from this study that strategies to improve health are different for various geographic and social subgroups within a metropolitan area. In particular, health status in the core city may be improved by dealing with nonhealth systems such as employment, housing, and social supports. One report of a study that links increases in unemployment with mortality notes, "Advances in the economic system have historically been the most important sources of improved health status both on international and national levels"[19]. Obviously, potential health consequences should be considered in the formulation of social and economic policy. Government officials, physicians, and other health care providers must consider the pressing need for greater investments in improving the social, environmental, and economic conditions that affect health.[20] These factors demand a higher priority than more dollars for more medical care if concerned health workers hope to alleviate the pressing problems that beset so many residents in the core city and other areas with similar characteristics. These and other differences must be taken into account by local boards of health and health planning agencies if they wish to develop effective programs for their various constituencies.

## SUMMARY

The association among social and economic characteristics, use of the health care system, health habits, life problems, and reported health status were examined in a survey of Greater Boston area residents. The respondents were classified according to their residence in the core city, the remainder of the city, the inner suburbs, or the outer suburban areas.

For all social and economic variables studied, significant differences among the four subgroups increased with increasing distance from the inner city, where respondents were most likely to be of lower socioeconomic status. No statistically significant differences were found with regard to use of health services, although the places where medical care was obtained differed. In terms of health habits, the findings suggest that outer suburban respondents exhibit somewhat healthier life styles, particularly with respect to smoking cigarettes and exercising. Respondents in the core city reported significantly more problems encountered, the greatest concern with their neighborhoods, and the least satisfaction with their neighborhoods. They were also most likely to report poorer health.

As to the relationship between the findings and health policy, strategies to improve health must be different for various geographic and social subgroups within a metropolitan area. Social, economic, and environmental conditions demand a higher priority than more dollars for medical care if the pressing problems of residents in the core city are to be alleviated. Health planners and government agencies must take these factors into account if they are to develop effective programs for their particular constituencies.

## REFERENCES

1. Lerner, M.: The non-health services' determinants of health levels: Conceptualization and public policy recommendations. Med Care 15: 74–83 (1977).

2. Aday, L. A., and Andersen, R.: Fostering access to medical care. *In* Health services: The local perspectives, edited by A. Levin. Proc Acad Pol Sci 32: 29–41 (1977).

3. Fuchs, V.: Who shall live? Basic Books, New York, 1974.

4. Lalonde, M.: A new perspective on the health of Canadians; a working document. Government of Canada, Ottawa, April 1974.

5. Belloc, N. B., and Breslow, L.: Relationships of physical health status and health practices. Prev Med 1: 409–421 (1972).

6. Knowles, J. H.: The responsibility of the individual. Daedalus 106: 45–80 (1977).

7. Antonovsky, A.: Social class, life expectancy and overall mortality. Milbank Mem Fund Q 45: 31–73 (1967).

8. Navarro, V.: The underdevelopment of health of working America: Causes, consequences and possible solutions. Am J Public Health 66: 538–546 (1976).

9. Newberger, E. H., Newberger, C. M., and Richmond, J. B.: Child health in America: Toward a rational public policy. Milbank Mem Fund Q 54: 249–289 (1976).

10. Jenkins, C. D.: Recent evidence supporting psychologic and social risk factors for coronary disease. N Engl J Med 294: 987–994 (pt. I), 1033–1038 (pt. II) (1976).

11. Kitagawa, E. M., and Hauser, P. M.: Differential mortality in the United States: A study in socioeconomic epidemiology. Harvard University Press, Cambridge, Mass.: 1973.

12. Syme, S. L., and Berkman, L. F.: Social class, susceptibility and sickness. Am J Epidemiol 104: 1–8 (1976).

13. Taeuber, K. E., and Taeuber, A. F.: White migration and socio-economic differences between cities and suburbs. Am Sociol Rev 29: 718–729 (1964).

14. Jenkins, C. D., Tuthill, R. W., Tannenbaum, S. I., and Kirby, C. R.: Zones of excess mortality in Massachusetts. N Engl J Med 296: 1354–1356 (1977).

15. Wechsler, H., Demone, H. W., Jr., and Gottlieb, N.: Drinking patterns of Greater Boston adults: Subgroup differences on the QFV index. J Stud Alcohol 39: 1158–1165 (1978).

16. Cahalan, D., Cisin, I. H., and Crossley, H. M.: American drinking practices: A national study of drinking behavior and attitudes. Rutgers Center of Alcohol Studies, New Brunswick, N.J., monograph No. 6, 1969.

17. American Cancer Society, Inc.: Adult use of tobacco—1975. Appendix to: Task Force on Tobacco and Cancer: Report to the Board of Directors. New York, 1976.

18. U.S. Department of Health, Education, and Welfare: Health, United States, 1975. DHEW Publication No. (HRA) 76-1232. U.S. Government Printing Office, Washington, D.C., 1976, pp. 448–449.

19. Brenner, M. H., cited in Evan, T. E.: Unemployment and health JAMA 237: 1965 (1977).

20.  Morse, A. E., Hyde, J. N., Jr., Newberger, E. H., and Reed, R. B.: Environmental correlates of pediatric social illness: Preventive implications of an advocacy approach. Am J Public Health 67: 612–615 (1977).

21.  Hollingshead, A. B.: Two-factor index of social position. Yale University, New Haven, Conn., 1957. Mimeographed.

*Chapter 24*

# COMMITMENT TO COMMUNITY MENTAL HEALTH AFTERCARE SERVICES

## Staffing and Structural Implications

## Allen Rubin

Recent reductions in state hospital populations have strained the capacity of community mental health centers to provide sufficient and effective aftercare services to the growing number of expatients who now reside in the community. Trends toward increased deinstitutionalization patterns have stimulated much controversy. One argument holds that insufficient resources exist to maintain adequately the large number of patients being discharged, and that many of these patients may receive better care in state hospitals. A conflicting view maintains that community agencies, including community mental health centers, have assigned insufficient priority to aftercare services and have therefore inadequately carried out their mandate in this area. Without advocating either of the above positions, community mental health centers may want to examine critically their efforts in aftercare and seek ways to improve their performance in it.

Hogarty (1971) and Zolik and Boyd (1972) have suggested that a partial explanation for the inadequacy of aftercare services may be found in the negative attitudes of mental health practitioners toward aftercare services or expatients. In contrast to more esoteric roles in psychotherapy or consultation, the provision of aftercare services may appear to be unimportant or unattractive to highly professionalized practitioners. Aftercare work tends to involve less lofty goals, less articulate or motivated clients, and a less sophisticated technology than do other mental health interventions. For example, current aftercare wisdom, as exemplified by Silverstein (1968), Glasscote (1969), Schwartz and Schwartz (1964), and Meyer and Borgotta (1959) recommends that aftercare workers should closely monitor medication maintenance, deemphasize verbalization and psychodynamics, aggressively reach out to motivate patients to utilize services, help patients secure suitable housing and finances, and facilitate patient resocialization in such basic living skills as personal hygiene and household management.

The contrast between concrete aftercare services and their clientele and other community mental health services and clients may be particularly problematic when aftercare services are delivered by highly professionalized practitioners in multipurpose units, since the interests of professionals are likely to be more consistent with other service options than with aftercare services. Practitioners may too often be prone toward viewing concrete aftercare services as superficial, and their resistance to such services may be rationalized in terms of the low potential of expatients to achieve meaningful psychosocial improvement. In such situations, practitioner commitment to aftercare services may be precarious. If so, this is likely to have a deleterious impact on the quantity and quality of aftercare services that these practitioners provide.

In the context of the above analysis, it is reasonable to ask whether community mental health aftercare services may be staffed or structured in such a way as to enhance practitioner commitment to aftercare. Three specific questions are implied, as follows:

1. Should aftercare services be delivered primarily by practitioners who have had little or no experience in the practice of psychotherapy?
2. Should aftercare services be delivered primarily by practitioners who have lower levels of professionalization?
3. Should aftercare services be delivered primarily by practitioners who specialize in aftercare and who are assigned to specialized aftercare units?

The following survey attempts to answer these questions.

## METHODOLOGY

A survey was conducted in the spring of 1975 to assess practitioner ratings of the importance of selected aftercare service recommendations and the capabilities of deinstitutionalized patients for improvement. The Aftercare Treatment Inventory was constructed to measure these views. By and large, only those recommendations of the literature on aftercare that contrast markedly with more esoteric forms of treatment for less impaired populations were selected for the inventory. The selected dimensions included persistent outreach to present and prospective clients, provision of concrete services, deemphasis of psychodynamics, optimism about patient capabilities, directiveness, and advocacy. Rubin (1976) presents a more detailed report of the development of the inventory, its acceptable reliability and validity, and internal analyses. A factor analysis identified four useful, distinct scales. The mean score on each of these scales constituted the dependent variables in this study. (Mean scores per respondent were computed so as to handle missing data on particular items.) The four scales were (1) general scale, (2) outreach scale, (3) psychodynamic scale, and (4) optimism scale. The general scale included 22 items, some of which appeared on the other scales, and some of which encompassed other dimensions involving concrete services, directiveness, and advocacy. The first three scales of the instrument covered a total of 27 items, each of which asked respondents for their views on how important it is that a specific service or practitioner behavior be included in aftercare treatment. Each item was followed by a 9-point rating scale of importance: (1) not at all, . . ., to (9) extremely. The 5-item optimism scale used a similar 9-point rating system, but asked how much improvement the respondent believed five categories of deinstitutionalized patients are capable of making. On all but the psychodynamic scale, higher responses were more consistent with the clinical recommendations discussed above. On the psychodynamic scale, however, lower importance ratings were more consistent with these recommendations. Therefore responses to psychodynamic scale items were scored in the reverse direction (10 minus the actual responses), so that higher scale scores would be more consistent with clinical recommendations for a deemphasis of psychodynamics. A sample of items in each scale is presented in Table 1.

The independent variables (for example, psychotherapy experience, professionalization, and aftercare specialization) in this study were assessed in a background questionnaire, which practitioners were instructed to complete before proceeding to the inventory. The questionnaire and inventory were mailed to each of the 361 mental health practitioners paid by county funds in the 11 community mental health centers of Allegheny County, Pennsylvania (which encompasses Pittsburgh and its suburbs). All returned instruments were coded, key punched, and electronically processed at the University of Pittsburgh.

## FINDINGS

Of the 361 surveyed practitioners, 192 (53%) returned appropriately completed instruments. Each of the major mental health professions was represented in the respondent group. The respondent

Table 1   Exemplary Items on Each of the Four Scales of
the Aftercare Treatment Inventory

| Scale | Exemplary items | Importance | | |
|---|---|---|---|---|
| | | Not at all | Moderately | Extremely |
| General | 2. Help patients secure employment | | | |
| | 17. Develop worker-patient rapport before state hospital discharge | | | |
| | 27. Give advice to patients about important decisions | 1 | 5 | 9 |
| Outreach | 11. See patients outside of an office setting . . . | | | |
| | 16. Always make more than one home visit to patients who continue to refuse to come to the clinic | 1 | 5 | 9 |
| Psycho-dynamic | 1. Understand in depth the patient's intrapsychic dynamics | | | |
| | 5. Be well trained in psychotherapeutic techniques | 1 | 5 | 9 |
| | | Capability for Improvement | | |
| | | Very little | Moderate | Extreme |
| Optimism | 28. Most patients discharged from state hospitals | | | |
| | 32. Most patients who were hospitalized for 10 years or longer | 1 | 5 | 9 |

group also reflected diversity in aftercare specialization in psychotherapeutic experience.

## Experience in Psychotherapy and Aftercare Views

Table 2 displays the Pearson product moment correlations between amount of experience in psychotherapy and mean scores on the aftercare scales. Table 3 shows the mean scale scores of those respondents with no experience in psychotherapy and those with some. Experience as a psychotherapist appears to be related to aftercare views. This is suggested by the negative correlations found with general scale scores ($p \leq .001$) and the significant $t$-test differences between scores of respondents in the some experience and no experience groups on the general scale ($p \leq .02$) and the outreach scale ($p \leq .01$). This indicates that respondents with more psychotherapeutic experience tended to assign less importance to the general aftercare recommendations in the scales. Although these correlations were small in terms of the extent to which variations in psychotherapy experience predict variations in aftercare views, the fact that significant relationships were found in the $t$ test as well as the correlational data would seem to suggest an inverse relationship between psychotherapy experience and the importance assigned to the selected aftercare recommendations.

Table 2   Correlations Between Each of Five Predictor
Variables and Mean Scores on Each of Four Aftercare Scales

| | Scale | | | |
|---|---|---|---|---|
| Predictor variable | General | Outreach | Psychodynamic | Optimism |
| Months of Psycho- | −.30*** | −.14 | −.05 | −.00 |
| therapy Experience | (n = 187) | (n = 187) | (n = 187) | (n = 177) |
| Highest Educational | −.19** | −.27*** | −.07 | −.04 |
| Degree Earned | (n = 185) | (n = 185) | (n = 185) | (n = 176) |
| Unit Aftercare | .04 | .15* | −.11 | .25*** |
| Percentage | (n = 164) | (n = 164) | (n = 164) | (n = 159) |
| Caseload Aftercare | .14 | .28*** | −.04 | .18* |
| Percentage | (n = 153) | (n = 153) | (n = 152) | (n = 148) |
| Work Time Aftercare | .07 | .19* | .11 | .14 |
| Percentage | (n = 153) | (n = 153) | (n = 152) | (n = 148) |

*$p \leq .05$
**$p \leq .01$
***$p \leq .001$

## Professional Affiliation and Aftercare Views

The relationship between professional affiliation and mean after-care scale scores was examined in an analysis of variance. As displayed in Table 4, significant differences between the professional groups were found on the general and outreach scale ($p \leq .025$). Administrators and aides had the highest mean group scores on the above two scales, whereas psychiatrists and psychologists had the lowest. Using the Scheffé multiple comparisons method, the scores of administrators and aids were significantly higher than the scores of psychiatrists and psychologists on the general scale ($p \leq .001$) and the outreach scale ($p \leq .05$). Thus administrators and aides assigned the most importance to the selected recommendations, whereas psychiatrists and psychologists assigned the least importance to them. This is rather intriguing, since the occupational status of administrators would seem to be high, whereas that of aides is generally consid-

Table 3  Mean Scores on Each of Four Aftercare Scales Among Respondents With and Without Experience in Psychotherapy

| Amount of experience | Scale | | | |
|---|---|---|---|---|
| | General | Outreach | Psychodynamic | Optimism |
| None (n = 50) | 6.48 | 6.65 | 4.22 | 4.35 |
| Some (n = 139) | 6.03 | 6.00 | 3.98 | 4.38 |
| t | 2.46* | 2.67** | 1.38 | −0.15 |

$*p \leqslant .02$
$**p \leqslant .01$

Table 4  Mean Scores of Each of Seven Professions on Each of Four Aftercare Scales

| Profession | Scale | | | |
|---|---|---|---|---|
| | General | Outreach | Psychodynamic | Optimism |
| Psychiatrists (n = 11) | 5.4 | 5.6 | 4.2 | 3.9 |
| Psychologists (n = 22) | 5.4 | 5.2 | 4.1˙ | 4.0 |
| Social Workers (n = 59) | 6.1 | 6.1 | 4.1 | 4.3 |
| Nurses (n = 13) | 6.3 | 6.6 | 4.1 | 5.1 |
| Administrators (n = 26) | 6.8 | 6.7 | 4.3 | 5.0 |
| Counselors (n = 21) | 6.0 | 5.8 | 3.7 | 4.3 |
| Aides (n = 9) | 6.7 | 7.2 | 3.9 | 4.6 |
| F | 2.44* | 2.48* | .45 | 1.58 |

$*p \leqslant .025$

Table 5   First-Order Partial Correlations Between Mean Scores
on Each of Four Aftercare Scales and Months of Psychotherapy
Experience (Controlling for Highest Educational Degree Earned)
and Highest Educational Degree Earned (Controlling for
Months of Psychotherpy Experience)

| Independent and control variables | Scale | | | / |
| --- | --- | --- | --- | --- |
| | General | Outreach | Psychodynamic | Optimism |
| Months of Psychotherapy Experience (Controlling Highest Educational Degree Earned) | −.26* (n = 184) | −.07 (n = 184) | −.07 (n = 184) | .01 (n = 175) |
| Highest Educational Degree Earned (Controlling for Months of Psychotherapy Experience) | −.11 (n = 184) | −.24* (n = 184) | .09 (n = 184) | .04 (n = 175) |

*$p \leqslant .001$

ered to be low. It is conceivable that the high scores of administrators can be attributed to their close involvement with current policy trends in deinstitutionalization. Also plausible, however, is the explanation that the professions which do little or no psychotherapy (aides and administrators) had the highest scores, whereas those that are most associated with a psychotherapeutic technology (psychiatrists and psychologists) had the lowest scores.

## Educational Level and Aftercare Views

As is shown in Table 2, highest degree earned was negatively correlated with mean general scale scores ($p \leq .01$) and mean outreach scale score ($p \leq .001$). Thus respondents with higher earned educational degrees tended to assign lower importance to the selected aftercare recommendations. (The assigned order of degrees, from highest to lowest, was (1) M.D. or Ph.D.; (2) master's degree; (3) baccalaureate degree; (4) nursing diploma; (5) associate degree, and (6) high school or lower.)

The correlation between months of psychotherapy experience and educational degree was .29 ($p \leq .01$). Therefore first-order partial correlations were computed in order to determine whether the relationship found between psychotherapy experience and scale scores could be explained by the possibility that the experienced psychotherapists may be the more highly educated. These partial correlations are displayed in Table 5. When highest degree earned is controlled, the negative correlation between psychotherapy experience and mean general scale scores remains significantly different from zero. When psychotherapy experience is controlled, the correlation between highest degree earned and mean general scale scores no longer significantly differs from zero, whereas the correlation on the outreach scale still does. Thus the relationship between psychotherapy experience and aftercare views does not appear to be explained by educational level. The relationship between educational level and aftercare views appears to involve primarily outreach and to be largely explained by differential psychotherapy experience with regard to the general scale.

## Aftercare Specialization and Aftercare Views

Pearson product-moment correlations were computed between each of the three measures of aftercare specialization and mean aftercare scale scores. Table 2 shows that specialization in aftercare appears to be related to scores on the outreach and optimism scales. Unit aftercare percentage and caseload aftercare percentage each had positive correlations that significantly differed from zero on each of the above two scales. Work-time aftercare percentage had a significant positive correlation with outreach scale scores and a near-significant positive correlation with optimism scale scores. The above data suggest that respondents who do more aftercare work or who work in units that do the same tend to assign more importance to outreach and express more optimism regarding aftercare.

To separate aftercare specialists from nonspecialists, each of the above three predictor variables was collapsed into specialized and nonspecialized categories. Analyses of variances were done on these categories, as displayed in Tables 6 through 8. Table 6 shows a significant association between the type of unit in which respondents work and their optimism about aftercare patients. In this analysis, specialized aftercare units were defined as those in which at least 90% of staff time is allocated to aftercare. Using the Scheffé multiple comparisons method, respondents who only work in specialized aftercare units had significantly higher optimism scale scores than did respondents in units that do not specialize in aftercare ($p \leq .025$). Tables 7 and 8 indicate that worker specialization in aftercare is associated with outreach scale scores. In these analyses, aftercare specialists were defined as respondents who report that at least 85% of their caseloads or work time is accounted for by aftercare. In each of these analyses the Scheffé multiple comparisons method found

that the outreach scale scores of aftercare specialists were significantly higher than the outreach scale scores of respondents who do
some aftercare, but who do not specialize in it ($p \leq .025$).

Each of the above measures of specialization was negatively
correlated with highest educational degree earned ($p \leq .0010$. This
suggested the possibility that the relationships found between aftercare specialization and outreach and optimism scale scores could be

Table 6    Mean Scale Scores of Each of Four Unit Types
on Each of Four Aftercare Scales

| | Scale | | | |
|---|---|---|---|---|
| Type of unit | General | Outreach | Psychodynamic | Optimism |
| 1. No Aftercare (n = 32) | 6.48 | 6.45 | 4.09 | 4.22 |
| 2. Some Aftercare (n = 110) | 5.98 | 5.83 | 4.08 | 4.27 |
| 3. Respondent in Specialized After-care Plus Another Unit(s) (n = 12) | 6.39 | 6.52 | 4.20 | 4.67 |
| 4. Specialized After-care Unit, Only (n = 14) | 6.32 | 6.56 | 3.87 | 5.39 |
| F | 1.82 | 2.27 | 0.20 | 3.61* |

*$p \leq .025$

Table 7    Mean Scores of Each of Three Levels of Case-Load
Aftercare Percentage on Each of Four Aftercare Scales

| | Scale | | | |
|---|---|---|---|---|
| Caseload aftercare percentage | General | Outreach | Psychodynamic | Optimism |
| 1. No Aftercare Cases (n = 44) | 5.88 | 5.99 | 4.03 | 4.39 |
| 2. Some Aftercare Cases (n = 86) | 6.00 | 5.83 | 3.98 | 4.20 |
| 3. Specialized After-care Caseloads (n = 23) | 6.42 | 6.93 | 4.06 | 4.89 |
| F | .97 | 3.17* | .16 | 1.69 |

*$p \leq .025$

explained by the fact that the more highly educated respondents tended to do less aftercare work. Therefore first-order partial correlations were computed between aftercare specialization and aftercare scale scores, controlling for highest educational degree earned. These partial correlations are displayed in Table 9. When highest degree earned is controlled, unit aftercare percentage is still significantly correlated with optimism scale scores ($p \leq .001$), but not with outreach scale scores; caseload aftercare percentage is still significantly correlated with outreach scale scores ($p \leq .01$) and optimism scale scores ($p \leq .05$); and work time aftercare percentage is still significantly correlated with outreach scale scores ($p \leq .05$). By and

Table 8   Mean Scores of Each of Three Levels of Work Time Aftercare Percentage on Each of Four Aftercare Scales

| Work time aftercare percentage | Scale | | | |
|---|---|---|---|---|
| | General | Outreach | Pstchodynamic | Optimism |
| 1. No Aftercare (n = 47) | 6.30 | 6.39 | 4.07 | 4.29 |
| 2. Some Aftercare (n = 110) | 6.06 | 5.91 | 4.04 | 4.30 |
| 3. Aftercare Specialists (n = 19) | 6.42 | 6.95 | 3.98 | 4.81 |
| F | .90 | 3.96* | .03 | 1.26 |

*$p \leq .025$

Table 9   First-Order Partial Correlations Between Each of Three Measures of Aftercare Specialization and Mean Scores on Each of Four Aftercare Scales, Controlling for Highest Educational Degree Earned

| Measure of aftercare specialization | Scale | | | |
|---|---|---|---|---|
| | General | Outreach | Psychodynamic | Optimism |
| Unit Aftercare Percentage | −.01 (n = 163) | .09 (n = 163) | −.10 (n = 163) | .25*** (n = 158) |
| Caseload Aftercare Percentage | .09 (n = 152) | .21** (n = 152) | −.02 (n = 152) | .18* (n = 147) |
| Work Time Aftercare Percentage | .04 (n = 152) | .18* (n = 152) | .07 (n = 152) | .12 (n = 147) |

*$p \leq .05$
**$p \leq .01$
***$p \leq .001$

large, then, the relationships found between aftercare specialization and outreach or optimism scale scores tended also to be found among given educational levels. This means that the fact that the more highly educated respondents may tend to do less aftercare work does not explain the relationship found between aftercare specialization and aftercare scale scores. Months of psychotherapy experience did not correlate with any of the three measures of aftercare specialization. Consequently, it would appear that specialization in aftercare is related to views about aftercare—with workers in units that do more aftercare appearing to be more optimistic and with workers who do more aftercare assigning more importance to outreach.

## IMPLICATIONS FOR STAFFING AND STRUCTURING AFTERCARE SERVICES

The above findings tend to imply an affirmative answer to each of the questions examined in this study; that is, community mental health aftercare services should be delivered primarily by practitioners who have had little or no experience in psychotherapy, who have lower levels of professionalization, and who are assigned to specialized aftercare units in which they can maintain a predominant focus on aftercare work. However, the above implications are valid only in the context of the following assumptions:

1.  That program developers want an aftercare program that is characterized by emphasis on persistent outreach, concrete services, deemphasis of psychodynamics, directiveness, advocacy, and practitioner optimism.
2.  That the above emphases are important attributes of effective aftercare services.
3.  That the views of practitioners accurately predict their actual clinical behavior.

The findings of this study have attendant implications for reducing the costs of aftercare programs by staffing them with practitioners who command relatively low salaries. In so doing, the ability of centers to meet present demands for more aftercare services would be enhanced. By staffing aftercare programs with practitioners who are less professionalized and less experienced in psychotherapy, there may be less disparity between what practitioners prefer to do and what deinstitutionalized patients need. Under such a set up, aftercare services are likely to appear less superficial to the practitioners who are responsible for delivering them, and deinstitutionalized patients are likely to be perceived with less pessimism by practitioners to whom they are assigned. Moreover, by assigning these practitioners to units that specialize exclusively in aftercare, and by restricting their caseload assignments to deinstitutionalized patients, there may be less likelihood that their commitment to aftercare services will be impeded by preferences for more prestigious or attractive interventions or clients. A related tenet of organizational theory holds that commitment by personnel to formal organizational goals is often impeded by competing identifications with previously learned technologies, professional reference groups, and subunits within the organization. This study has examined how such organizational phenomena may impact on commitment to aftercare services. It has found that community mental health centers may be able to increase commitment to aftercare by developing staffing and structural patterns that tend to decrease the prevalence of competing latent identities among practitioners who deliver aftercare services.

## REFERENCES

Glasscote, R. M. *Rehabilitating the mentally ill in the community.* Washington, D.C.: The Joint Information Service of the American Psychiatric Association and the National Association for Mental Health, 1969.

Hogarty, G. E. The plight of schizophrenics in modern treatment programs. *Hospital and Community Psychiatry,* 1971, *22,* 197–203.

Meyer, H., & Borgotta, E. F. *An experiment in mental patient rehabilitation: Evaluating a social agency program.* New York: Russell Sage Foundation, 1959.

Rubin, A. *Perspectives on aftercare.* Dissertation, University of Pittsburgh, 1976.

Schwartz, M., & Schwartz, C. G. *Social approaches to mental patient care.* New York: Columbia University Press, 1964.

Silverstein, M. *Psychiatric aftercare.* Philadelphia: University of Pennsylvania Press, 1968.

Zolik, E. S., & Boyd, R. J. Attitudes toward patients and service delivery. *Proceedings of the Annual Convention of the American Psychological Association,* 1972, *7,* 797–798.

*Chapter 25*

# DISCUSSION OF THE SELECTED STUDIES

## Joseph M. Regan
## Helen Z. Reinherz

### FRAIBERG: THE MUSE IN THE KITCHEN (PART B)

The analysis of this portion of the study, which had grown from the single case study of one child, involves the complex task of sorting and tabulating of observational material that had to be placed in one of 400 categories, but had also to be recorded chronologically, so that the sequence and connection of one behavior with another could be understood.

This section of the study (Part B) also shows additional and appropriate concern with issues of reliability and validity. It should be noted that *two* observers were deployed for the complicated observation and recording sessions with each child. As a further safeguard of the validity of the study's method, the author emphasizes the use of highly trained clinicians as the major means of insuring that there is accuracy and freedom from bias in data-gathering. Here the skilled clinical observer, a nonstatistical tool, is presented as the major weapon against threats to validity of findings.

Fraiberg's use of case illustrations, particularly that of Robbie and his garrulous mother, provides an enrichment to the reader's understanding of the data. The use of case examples (raw data) can provide additional insights in analysis both for the researcher and reader.

This study is notable in the era of the computer for its lack of reliance on computer analysis of its complex and extensive data. However, Fraiberg was seeking to use clinical imagination and experience for all phases of the study believing that the associative connections of the experienced therapist surpassed the power of the computer. Since her study was breaking new territory in understanding the development of blind infants as well as creating appropriate clinical intervention her approach was appropriate and highly productive of usable results.

## WECHSLER, GOTTLIEB, AND DEMONE: LIFESTYLE, CONDITIONS OF LIFE, AND HEALTH CARE IN URBAN AND SUBURBAN AREAS

This study illustrates the importance of a clearly developed problem statement and the choice of an appropriate methodology as a foundation for effective and efficient analysis and presentation of results. The study's focus is on such factors as socioeconomic status, life-style behaviors, and environmental issues as well as aspects of the health service delivery system as health determinants. The choice of data collected by a household survey using area probability sampling within the local standard metropolitan statistical area allows the study both to classify the respondents into four neighborhood areas with different social and demographic characteristics and to generalize the results obtained from its sample to the entire area population.

The study then presents its results within this framework. The four tables that are used allow the reader to appreciate visually the impact of the data's distribution. The tables also delineate what aspects of socioeconomic status, lifestyle, and neighborhood concerns were examined by the study as well as significant differences found in the four neighborhoods in socioeconomic status, problems encountered, and level of concern with neighborhood conditions.

The study reveals an economy in its use of statistical operations. The statistics are adequate to the study's needs of presentation and inference but do not needlessly go beyond these requirements. Percentages and means are used to describe the distributions of the data. Chi square and analysis of variance are employed to test differences between groups. Thus, statistical analysis is used to answer the questions posed by the authors and facilitate subsequent interpretation.

The discussion section of the study summarizes the results but it also puts certain aspects of the findings in perspective and highlights areas of special significance. Although lifestyle differences and their implications are discussed, the study underlines the areas of most notable difference, socioeconomic and environmental conditions. The discussion section also presents the limitations of the study. The authors state that their work here does not allow them to draw a causal link between these conditions and heightened mortality rates. However, there are clear implications for health care strategies. The impact of non-health systems particularly economic opportunity on health status in the core city is emphasized. Increased attention to these areas should be reflected in policy and planning priorities. In this manner, the analysis and interpretation of the study are logically connected to the problem from which it began and some important issues, often ignored in health policy and planning, are identified.

### RUBIN: COMMITMENT TO COMMUNITY MENTAL HEALTH AFTERCARE SERVICES: STAFFING AND STRUCTURAL IMPLICATIONS

The goal of this study is to provide empirical answers to three questions concerning the optimal structure and staffing patterns of aftercare services. This important component of deinstitutionalization has tended to remain poorly developed. Taking its cue from a review of the literature the study points out that certain negative practitioner attitudes may account for this underdevelopment. The analysis of the study's results is set up to determine the degree to which lower levels of experience with psychotherapy and of professionalization and higher levels of aftercare specialization are associated with more positive attitudes towards aftercare services.

An Aftercare Treatment Inventory, designed and tested by the author, attempted to measure the dependent variable, attitude towards aftercare. The four subscales of this instrument: the general scale, the outreach scale, the psychodynamic scale, and the optimism scale become the categories by which the operation of the independent variables, psychotherapy experience, professionalization, and specialization, are analyzed. The coherence of the problem formulation and the explicit structure of the study's methodology greatly assist its ability to organize its collected data.

Measures of association are most appropriate to the statistical needs of the study. Table 2, which presents correlations between the various predictor variables and aftercare mean scores, contains the data by which all three study questions are answered. The author uses the $t$-test and analysis of variance to test the significance of these relationships and to examine them in more detail. The use of partial correlation allows the study to analyze the unique impact of two closely related variables, educational level and experience in psychotherapy. The results discussed by the author are also presented to the reader in the study's tables. The reader may find additional information in the tables, however, that are not directly alluded to in the discussion. For example, readers of this volume may be interested particularly in the aftercare scores of social workers and how they compare with the other professions presented in Table 4.

On the basis of its analysis, the study concludes that all three of its major questions could be answered affirmatively. The delivery of aftercare services would be enhanced if they were staffed by persons with less experience in the practice of psychotherapy and not as highly professionally educated, and if such services were offered in specialized units. The study identifies certain benefits that might ensue. Reduced cost of aftercare services may facilitate agencies' ability to supply them. There might be less disparity in outlook between client and service provided. Last, the aftercare clinician in specialized units may have a more consistent professional identification. It should be noted that the author states his conclusions with a note of caution by saying that the results "tend to suggest" answers and by his explicit awareness that his answers are affected by the validity of certain assumptions. Such caution and qualification is appropriate. Every study of social relationships exists within the context of varying values and interest. The aim of any particular study is to make as cogent a statement as possible that will increase both our understanding of an issue and our options for responding to it.

## ARTICLES REPRINTED

Fraiberg, S. The muse in the kitchen: A case study in clinical research. *Smith College Studies in Social Work,* 1970, *40*(2), 101–115.

Rubin, A. Commitment to community mental health aftercare services: Staffing and structural implications. *Community Mental Health Journal,* 1978, *14*(3), 199–208.

Wechsler, H., Gottlieb, N. H., and Demone, H. W. Lifestyle, conditions of life, and health care in urban and suburban areas. *Public Health Reports,* 1979, *94*(5), 477–482.

# INDEX

# INDEX